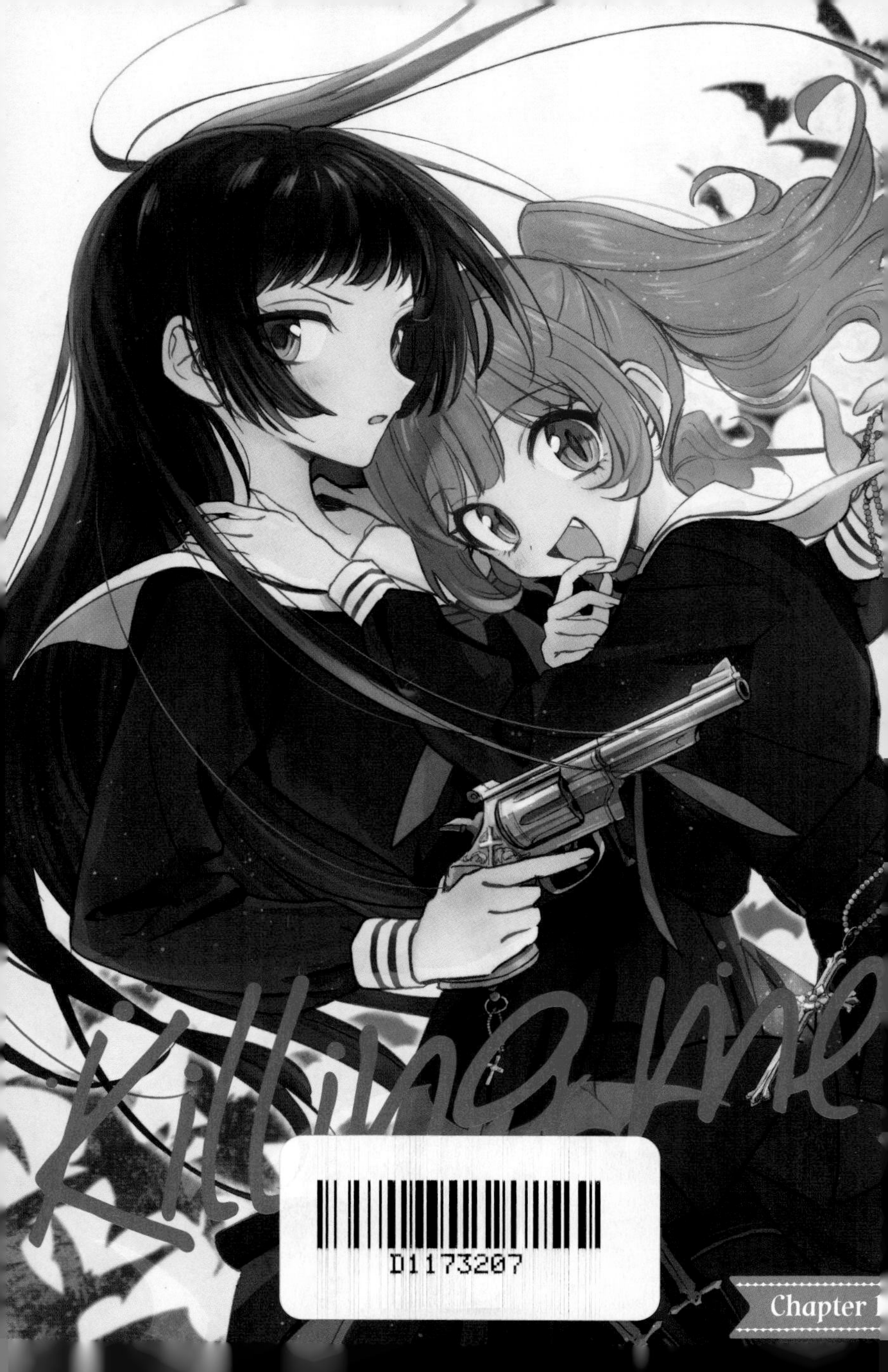
Chapter 1

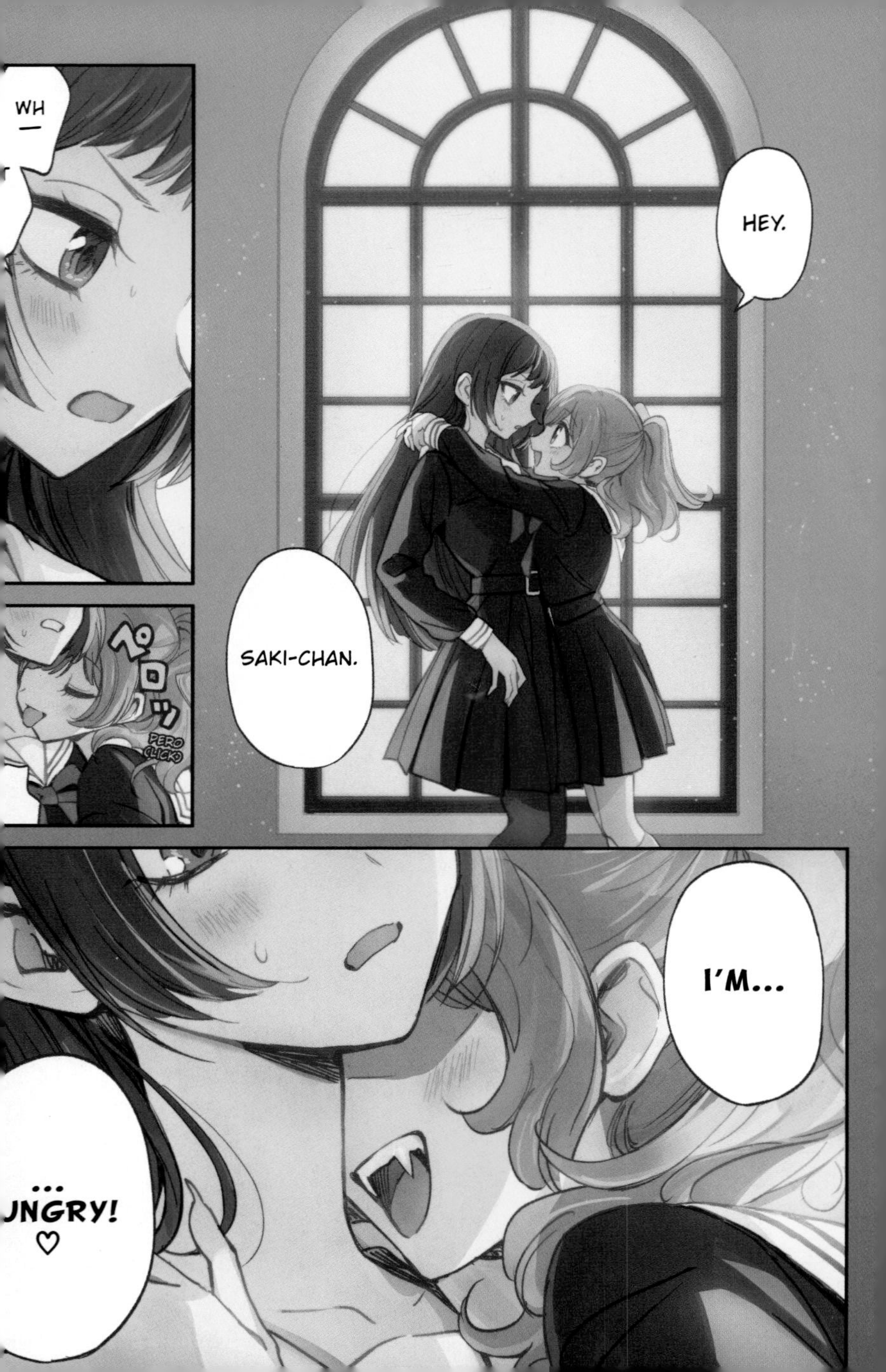
HEY.
SAKI-CHAN.
WH—
ペロッ
PERO (LICK)
I'M...
...UNGRY! ♡

Killing me!

AKIYAMA

···1···

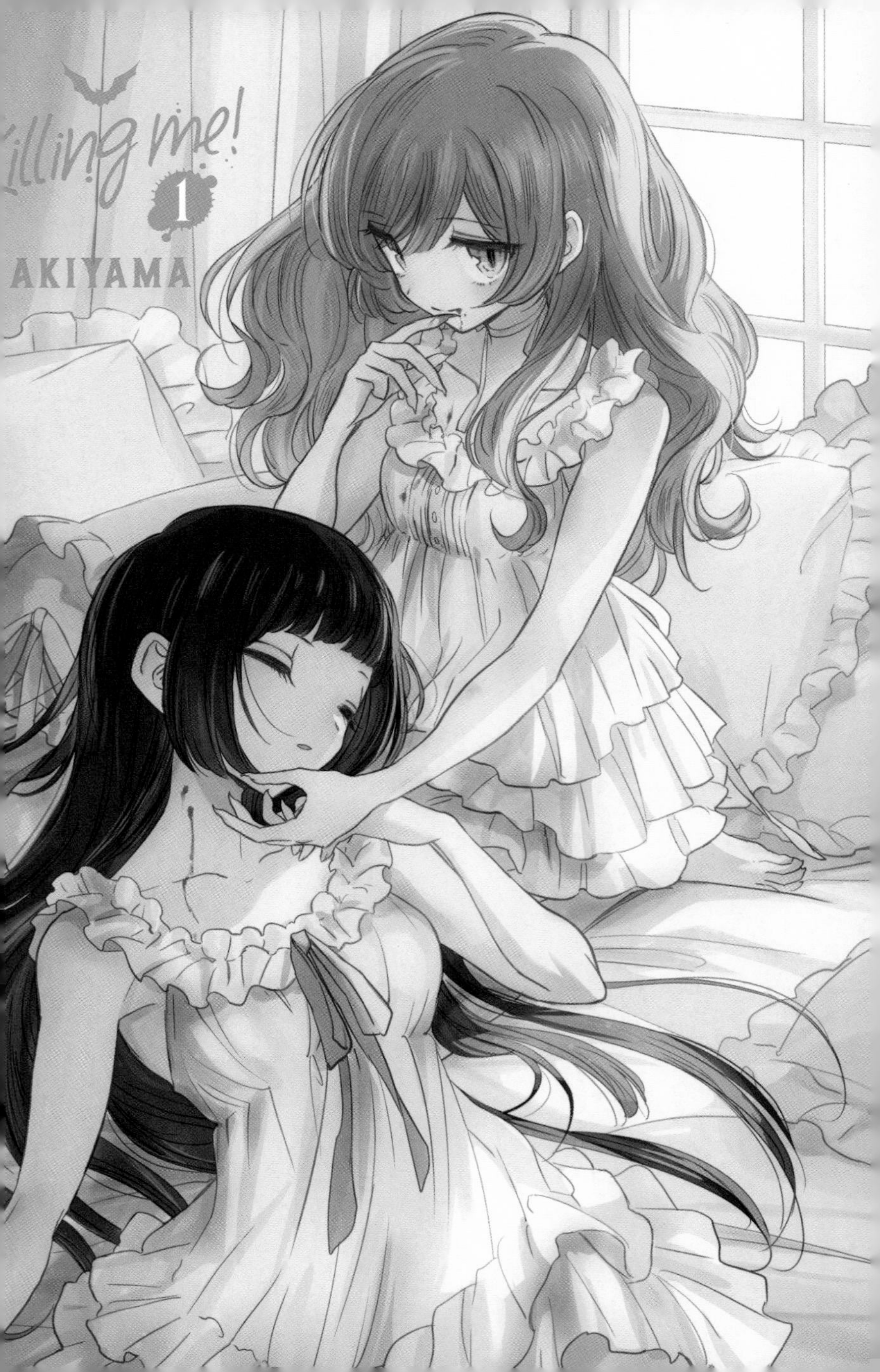
illing me!
1
AKIYAMA

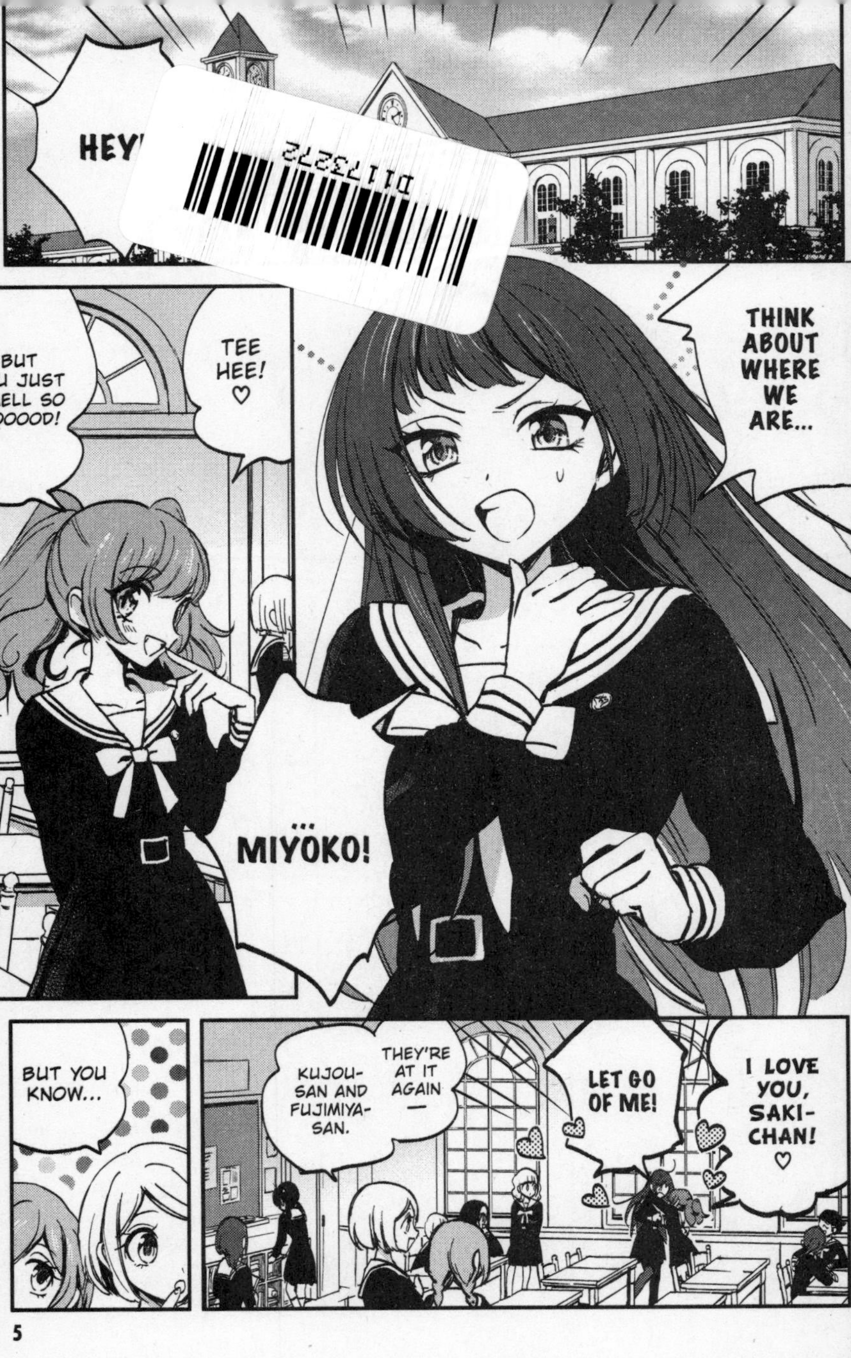
HEY
THINK ABOUT WHERE WE ARE...
...MIYOKO!
TEE HEE! ♡
BUT YOU JUST SMELL SO GOOOOD!
I LOVE YOU, SAKI-CHAN! ♡
LET GO OF ME!
THEY'RE AT IT AGAIN—
KUJOU-SAN AND FUJIMIYA-SAN.
BUT YOU KNOW...

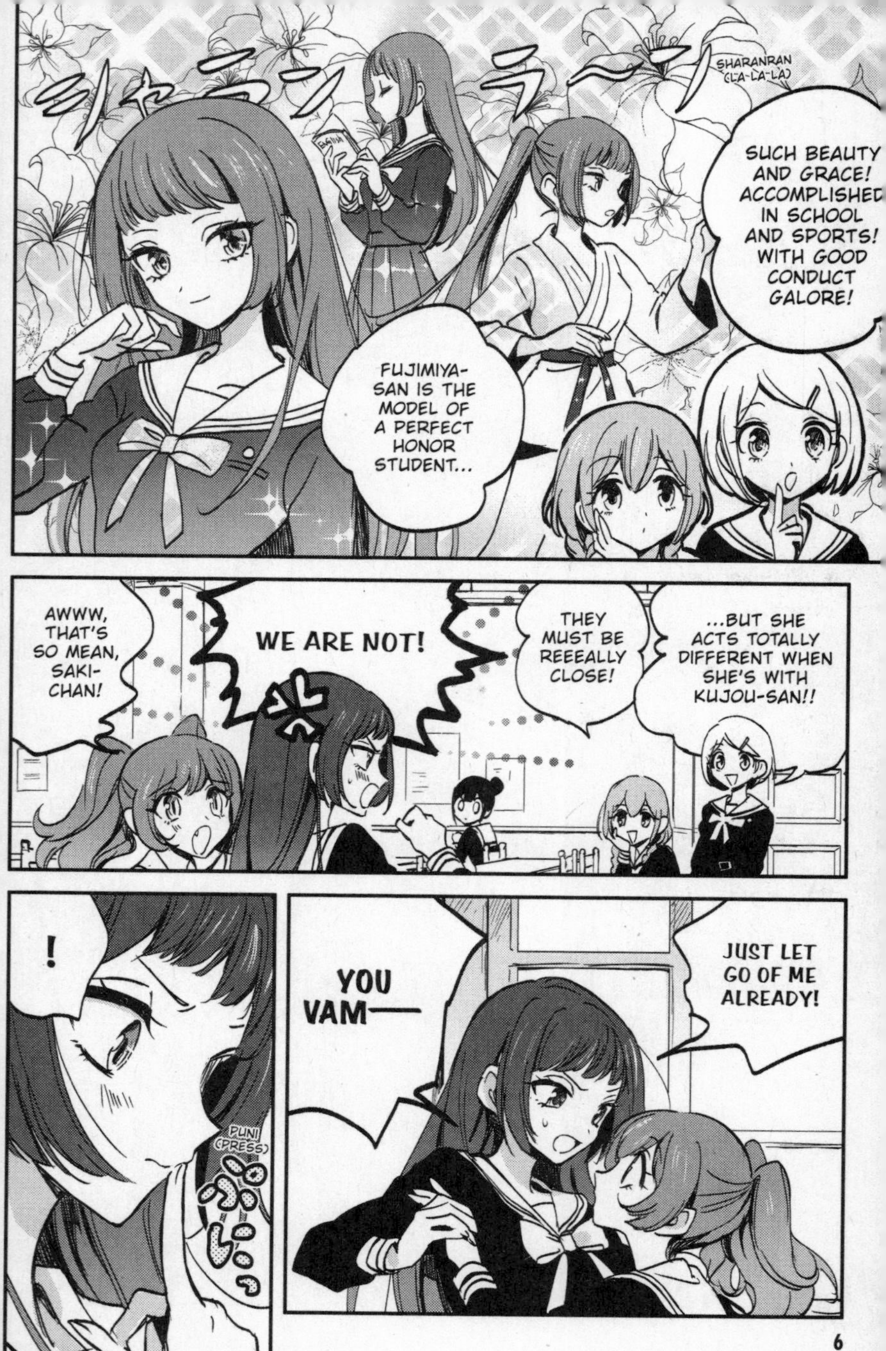
SHARANRAN (LA-LA-LA)
SUCH BEAUTY AND GRACE! ACCOMPLISHED IN SCHOOL AND SPORTS! WITH GOOD CONDUCT GALORE!
FUJIMIYA-SAN IS THE MODEL OF A PERFECT HONOR STUDENT...
...BUT SHE ACTS TOTALLY DIFFERENT WHEN SHE'S WITH KUJOU-SAN!!
THEY MUST BE REEEALLY CLOSE!
WE ARE NOT!
AWWW, THAT'S SO MEAN, SAKI-CHAN!
JUST LET GO OF ME ALREADY!
YOU VAM—
!
PUNI (PRESS)

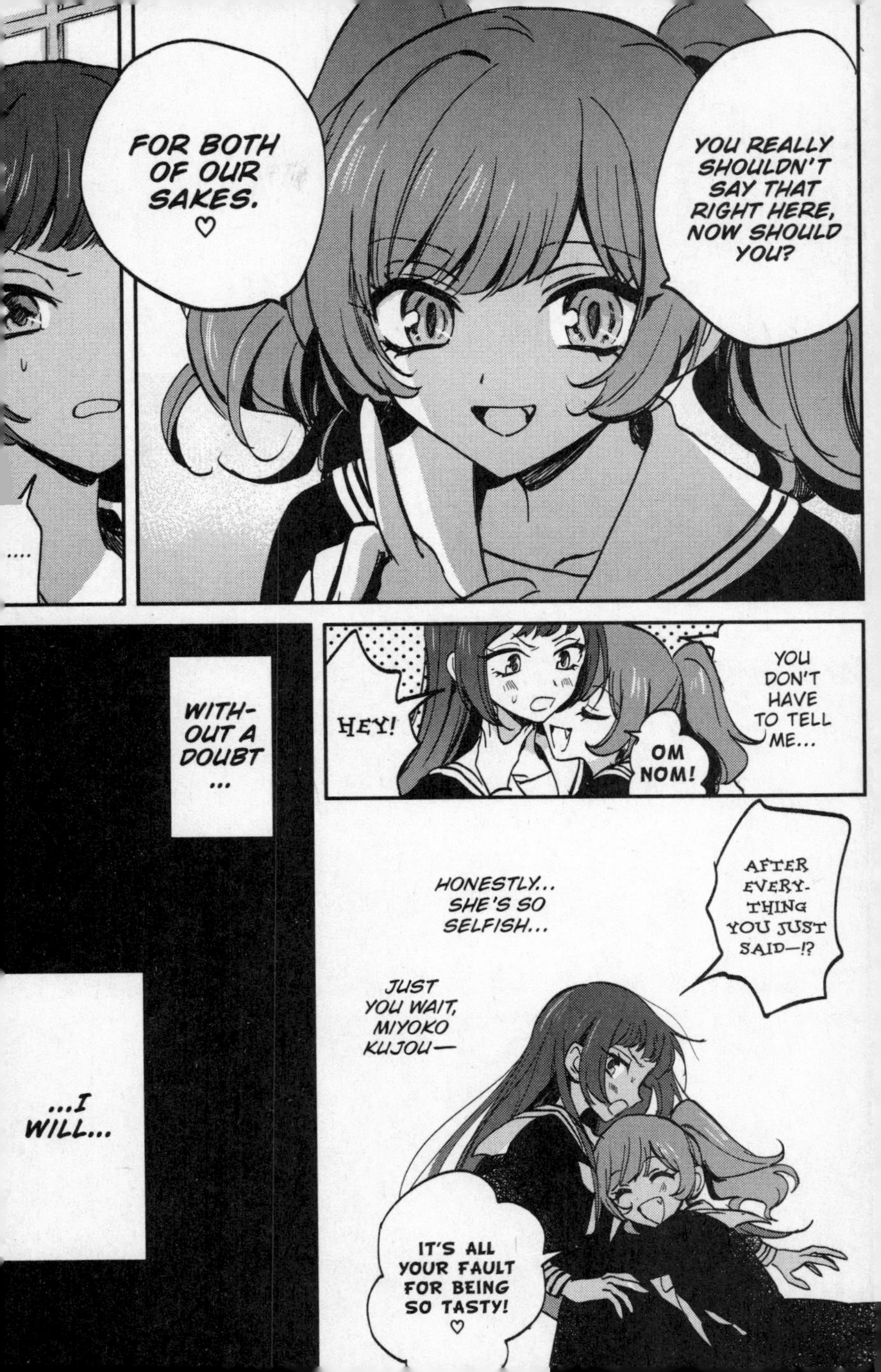
YOU REALLY SHOULDN'T SAY THAT RIGHT HERE, NOW SHOULD YOU?
FOR BOTH OF OUR SAKES. ♡
....
YOU DON'T HAVE TO TELL ME...
OM NOM!
HEY!
AFTER EVERY-THING YOU JUST SAID—!?
HONESTLY... SHE'S SO SELFISH...
JUST YOU WAIT, MIYOKO KUJOU—
IT'S ALL YOUR FAULT FOR BEING SO TASTY! ♡
WITH-OUT A DOUBT ...
...I WILL...

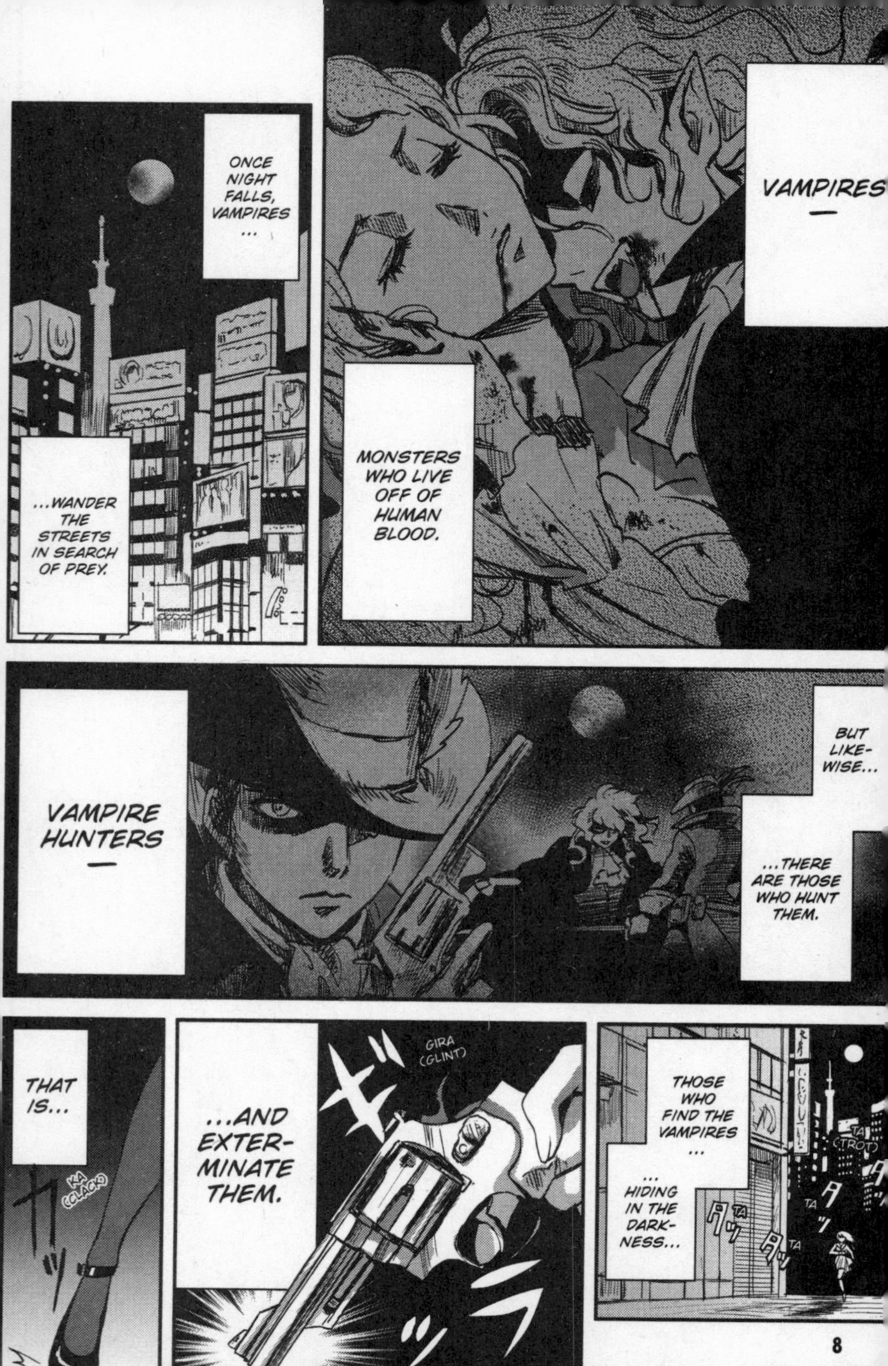
VAMPIRES —
MONSTERS WHO LIVE OFF OF HUMAN BLOOD.
ONCE NIGHT FALLS, VAMPIRES ...
...WANDER THE STREETS IN SEARCH OF PREY.
BUT LIKE-WISE...
...THERE ARE THOSE WHO HUNT THEM.
VAMPIRE HUNTERS —
THOSE WHO FIND THE VAMPIRES ...
... HIDING IN THE DARK-NESS...
TA (TROT)
TA
TA
TA
GIRA (GLINT)
...AND EXTER-MINATE THEM.
THAT IS...
KA (CLACK)

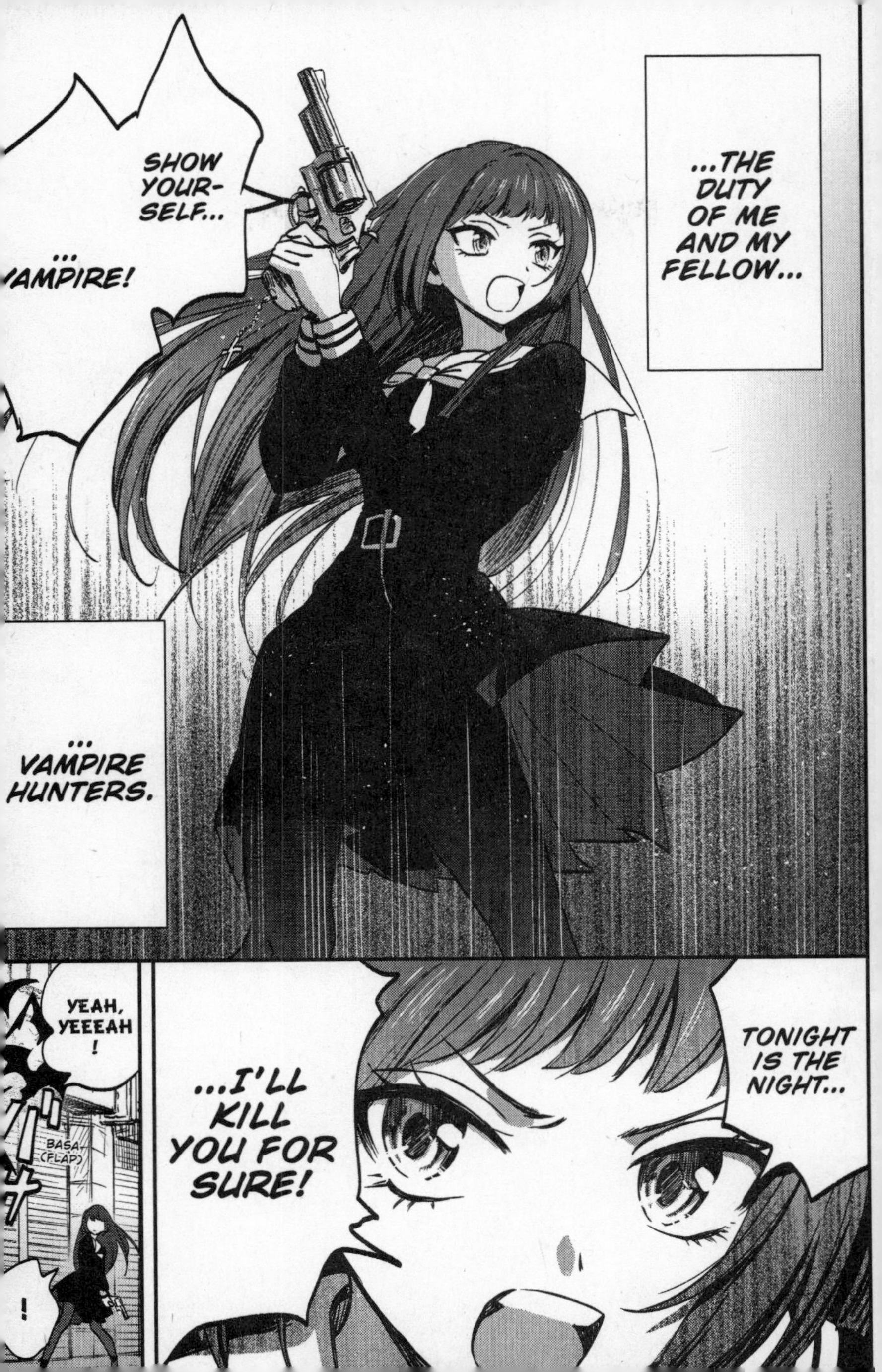
...THE DUTY OF ME AND MY FELLOW...
SHOW YOUR-SELF...
...VAMPIRE!
...VAMPIRE HUNTERS.
TONIGHT IS THE NIGHT...
...I'LL KILL YOU FOR SURE!
YEAH, YEEEAH!
BASA (FLAP)
!

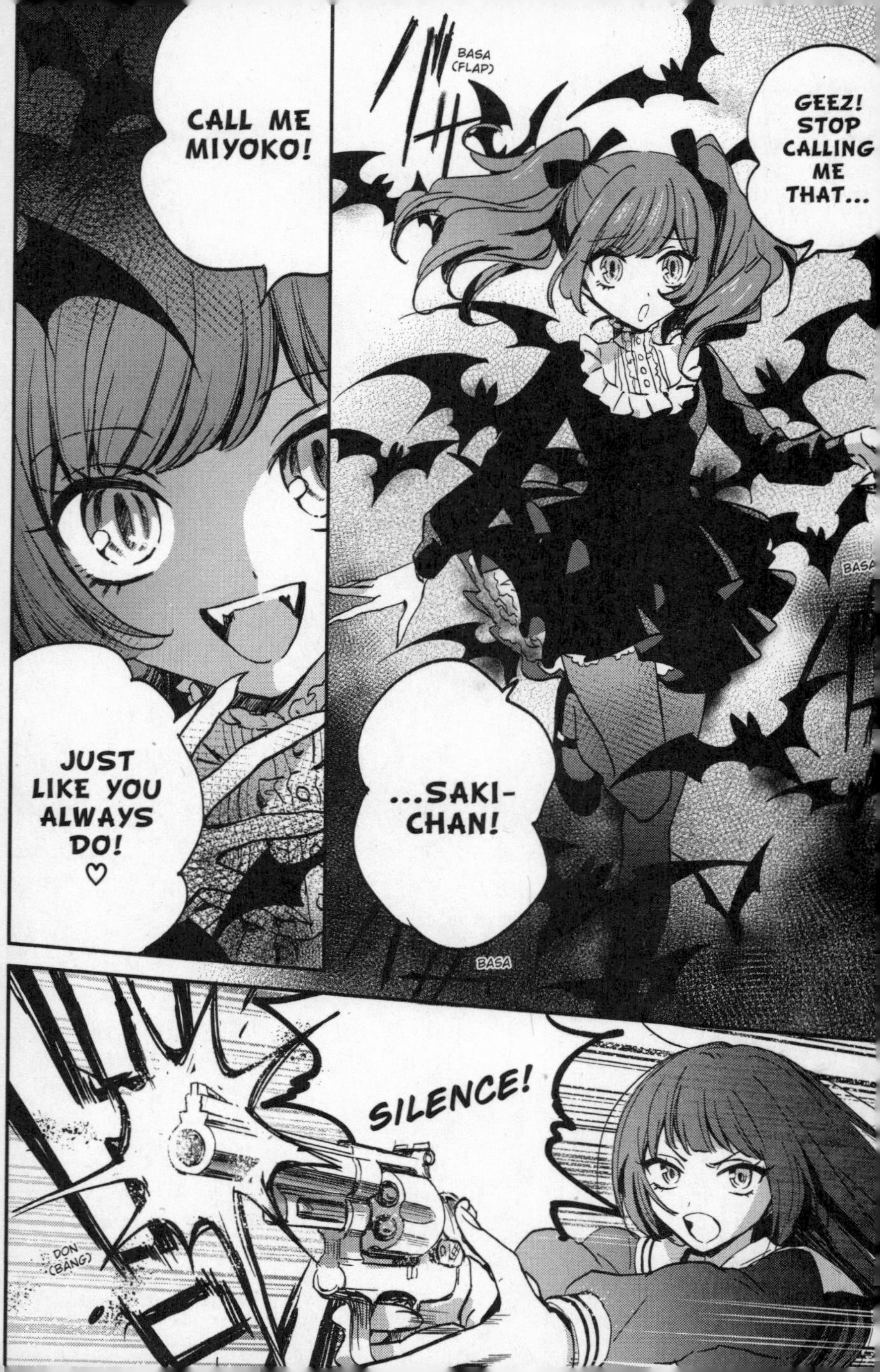
BASA (FLAP)
GEEZ! STOP CALLING ME THAT...
BASA
...SAKI-CHAN!
BASA
CALL ME MIYOKO!
JUST LIKE YOU ALWAYS DO! ♡
SILENCE!
DON (BANG)

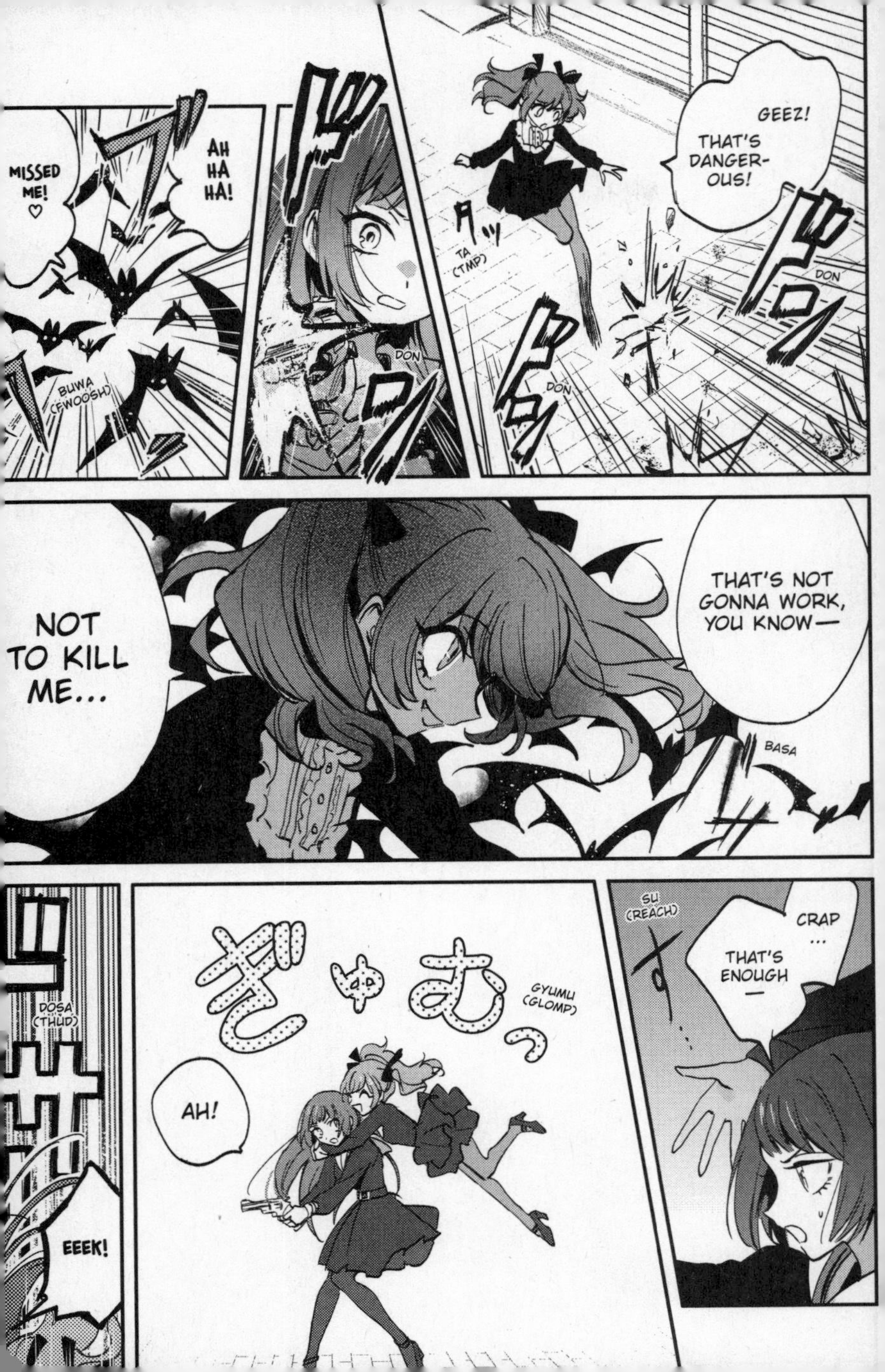
GEEZ! THAT'S DANGER-OUS!
DON
TA (TMP)
DON
DON
AH HA HA!
MISSED ME! ♡
BUWA (FWOOSH)
THAT'S NOT GONNA WORK, YOU KNOW—
BASA
NOT TO KILL ME...
SU (REACH)
CRAP ... THAT'S ENOUGH —
GYUMU (GLOMP)
AH!
DOSA (THUD)
EEEK!

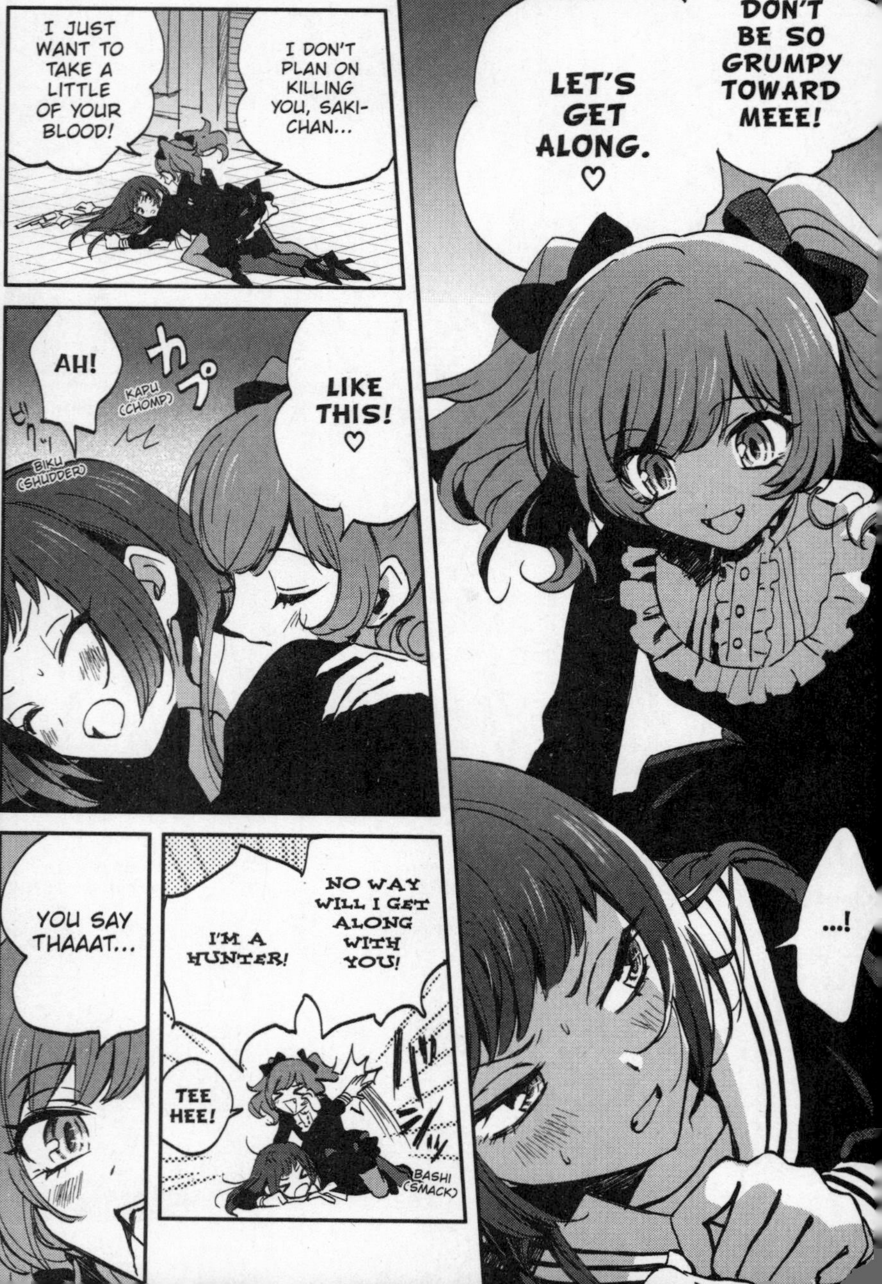
DON'T BE SO GRUMPY TOWARD MEEE!
LET'S GET ALONG. ♡
...!
I DON'T PLAN ON KILLING YOU, SAKI-CHAN...
I JUST WANT TO TAKE A LITTLE OF YOUR BLOOD!
LIKE THIS! ♡
KAPU (CHOMP)
AH!
BIKU (SHUDDER)
NO WAY WILL I GET ALONG WITH YOU!
I'M A HUNTER!
TEE HEE!
BASHI (SMACK)
YOU SAY THAAAT...

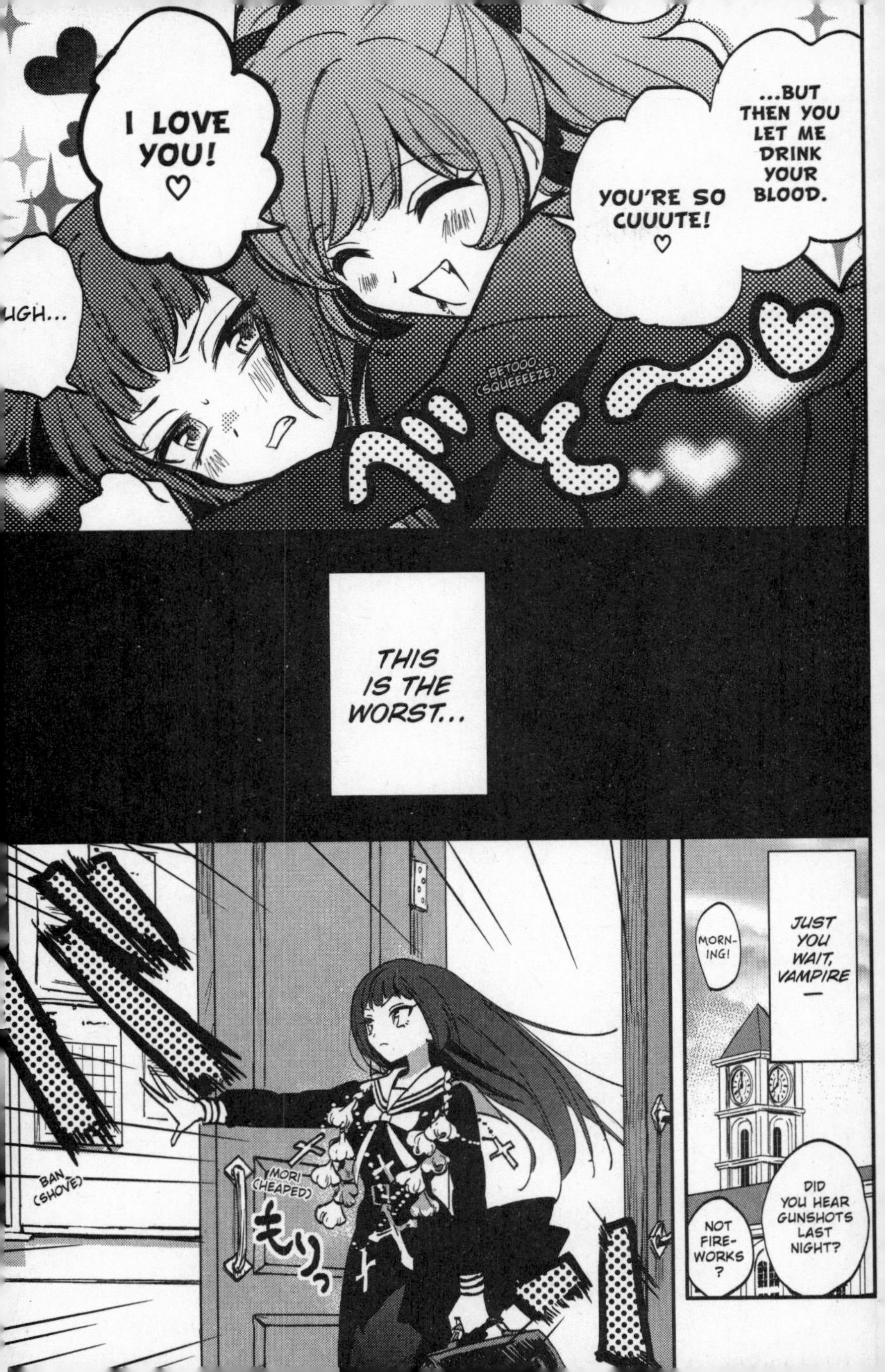
...BUT THEN YOU LET ME DRINK YOUR BLOOD.
YOU'RE SO CUUUTE! ♡
I LOVE YOU! ♡
UGH...
BETOOO (SQUEEEEZE)
THIS IS THE WORST...
JUST YOU WAIT, VAMPIRE—
MORN-ING!
DID YOU HEAR GUNSHOTS LAST NIGHT?
NOT FIRE-WORKS?
MORI (HEAPED)
BAN (SHOVE)

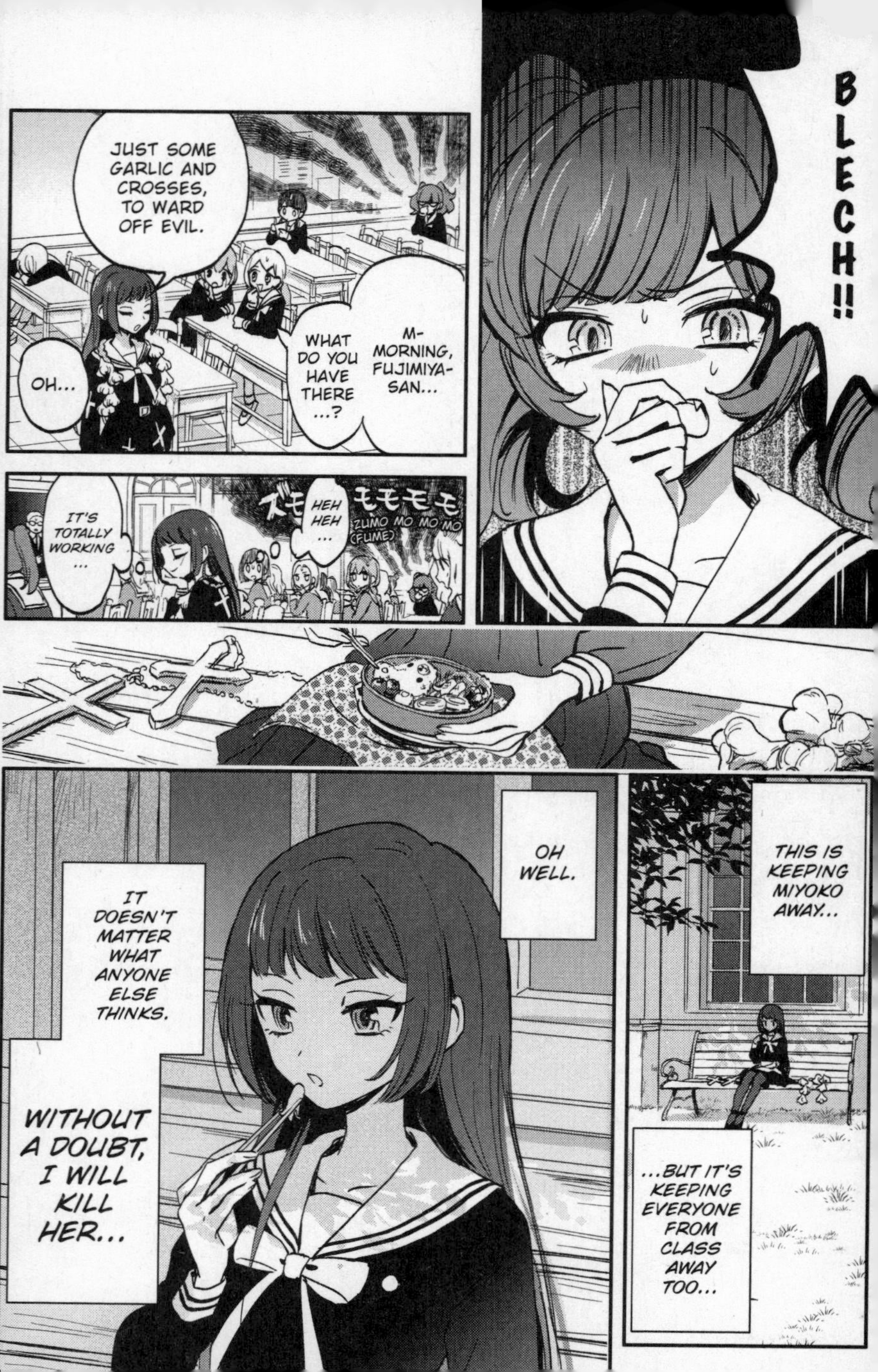
BLECH!!
M-MORNING, FUJIMIYA-SAN...
WHAT DO YOU HAVE THERE ...?
JUST SOME GARLIC AND CROSSES, TO WARD OFF EVIL.
OH...
ズモモモモ
ZUMO MO MO MO (FUME)
HEH HEH ...
IT'S TOTALLY WORKING ...
THIS IS KEEPING MIYOKO AWAY...
...BUT IT'S KEEPING EVERYONE FROM CLASS AWAY TOO...
OH WELL.
IT DOESN'T MATTER WHAT ANYONE ELSE THINKS.
WITHOUT A DOUBT, I WILL KILL HER...

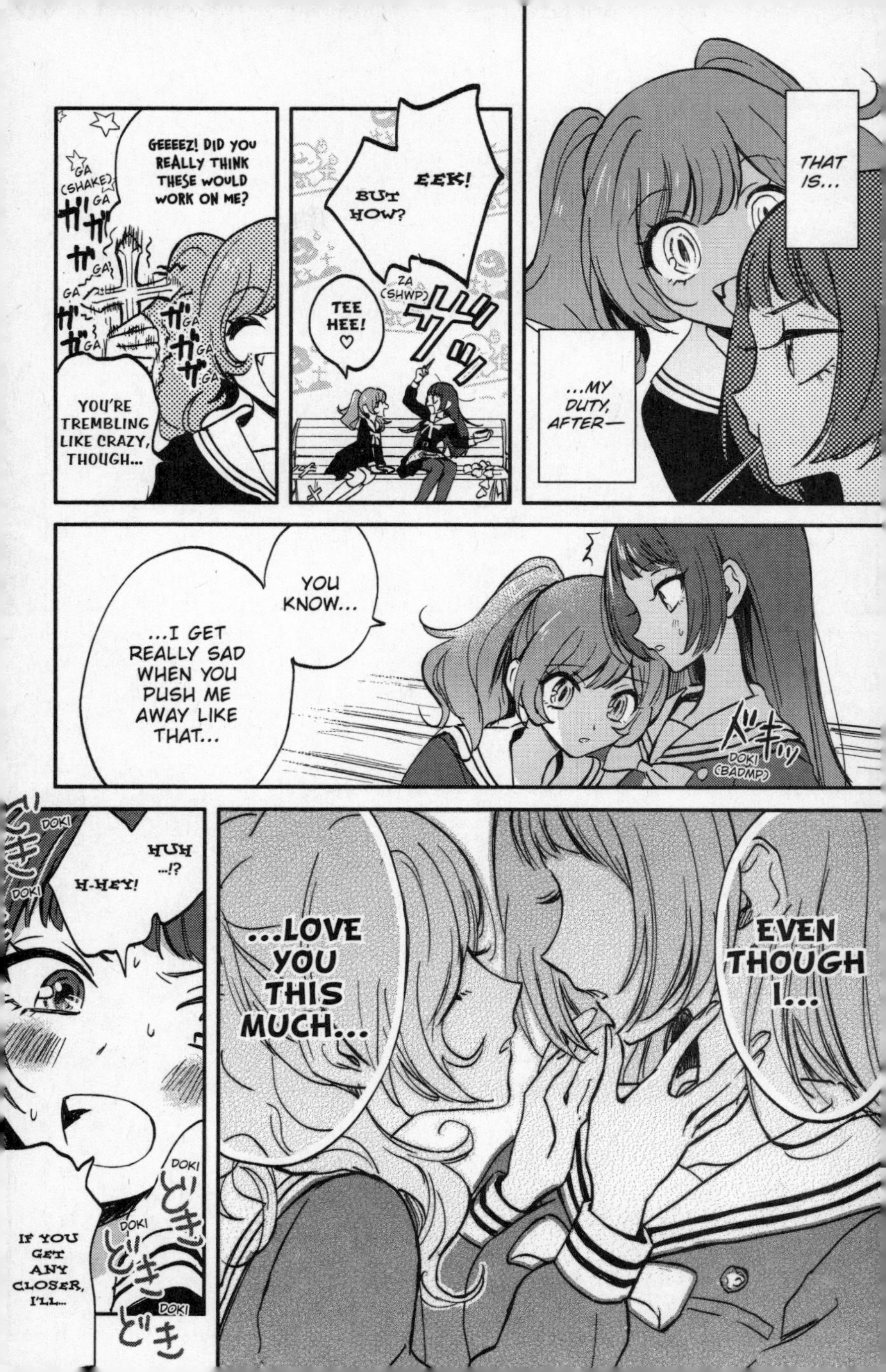
THAT IS...
...MY DUTY, AFTER—
EEK!
BUT HOW?
ZA (SHWP)
TEE HEE! ♡
GEEEZ! DID YOU REALLY THINK THESE WOULD WORK ON ME?
GA (SHAKE) GA
GA
GA
GA
GA
GA
YOU'RE TREMBLING LIKE CRAZY, THOUGH...
YOU KNOW...
...I GET REALLY SAD WHEN YOU PUSH ME AWAY LIKE THAT...
DOKI (BADMP)
EVEN THOUGH I...
...LOVE YOU THIS MUCH...
HUH ...!?
H-HEY!
DOKI
DOKI
DOKI
DOKI
DOKI
IF YOU GET ANY CLOSER, I'LL...

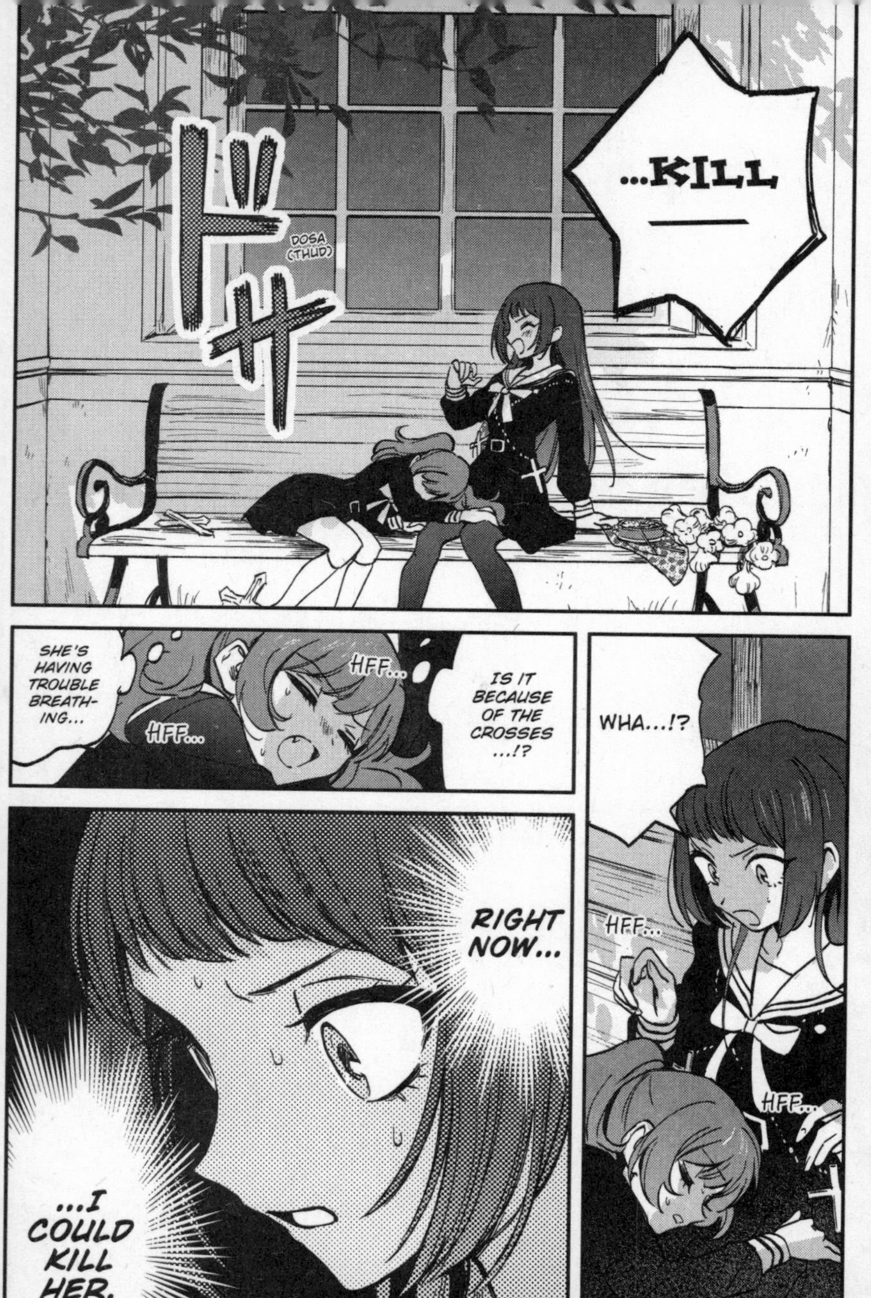
...KILL
DOSA (THUD)
WHA...!?
HFF...
HFF...
IS IT BECAUSE OF THE CROSSES ...!?
HFF...
SHE'S HAVING TROUBLE BREATHING...
HFF...
RIGHT NOW...
...I COULD KILL HER.

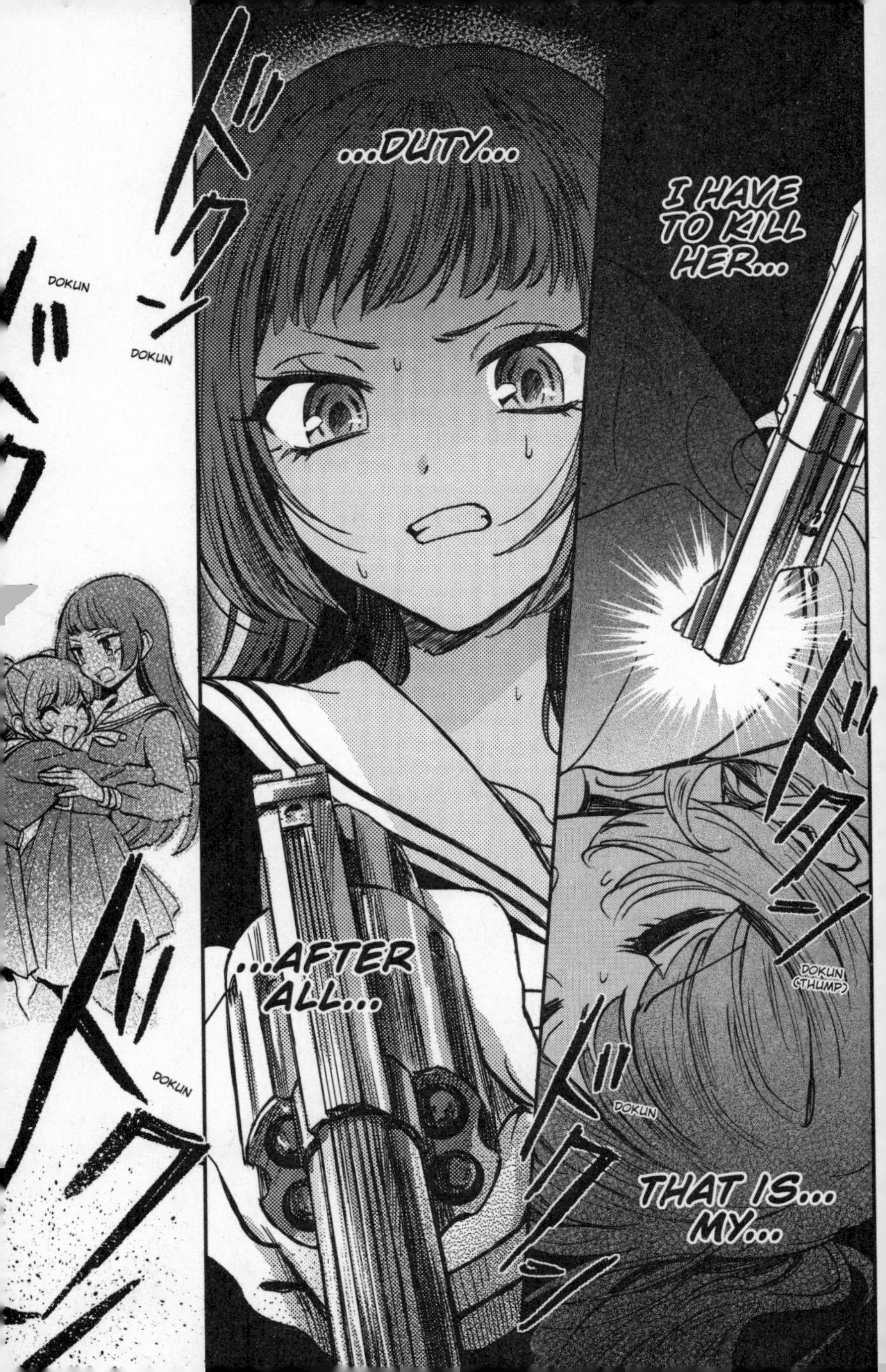
I HAVE TO KILL HER...
DOKUN (THUMP)
DOKUN
THAT IS... MY...
...DUTY...
...AFTER ALL...
DOKUN
DOKUN
DOKUN

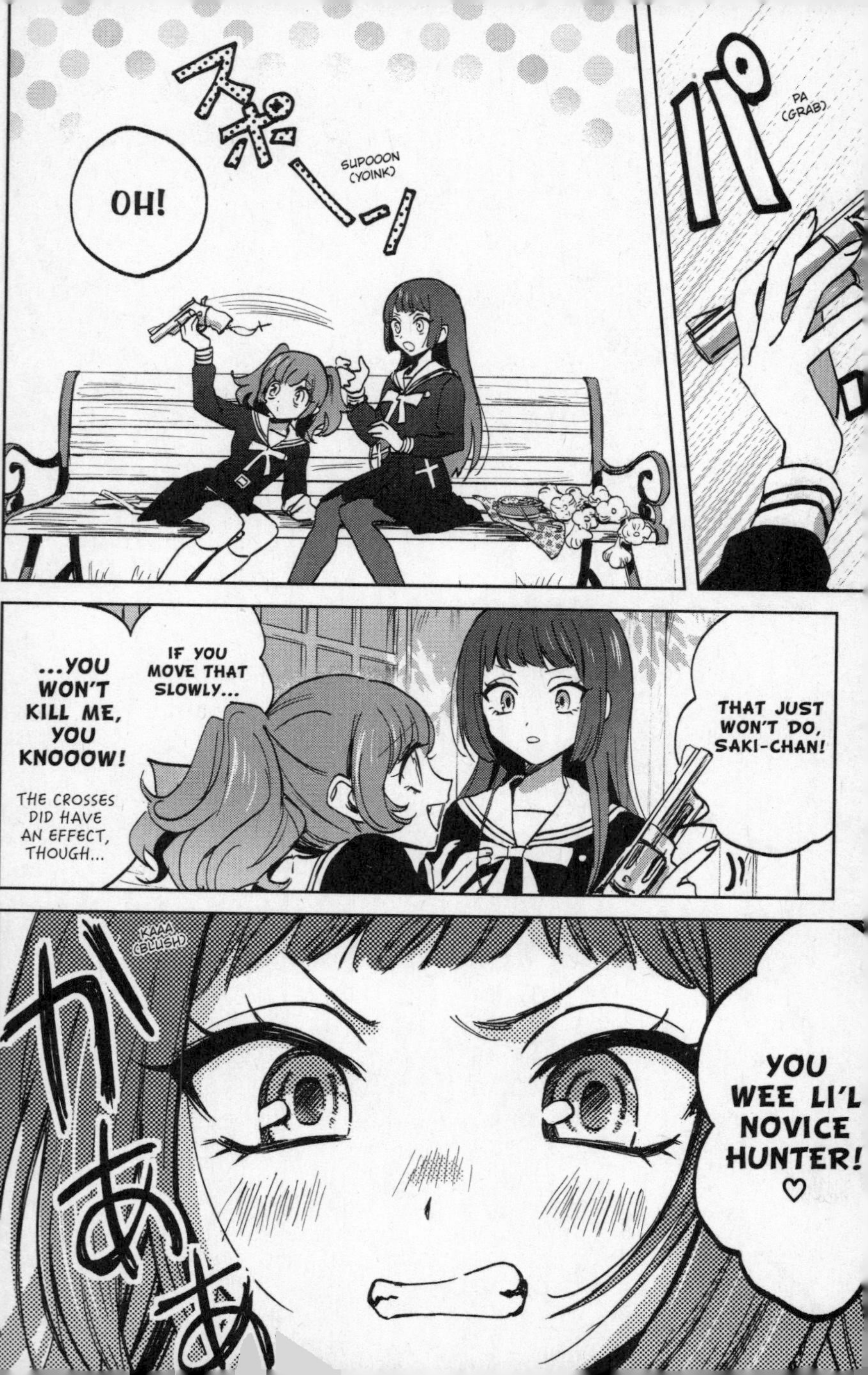
パ
PA (GRAB)
OH!
スポーーン
SUPOOON (YOINK)
THAT JUST WON'T DO, SAKI-CHAN!
IF YOU MOVE THAT SLOWLY...
...YOU WON'T KILL ME, YOU KNOOOW!
THE CROSSES DID HAVE AN EFFECT, THOUGH...
YOU WEE LI'L NOVICE HUNTER! ♡
KAAA (BLUSH)
かぁぁ

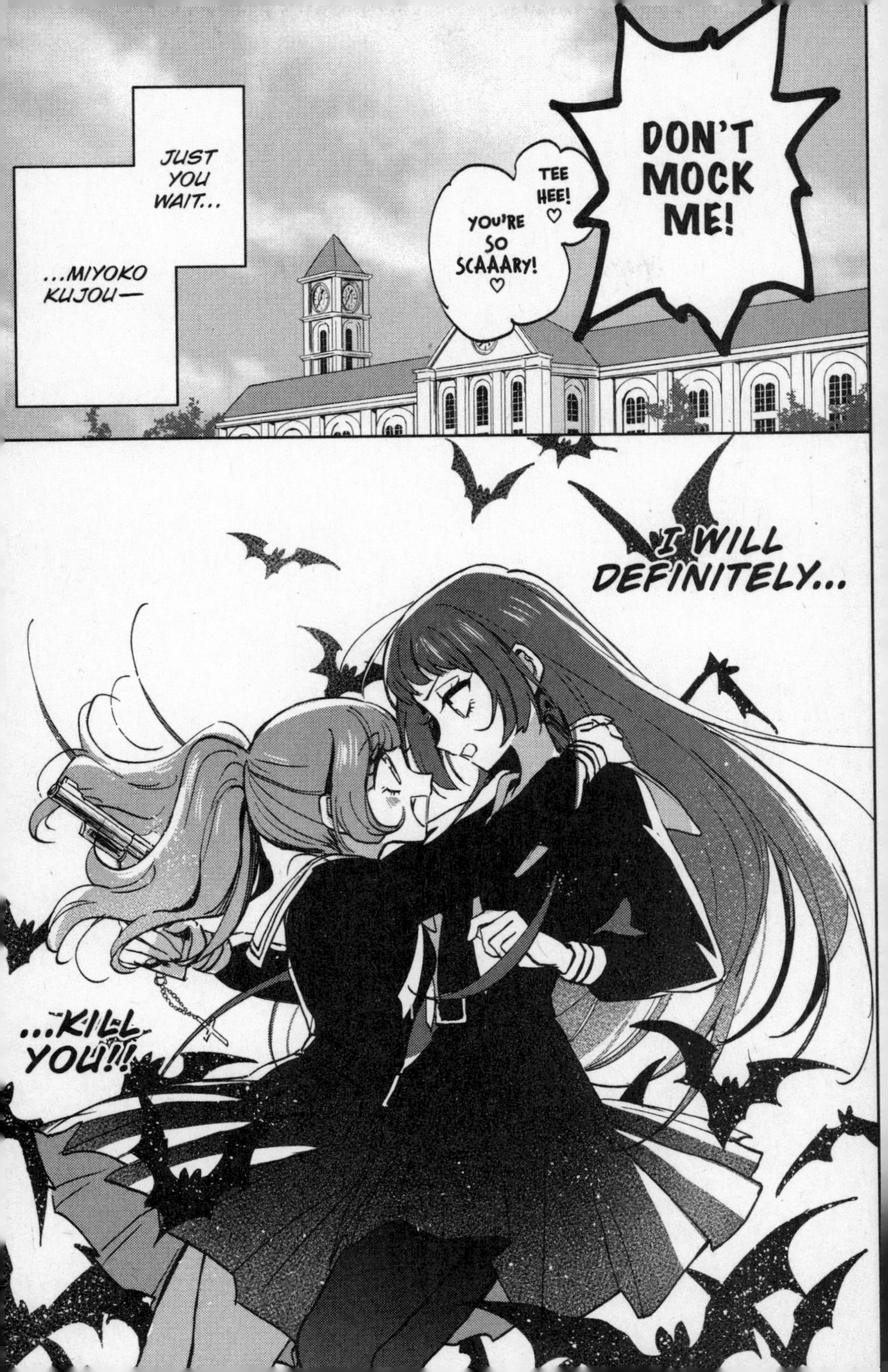
DON'T MOCK ME!
TEE HEE! ♡ YOU'RE SO SCAAARY! ♡
JUST YOU WAIT...
...MIYOKO KUJOU—
I WILL DEFINITELY...
...KILL YOU!!!

Killing me!

1

Chapter 2

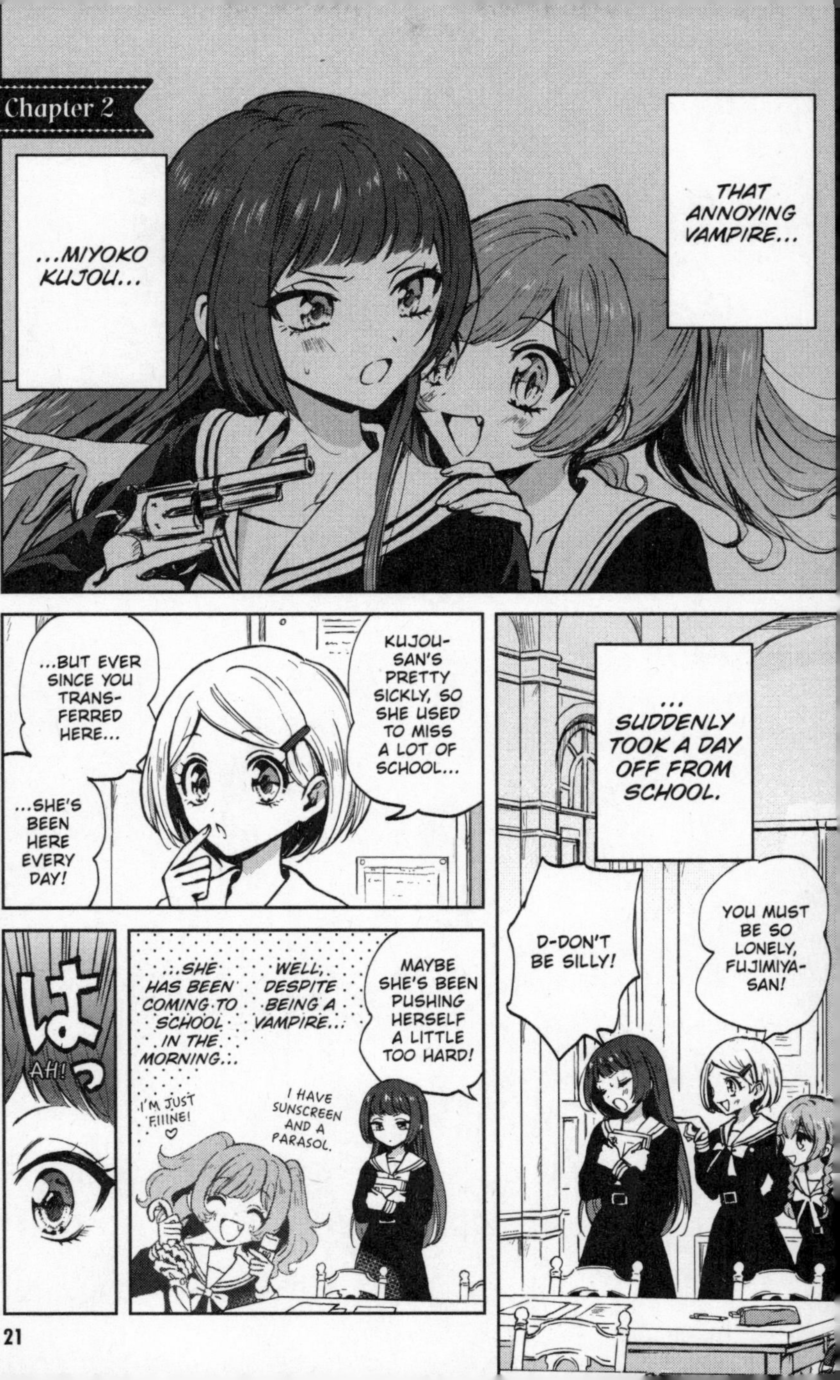
THAT ANNOYING VAMPIRE...
...MIYOKO KUJOU...
...SUDDENLY TOOK A DAY OFF FROM SCHOOL.
YOU MUST BE SO LONELY, FUJIMIYA-SAN!
D-DON'T BE SILLY!
KUJOU-SAN'S PRETTY SICKLY, SO SHE USED TO MISS A LOT OF SCHOOL...
...BUT EVER SINCE YOU TRANSFERRED HERE...
...SHE'S BEEN HERE EVERY DAY!
MAYBE SHE'S BEEN PUSHING HERSELF A LITTLE TOO HARD!
WELL, DESPITE BEING A VAMPIRE...
...SHE HAS BEEN COMING TO SCHOOL IN THE MORNING...
I HAVE SUNSCREEN AND A PARASOL.
I'M JUST FIIINE! ♡
はっ
AH!

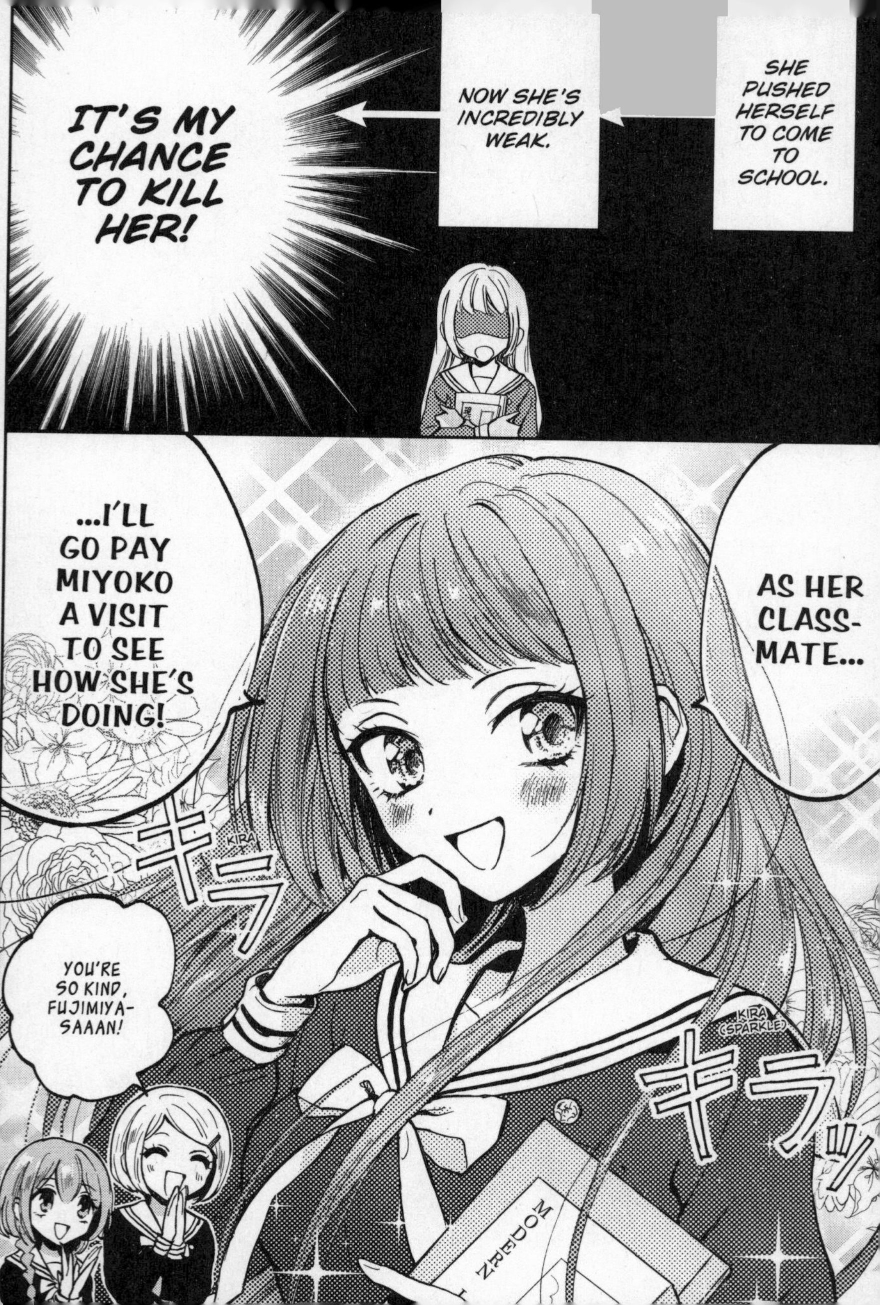
SHE PUSHED HERSELF TO COME TO SCHOOL.
NOW SHE'S INCREDIBLY WEAK.
IT'S MY CHANCE TO KILL HER!
AS HER CLASS-MATE...
...I'LL GO PAY MIYOKO A VISIT TO SEE HOW SHE'S DOING!
キラッ
KIRA (SPARKLE)
キラ
KIRA
YOU'RE SO KIND, FUJIMIYA-SAAAN!

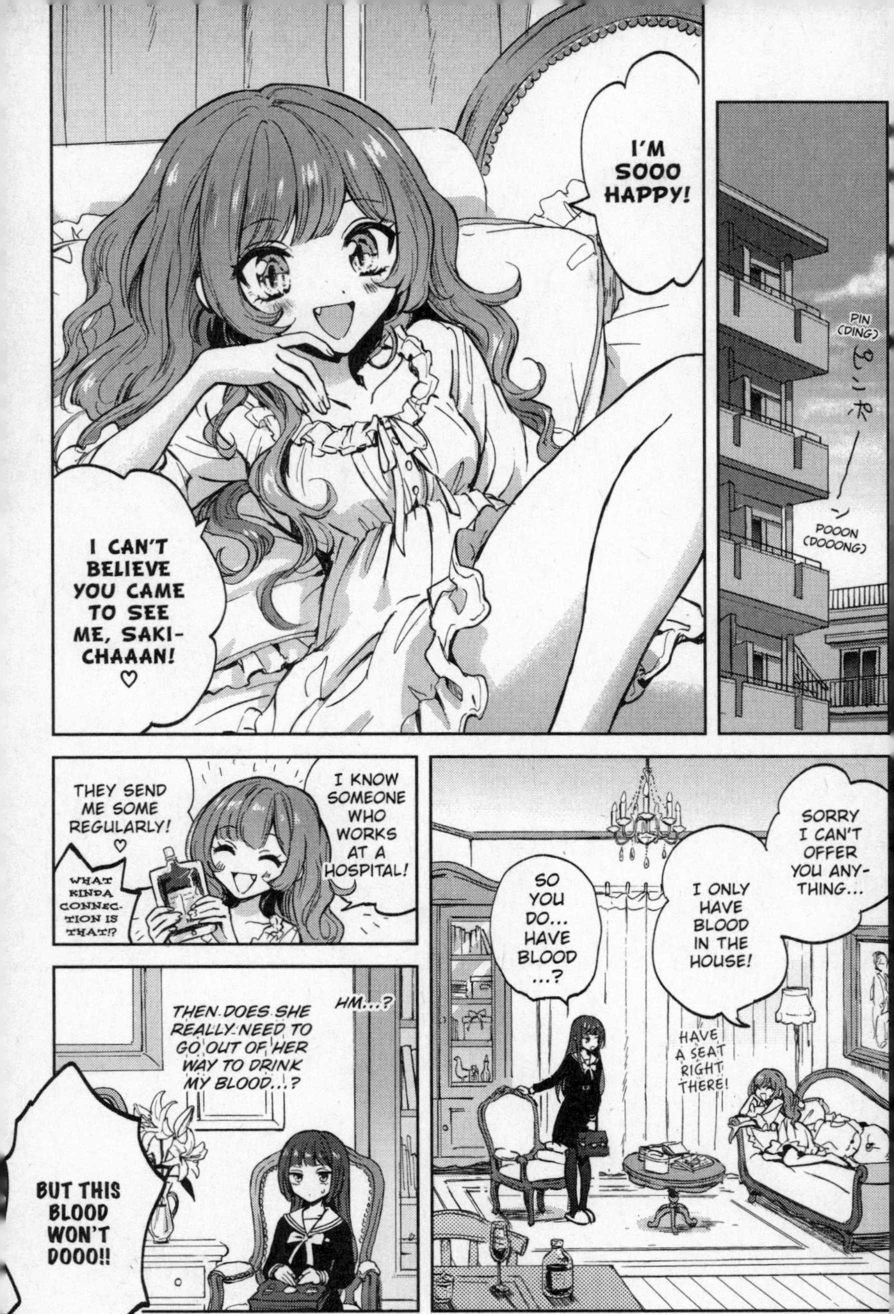
PIN (DING)
POOON (DOOONG)
I'M SOOO HAPPY!
I CAN'T BELIEVE YOU CAME TO SEE ME, SAKI-CHAAAN! ♡
SORRY I CAN'T OFFER YOU ANY-THING...
I ONLY HAVE BLOOD IN THE HOUSE!
SO YOU DO... HAVE BLOOD ...?
HAVE A SEAT RIGHT THERE!
I KNOW SOMEONE WHO WORKS AT A HOSPITAL!
THEY SEND ME SOME REGULARLY! ♡
WHAT KINDA CONNECTION IS THAT!?
HM...?
THEN DOES SHE REALLY NEED TO GO OUT OF HER WAY TO DRINK MY BLOOD...?
BUT THIS BLOOD WON'T DOOO!!

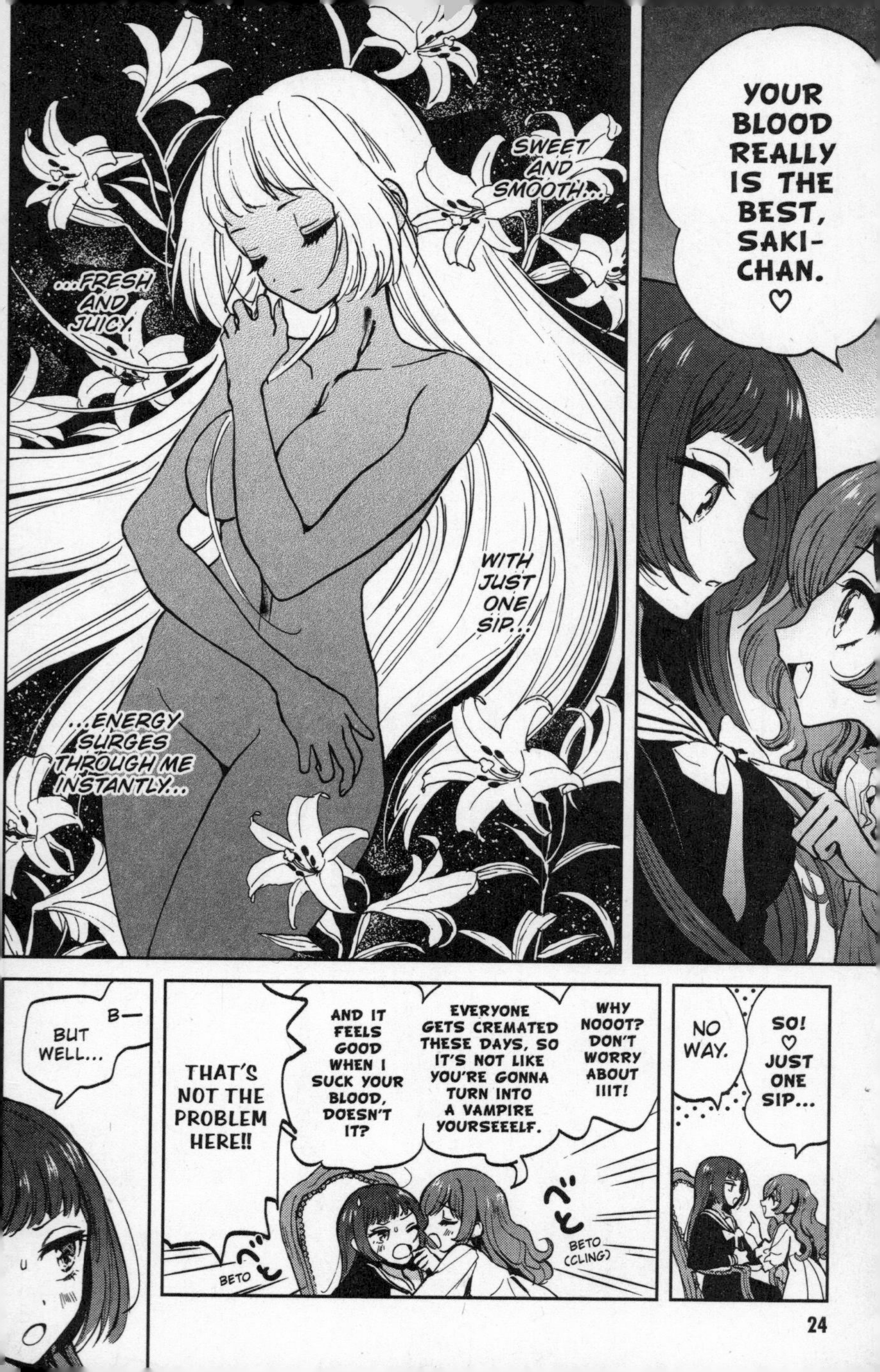
YOUR BLOOD REALLY IS THE BEST, SAKI-CHAN. ♡
SWEET AND SMOOTH...
...FRESH AND JUICY.
WITH JUST ONE SIP...
...ENERGY SURGES THROUGH ME INSTANTLY...
SO! ♡ JUST ONE SIP...
NO WAY.
WHY NOOOT? DON'T WORRY ABOUT IIIT!
EVERYONE GETS CREMATED THESE DAYS, SO IT'S NOT LIKE YOU'RE GONNA TURN INTO A VAMPIRE YOURSEEELF.
AND IT FEELS GOOD WHEN I SUCK YOUR BLOOD, DOESN'T IT?
THAT'S NOT THE PROBLEM HERE!!
BETO (CLING)
BETO
B—
BUT WELL...

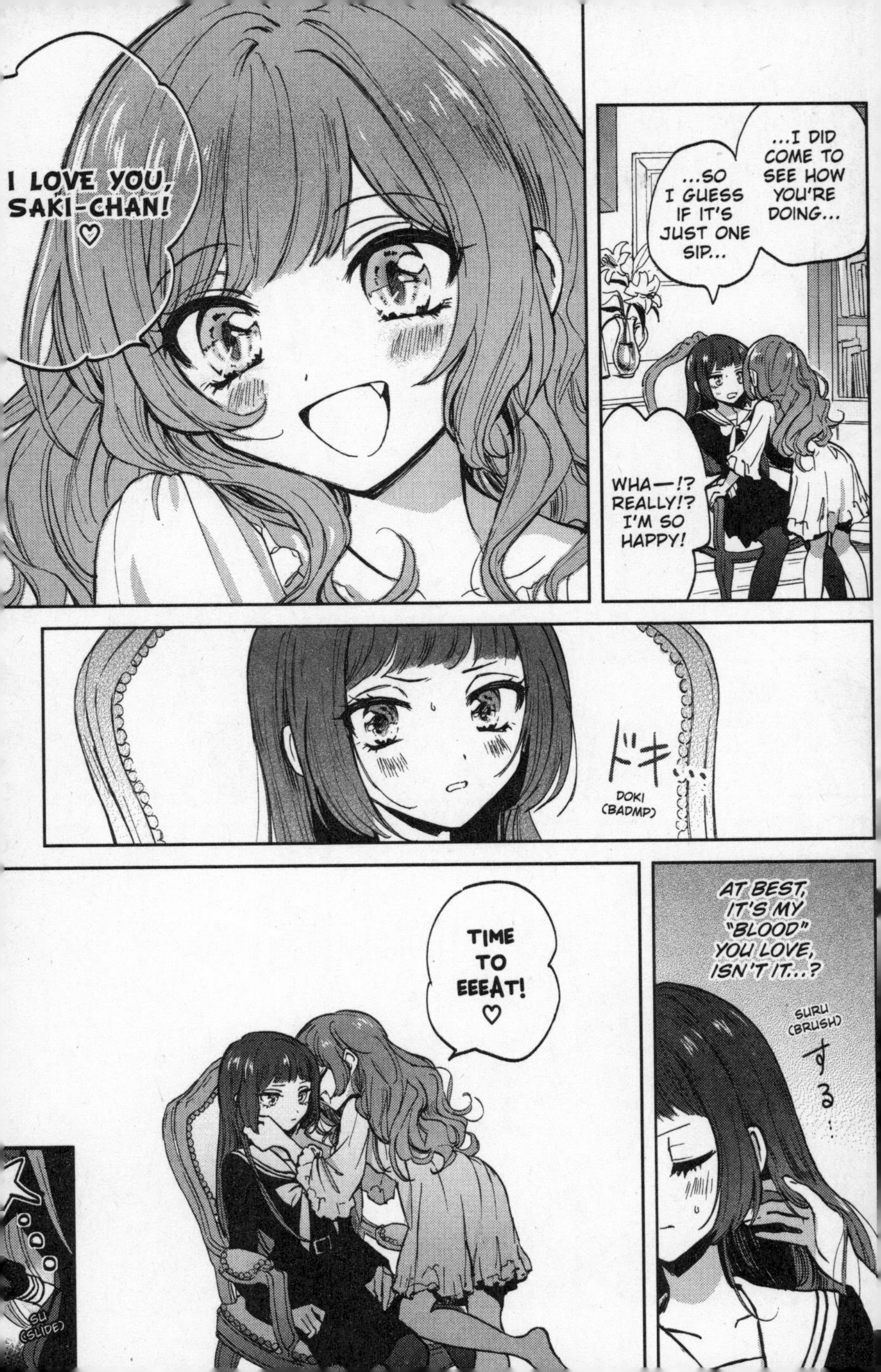
...I DID COME TO SEE HOW YOU'RE DOING...
...SO I GUESS IF IT'S JUST ONE SIP...
WHA—!? REALLY!? I'M SO HAPPY!
I LOVE YOU, SAKI-CHAN! ♡
ドキ
DOKI (BADMP)
AT BEST, IT'S MY "BLOOD" YOU LOVE, ISN'T IT...?
SURU (BRUSH)
する
TIME TO EEEAT! ♡
SU (SLIDE)

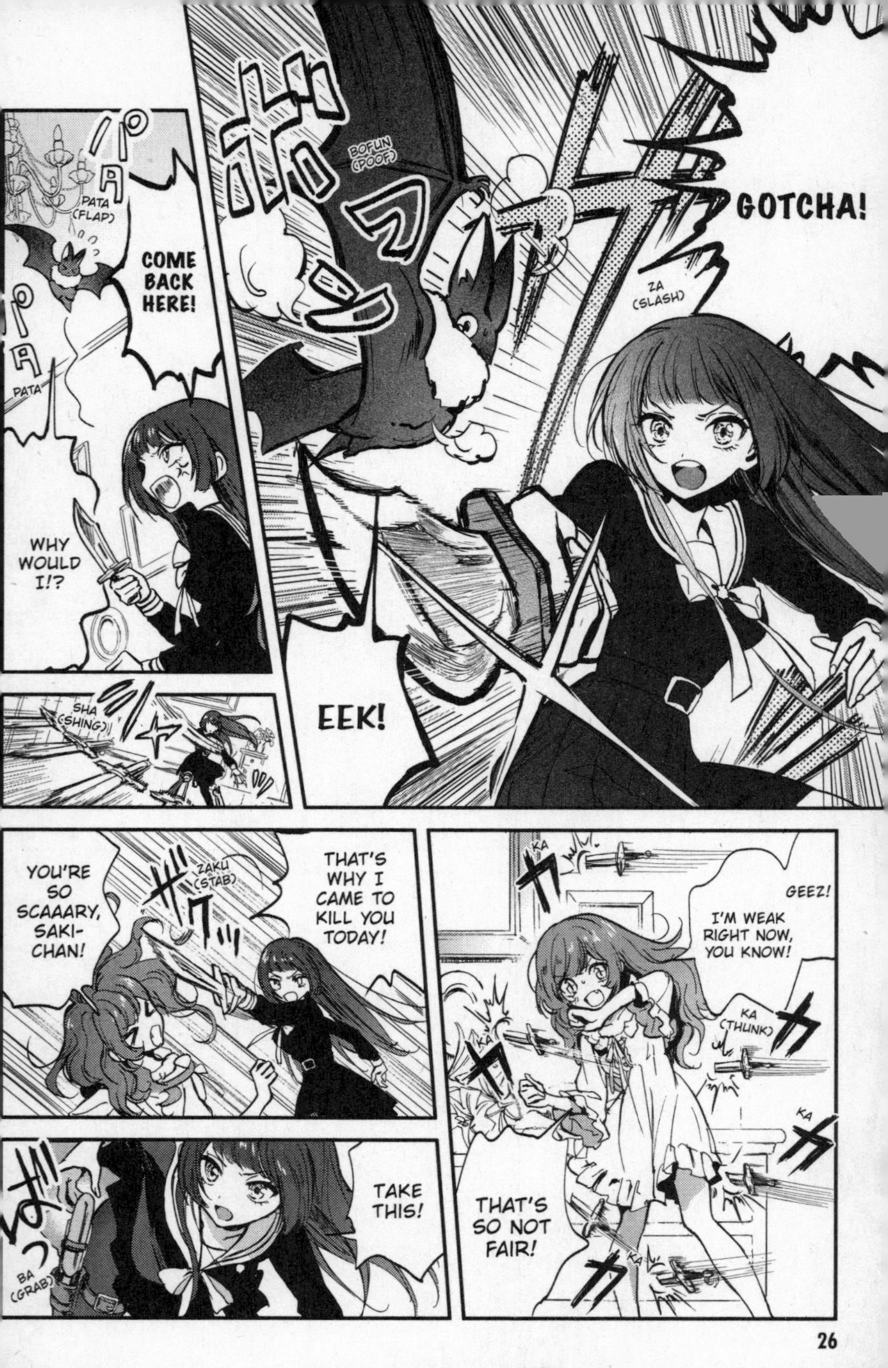
GOTCHA!
ZA (SLASH)
BOFUN (POOF)
EEK!
PATA (FLAP)
PATA
COME BACK HERE!
WHY WOULD I!?
SHA (SHING)
GEEZ!
I'M WEAK RIGHT NOW, YOU KNOW!
KA
KA (THUNK)
KA
KA
THAT'S SO NOT FAIR!
KA
THAT'S WHY I CAME TO KILL YOU TODAY!
ZAKU (STAB)
YOU'RE SO SCAAARY, SAKI-CHAN!
TAKE THIS!
BA (GRAB)

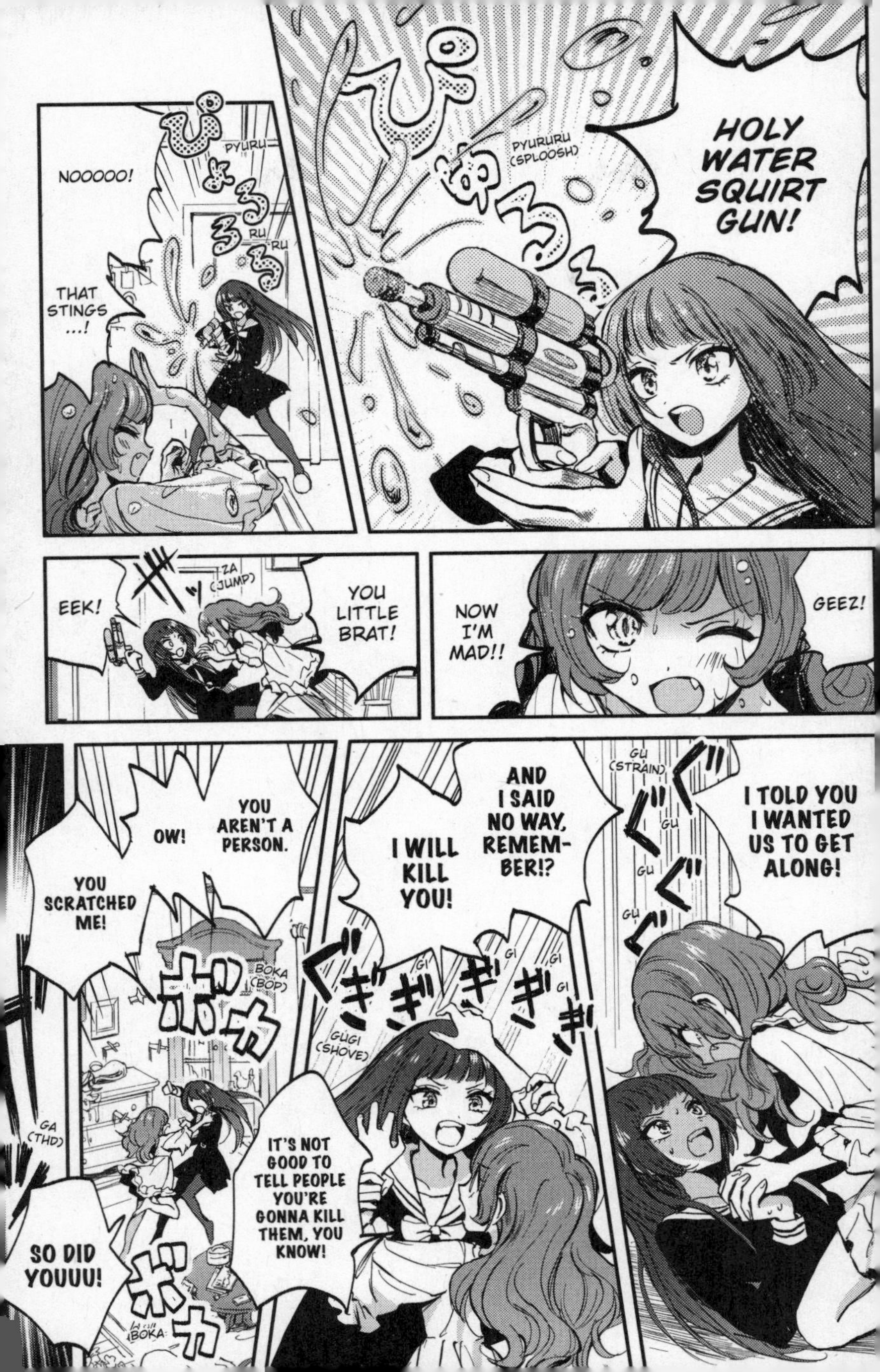
HOLY WATER SQUIRT GUN!
PYURURU (SPLOOSH)
PYURU
RU
RU
NOOOOO!
THAT STINGS ...!
GEEZ!
NOW I'M MAD!!
YOU LITTLE BRAT!
ZA (JUMP)
EEK!
I TOLD YOU I WANTED US TO GET ALONG!
GU (STRAIN)
GU
GU
GU
AND I SAID NO WAY, REMEMBER!?
I WILL KILL YOU!
GI
GI
GI
GUGI (SHOVE)
IT'S NOT GOOD TO TELL PEOPLE YOU'RE GONNA KILL THEM, YOU KNOW!
YOU AREN'T A PERSON.
OW!
YOU SCRATCHED ME!
BOKA (BOP)
GA (THD)
SO DID YOUUU!
BOKA

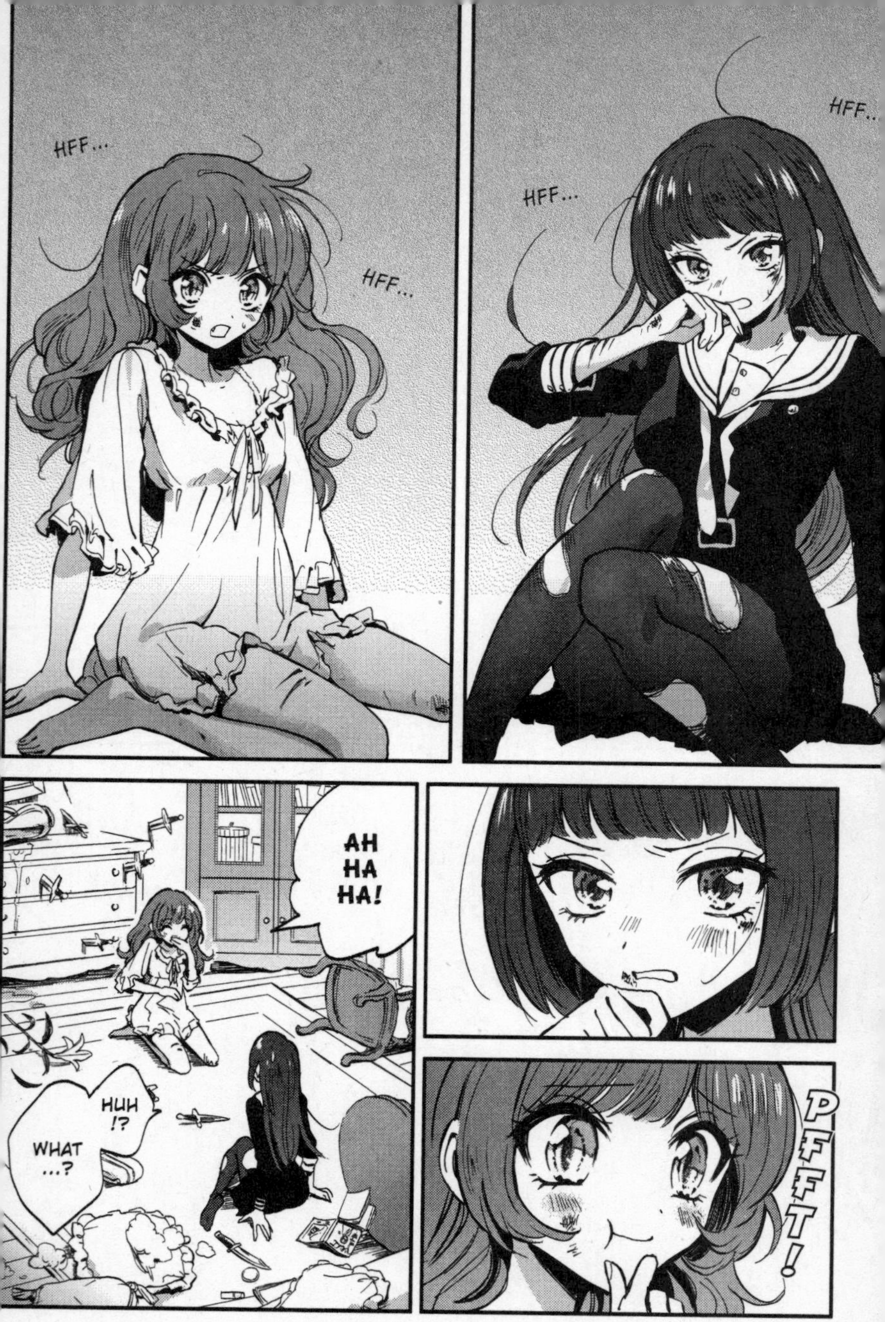
HFF...
HFF...
HFF...
HFF...
PFFFT!
AH HA HA!
HUH!?
WHAT...?

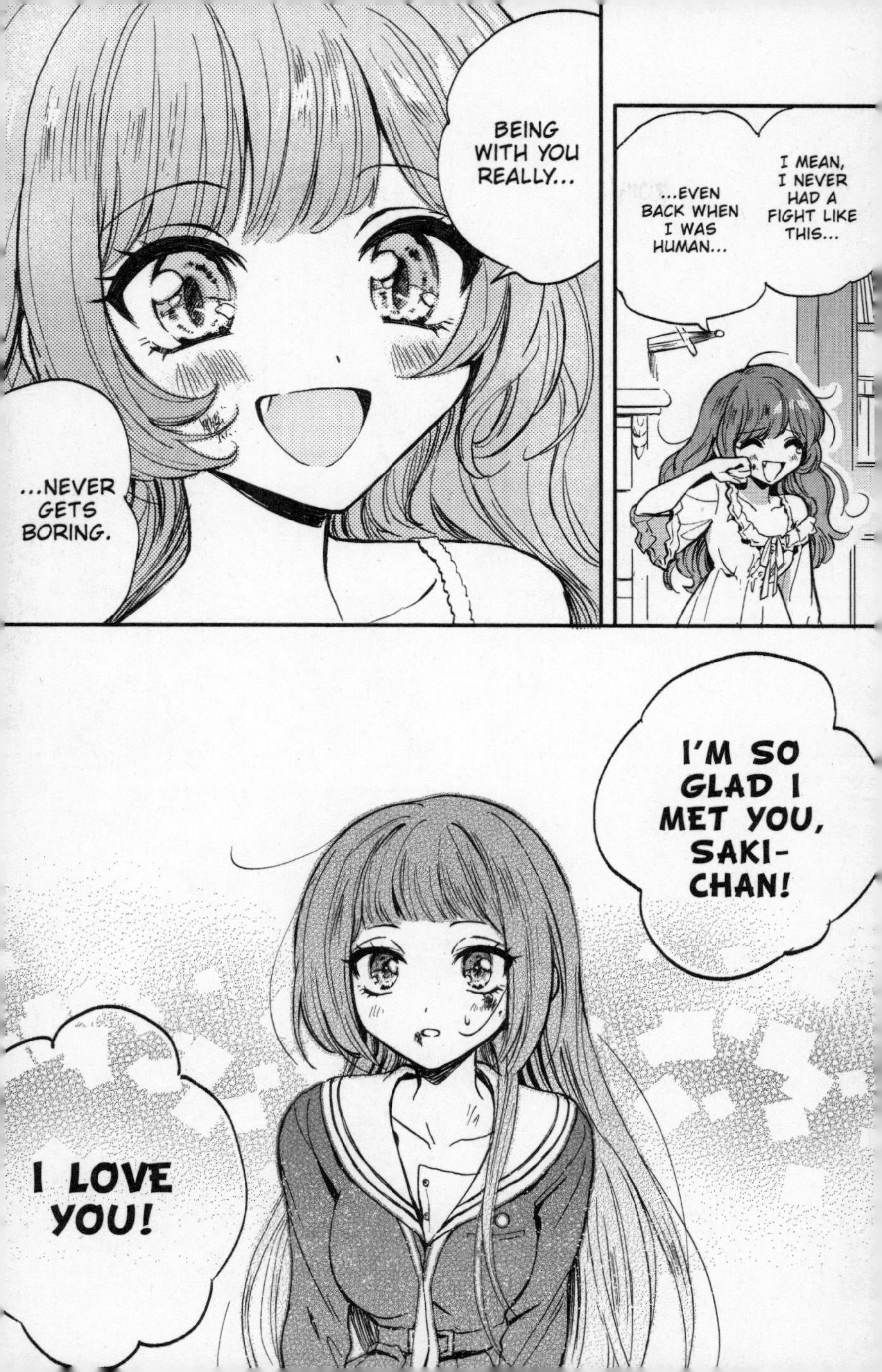
I MEAN, I NEVER HAD A FIGHT LIKE THIS...
...EVEN BACK WHEN I WAS HUMAN...
BEING WITH YOU REALLY...
...NEVER GETS BORING.
I'M SO GLAD I MET YOU, SAKI-CHAN!
I LOVE YOU!

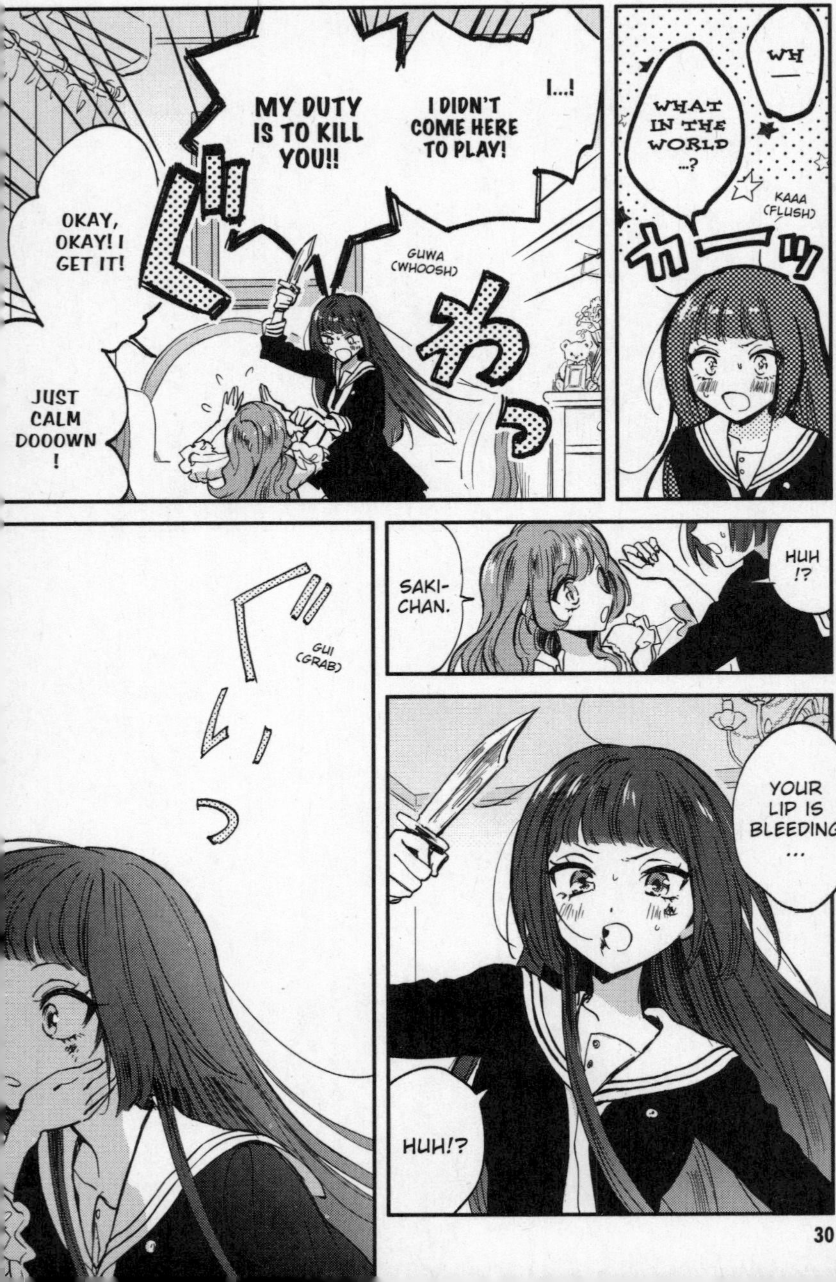
WH—
WHAT IN THE WORLD ...?
KAAA (FLUSH)
I...!
I DIDN'T COME HERE TO PLAY!
MY DUTY IS TO KILL YOU!!
GUWA (WHOOSH)
OKAY, OKAY! I GET IT!
JUST CALM DOOOWN!
HUH!?
SAKI-CHAN.
YOUR LIP IS BLEEDING ...
HUH!?
GUI (GRAB)

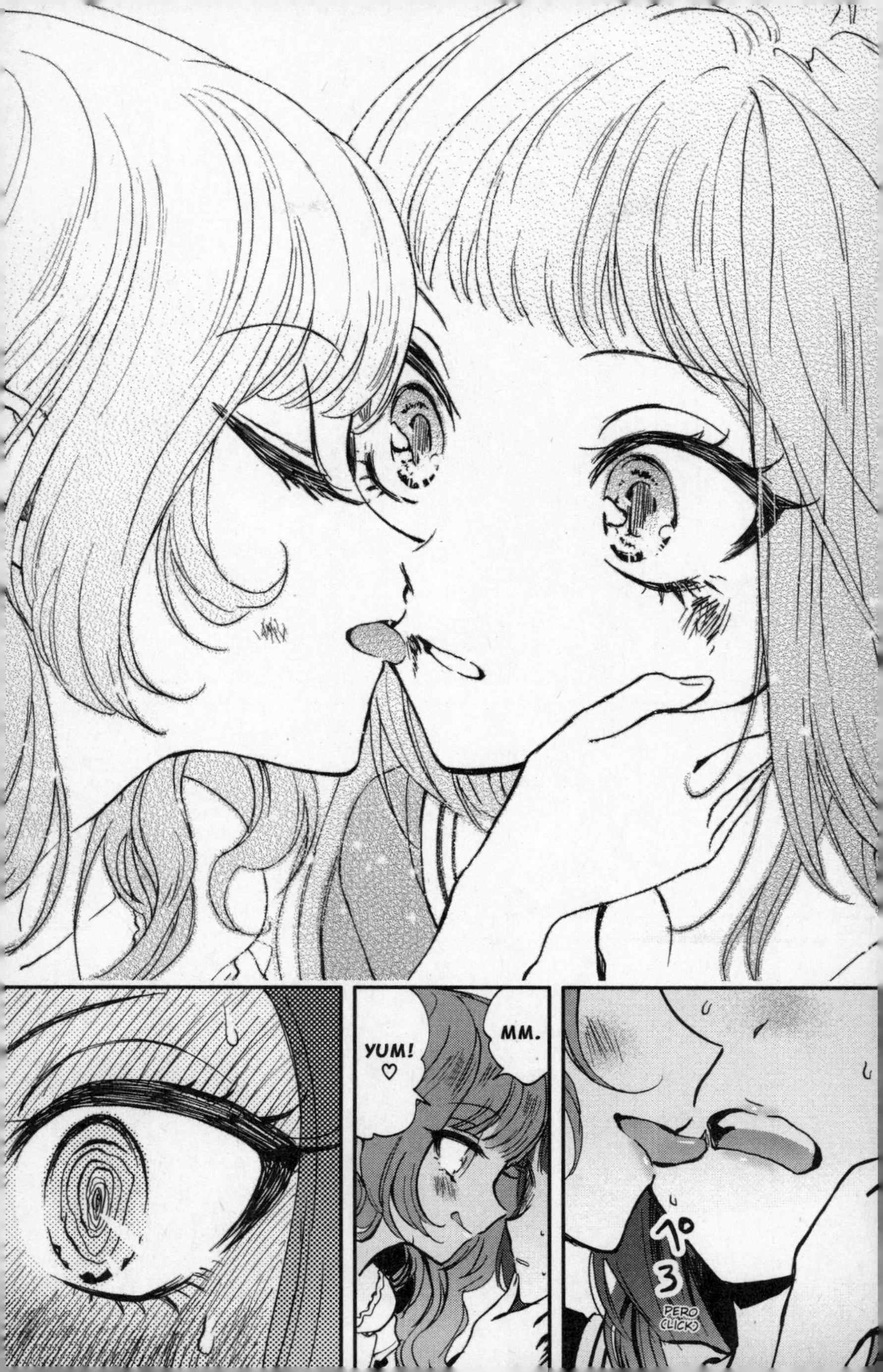
PERO (CLICK)
MM.
YUM! ♡

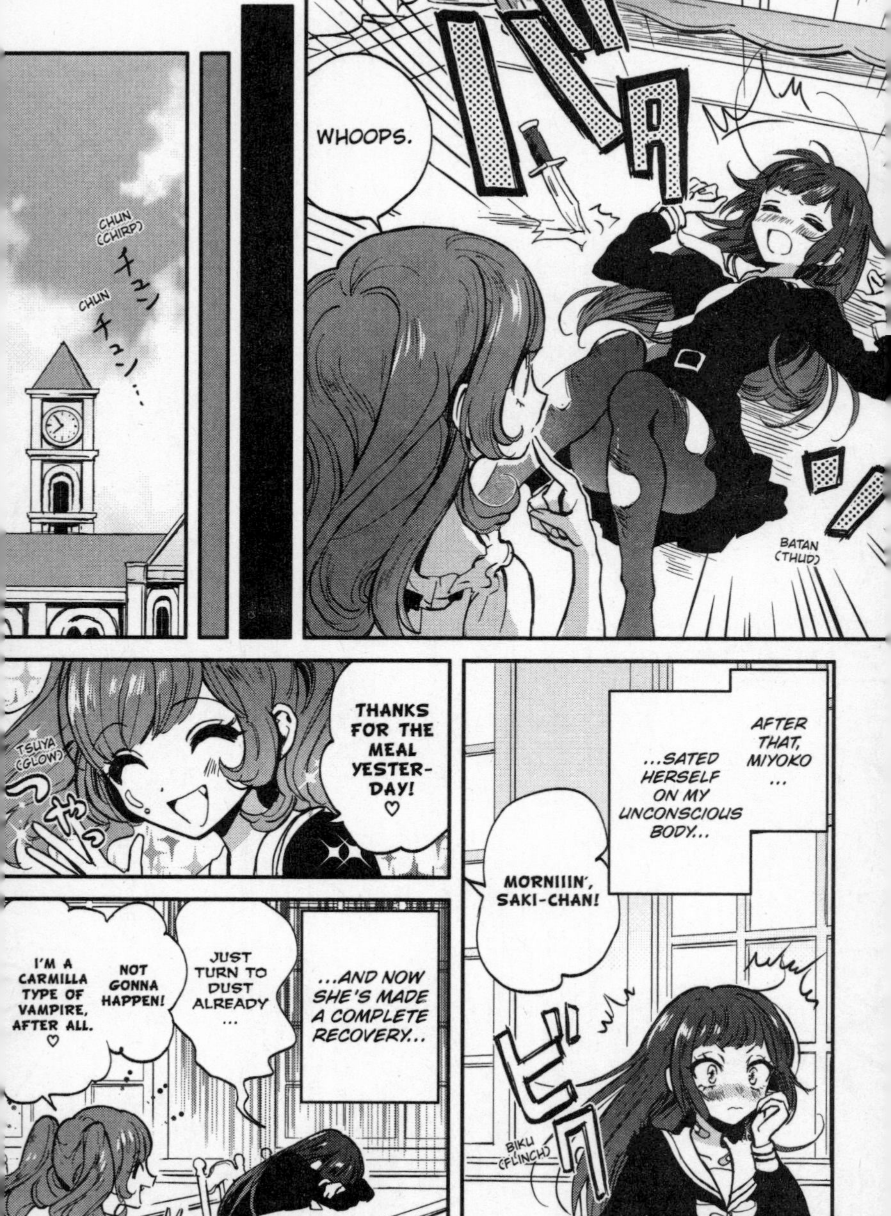
WHOOPS.
BATAN (THUD)
CHUN (CHIRP)
チュン
CHUN
チュン…
AFTER THAT, MIYOKO…
…SATED HERSELF ON MY UNCONSCIOUS BODY…
MORNIIIN', SAKI-CHAN!
BIKU (FLINCH)
THANKS FOR THE MEAL YESTER-DAY! ♡
TSUYA (GLOW)
…AND NOW SHE'S MADE A COMPLETE RECOVERY…
JUST TURN TO DUST ALREADY…
NOT GONNA HAPPEN!
I'M A CARMILLA TYPE OF VAMPIRE, AFTER ALL. ♡

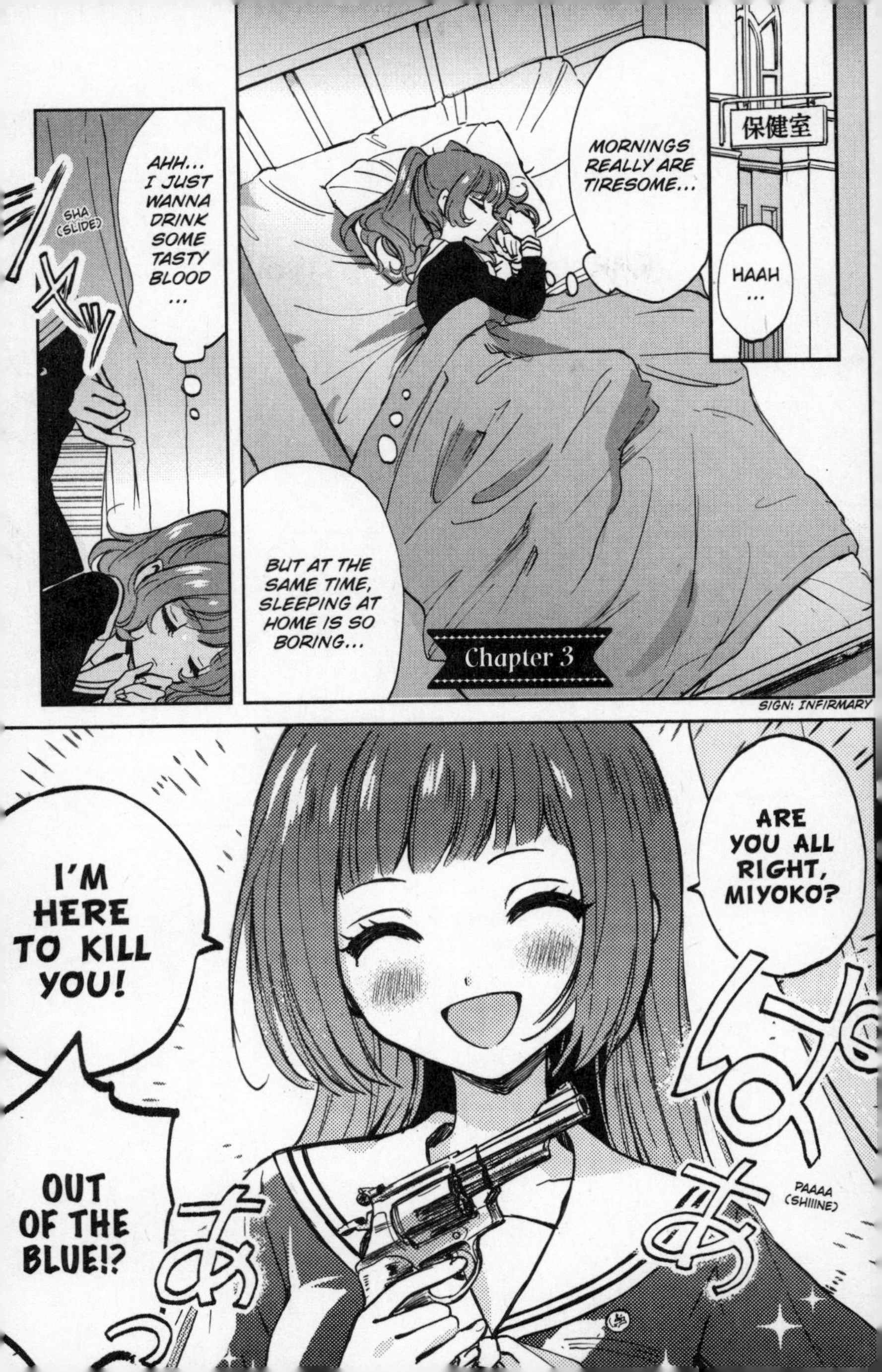
保健室
HAAH...
MORNINGS REALLY ARE TIRESOME...
BUT AT THE SAME TIME, SLEEPING AT HOME IS SO BORING...
Chapter 3
AHH... I JUST WANNA DRINK SOME TASTY BLOOD...
SHA (SLIDE)
SIGN: INFIRMARY
ARE YOU ALL RIGHT, MIYOKO?
PAAAA (SHIIINE)
I'M HERE TO KILL YOU!
OUT OF THE BLUE!?

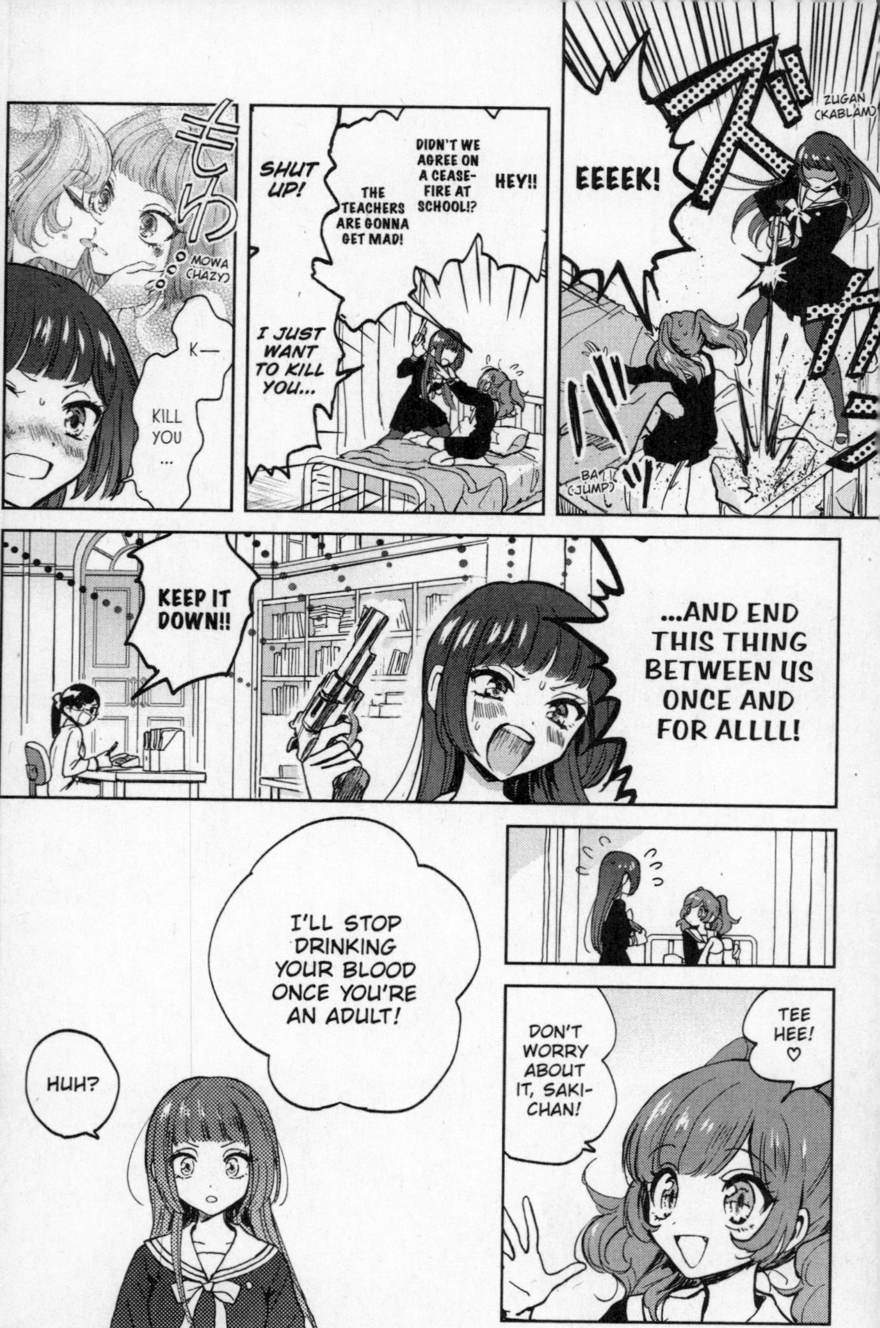
ZUGAN (KABLAM)
EEEEK!
BA (JUMP)
HEY!!
DIDN'T WE AGREE ON A CEASE-FIRE AT SCHOOL!?
THE TEACHERS ARE GONNA GET MAD!
SHUT UP!
I JUST WANT TO KILL YOU...
MOWA (HAZY)
K—
KILL YOU ...
...AND END THIS THING BETWEEN US ONCE AND FOR ALLLL!
KEEP IT DOWN!!
TEE HEE! ♡
DON'T WORRY ABOUT IT, SAKI-CHAN!
I'LL STOP DRINKING YOUR BLOOD ONCE YOU'RE AN ADULT!
HUH?

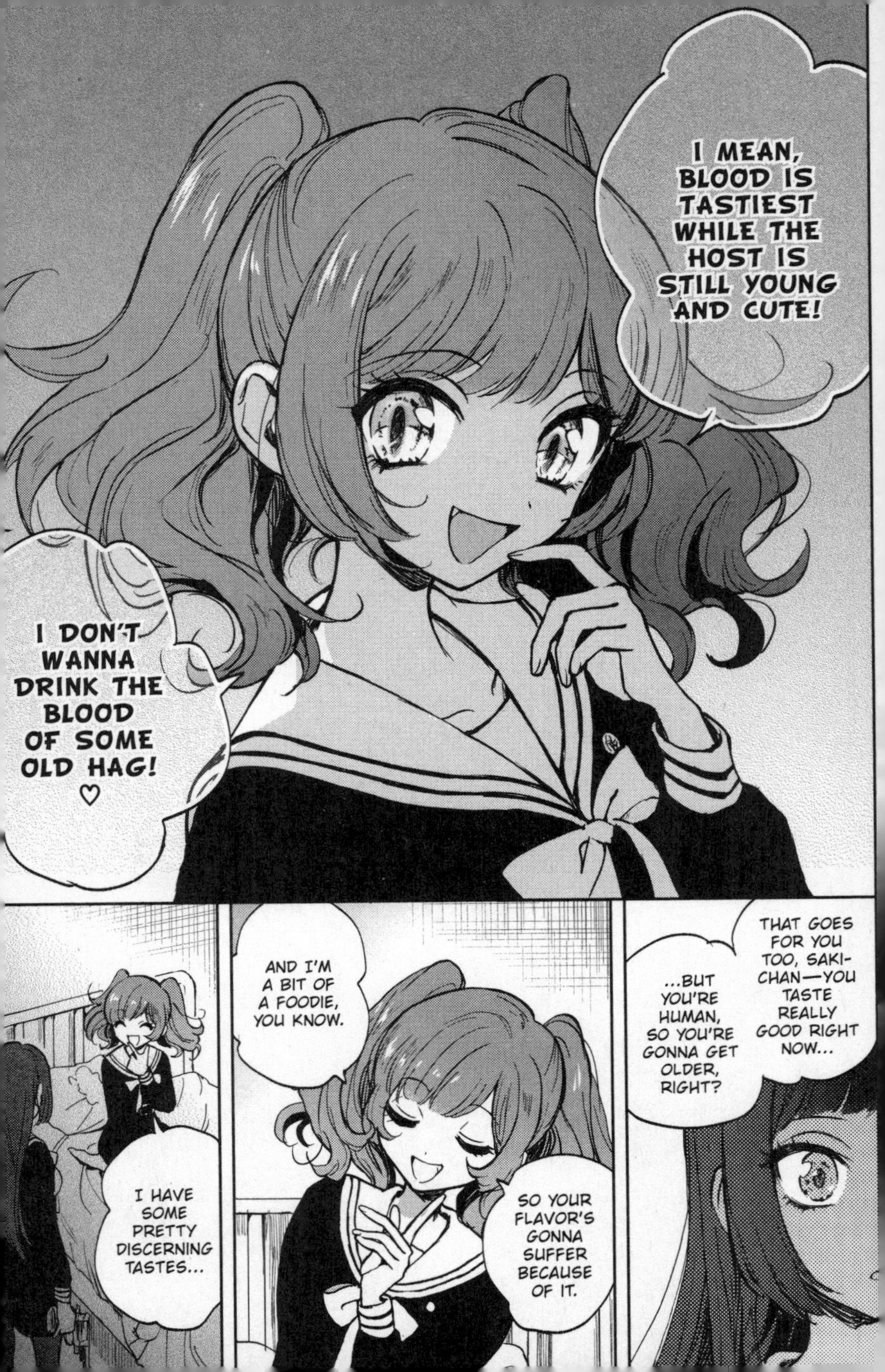
I MEAN, BLOOD IS TASTIEST WHILE THE HOST IS STILL YOUNG AND CUTE!
I DON'T WANNA DRINK THE BLOOD OF SOME OLD HAG! ♡
THAT GOES FOR YOU TOO, SAKI-CHAN—YOU TASTE REALLY GOOD RIGHT NOW...
...BUT YOU'RE HUMAN, SO YOU'RE GONNA GET OLDER, RIGHT?
SO YOUR FLAVOR'S GONNA SUFFER BECAUSE OF IT.
AND I'M A BIT OF A FOODIE, YOU KNOW.
I HAVE SOME PRETTY DISCERNING TASTES...

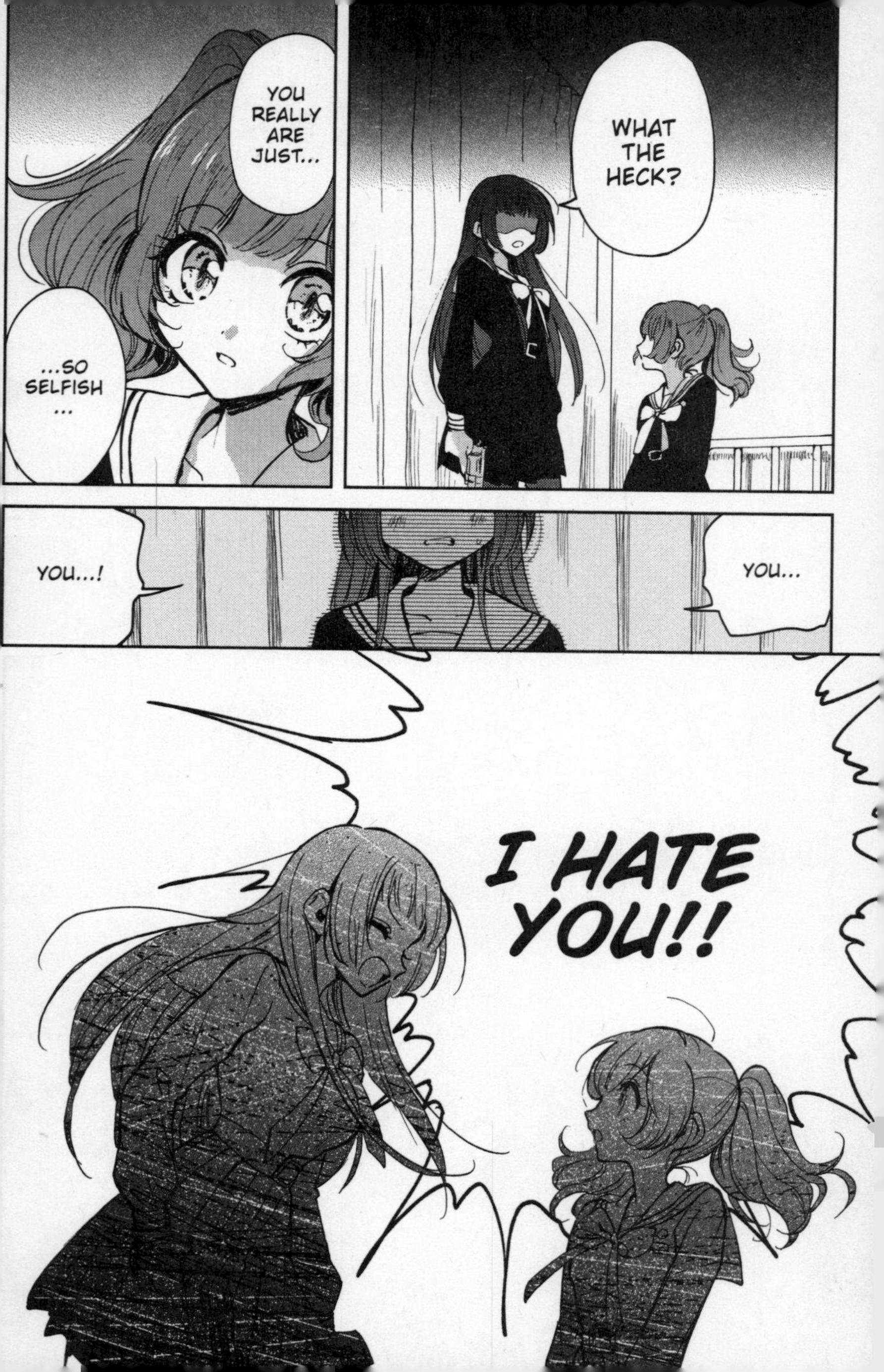
WHAT THE HECK?
YOU REALLY ARE JUST...
...SO SELFISH...
YOU...
YOU...!
I HATE YOU!!

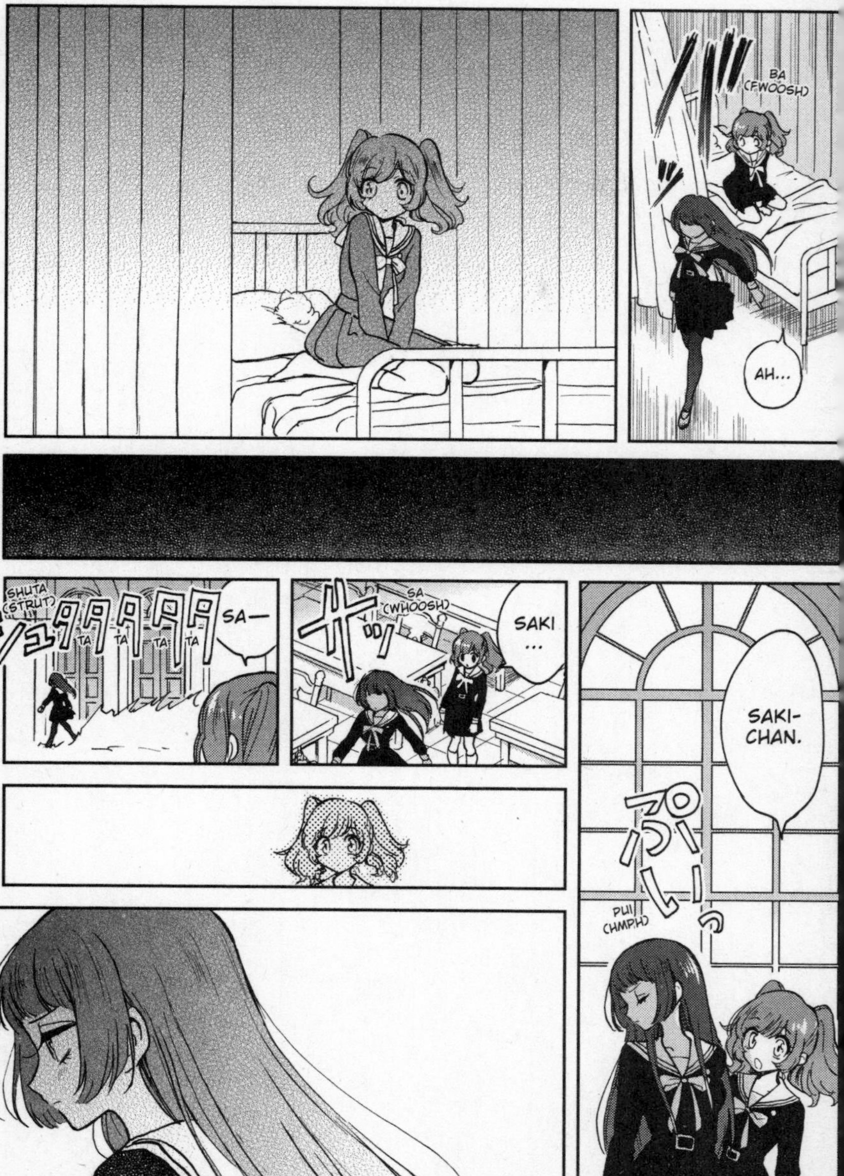
BA (F.WOOSH)
AH...
SAKI-CHAN.
PUI (HMPH)
SA (WHOOSH)
SAKI ...
SHUTA (STRUT)
TA TA TA TA
SA—

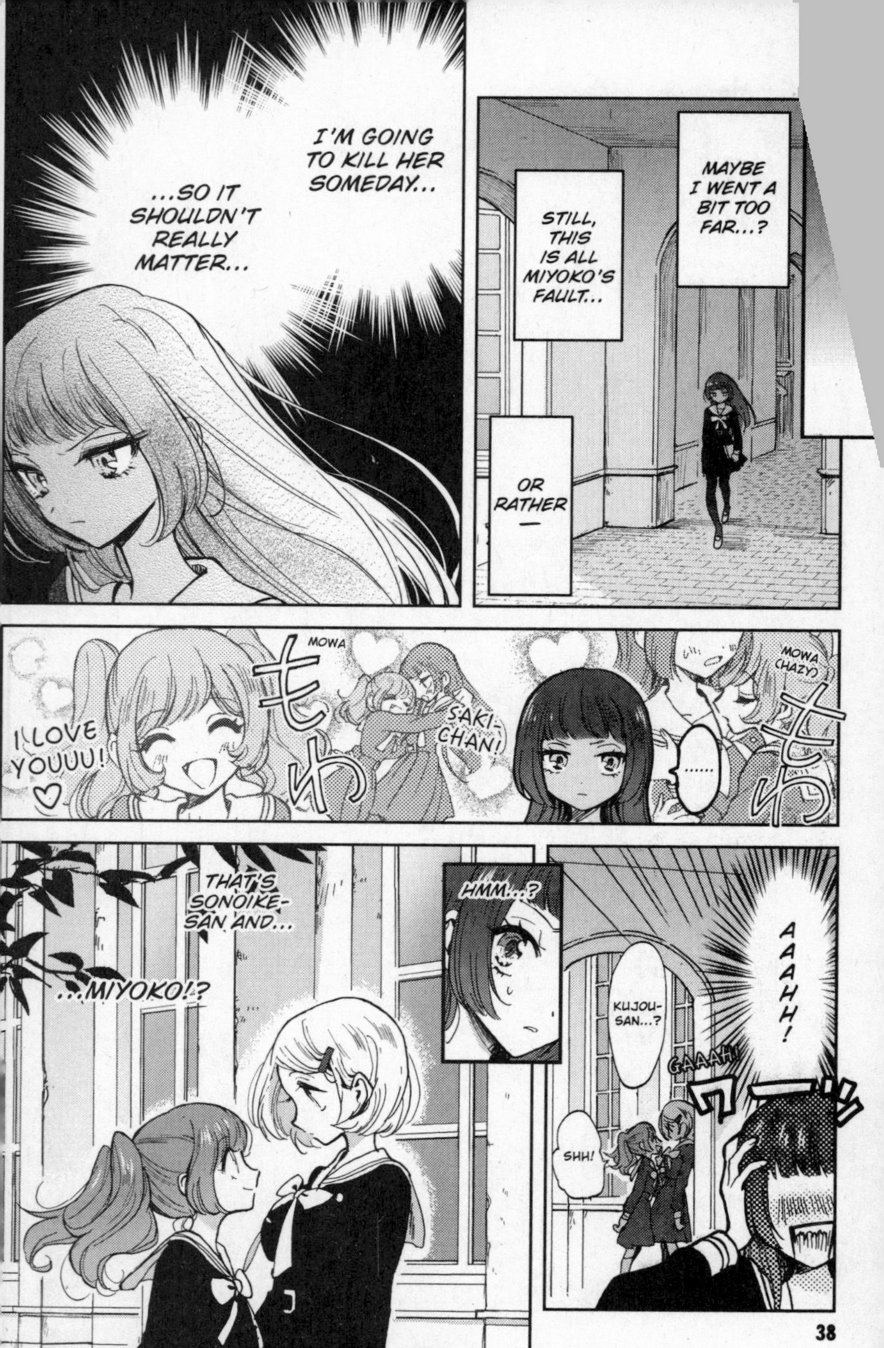
MAYBE I WENT A BIT TOO FAR...?
STILL, THIS IS ALL MIYOKO'S FAULT...
OR RATHER —
I'M GOING TO KILL HER SOMEDAY...
...SO IT SHOULDN'T REALLY MATTER...
MOWA (HAZY)
もわ
......
SAKI-CHAN!
MOWA
もわ
I LOVE YOUUU! ♡
AAAAHH!
GAAAH!
ワーッ
KUJOU-SAN...?
SHH!
HMM...?
THAT'S SONOIKE-SAN AND...
...MIYOKO!?

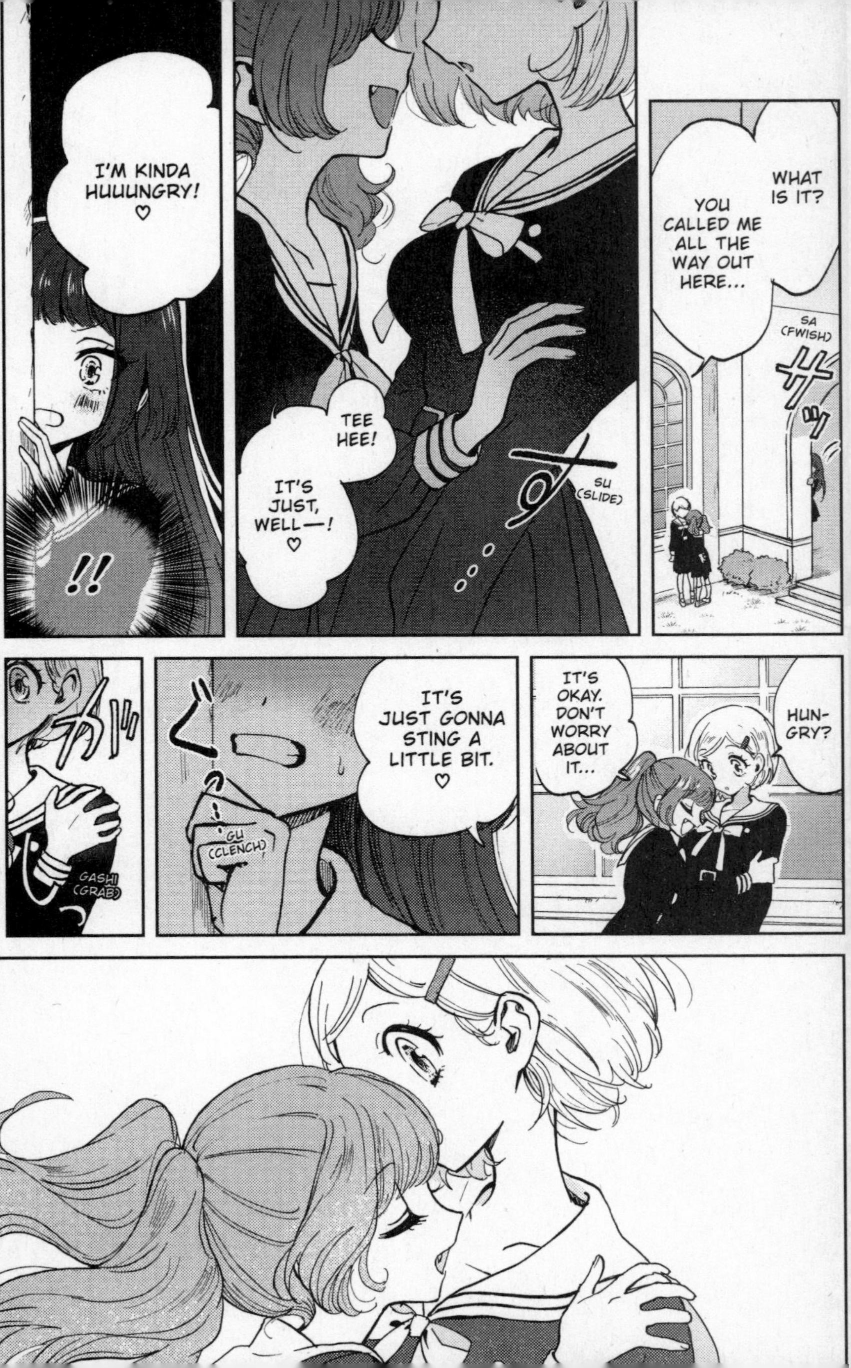
WHAT IS IT?
YOU CALLED ME ALL THE WAY OUT HERE...
SA (FWISH)
TEE HEE!
IT'S JUST, WELL—! ♡
SU (SLIDE)
I'M KINDA HUUUNGRY! ♡
!!
HUN-GRY?
IT'S OKAY. DON'T WORRY ABOUT IT...
IT'S JUST GONNA STING A LITTLE BIT. ♡
GU (CLENCH)
GASHI (GRAB)

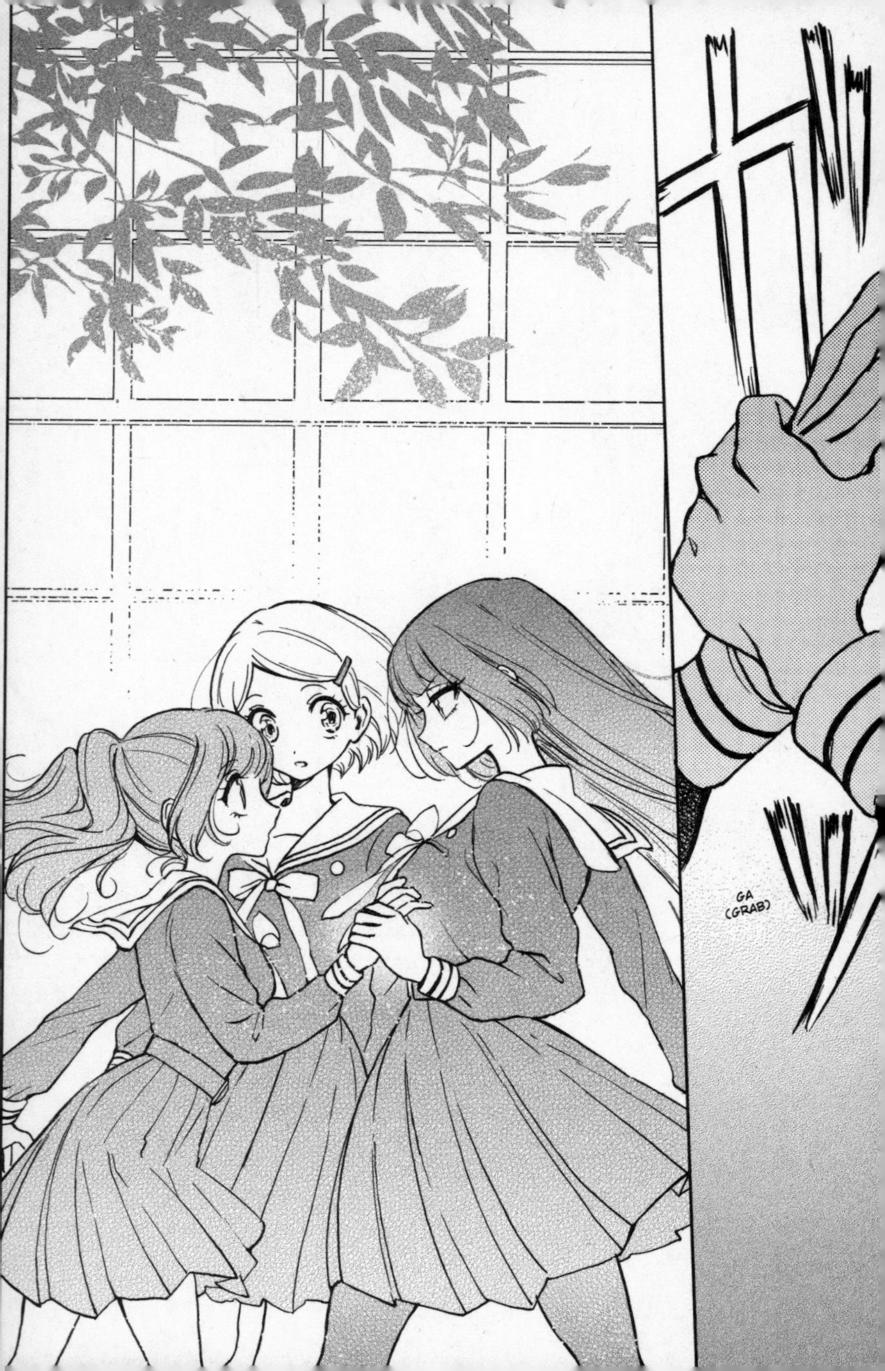
GA
(GRAB)

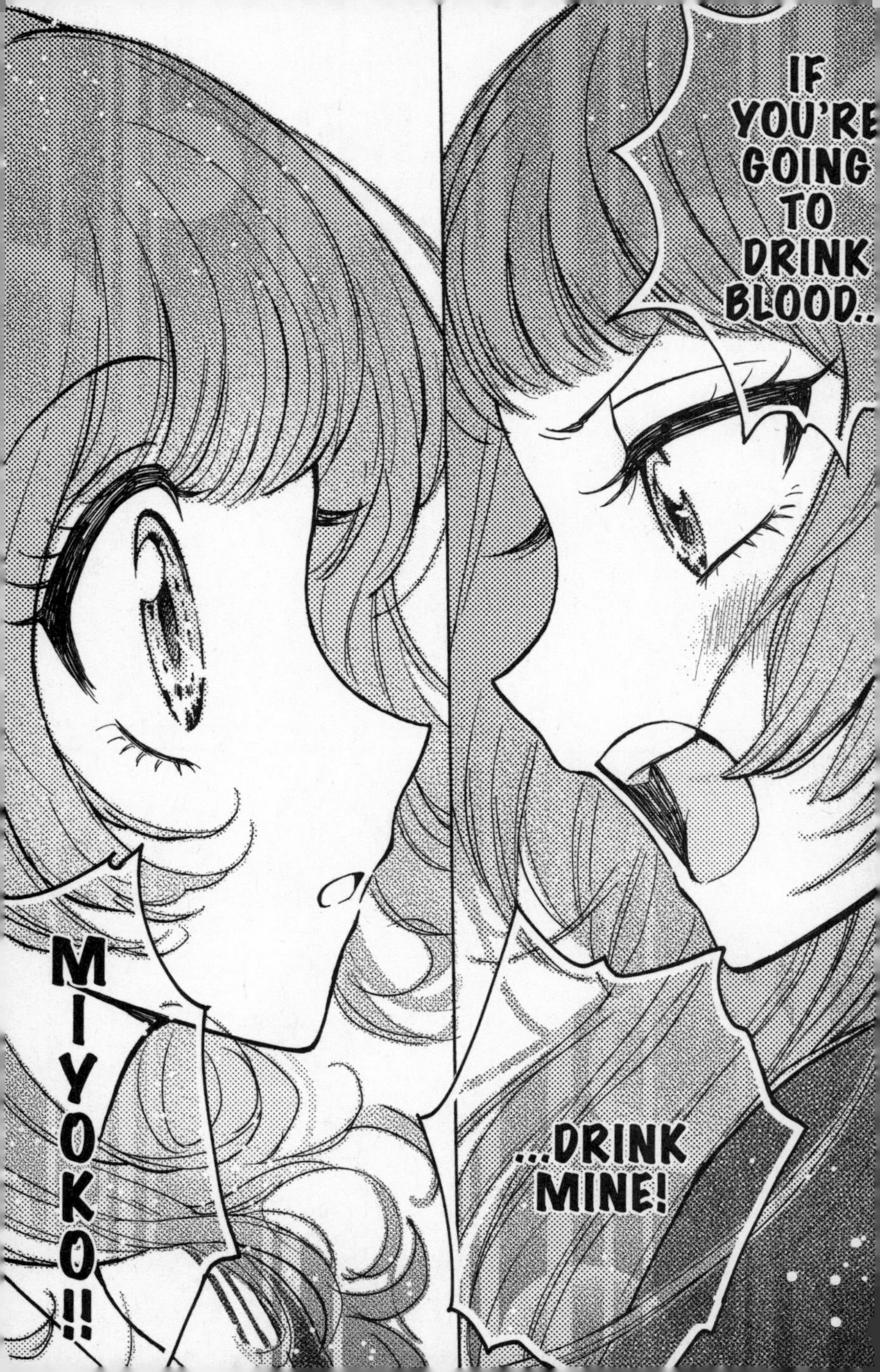
IF YOU'RE GOING TO DRINK BLOOD...
...DRINK MINE!
MIYOKO!!

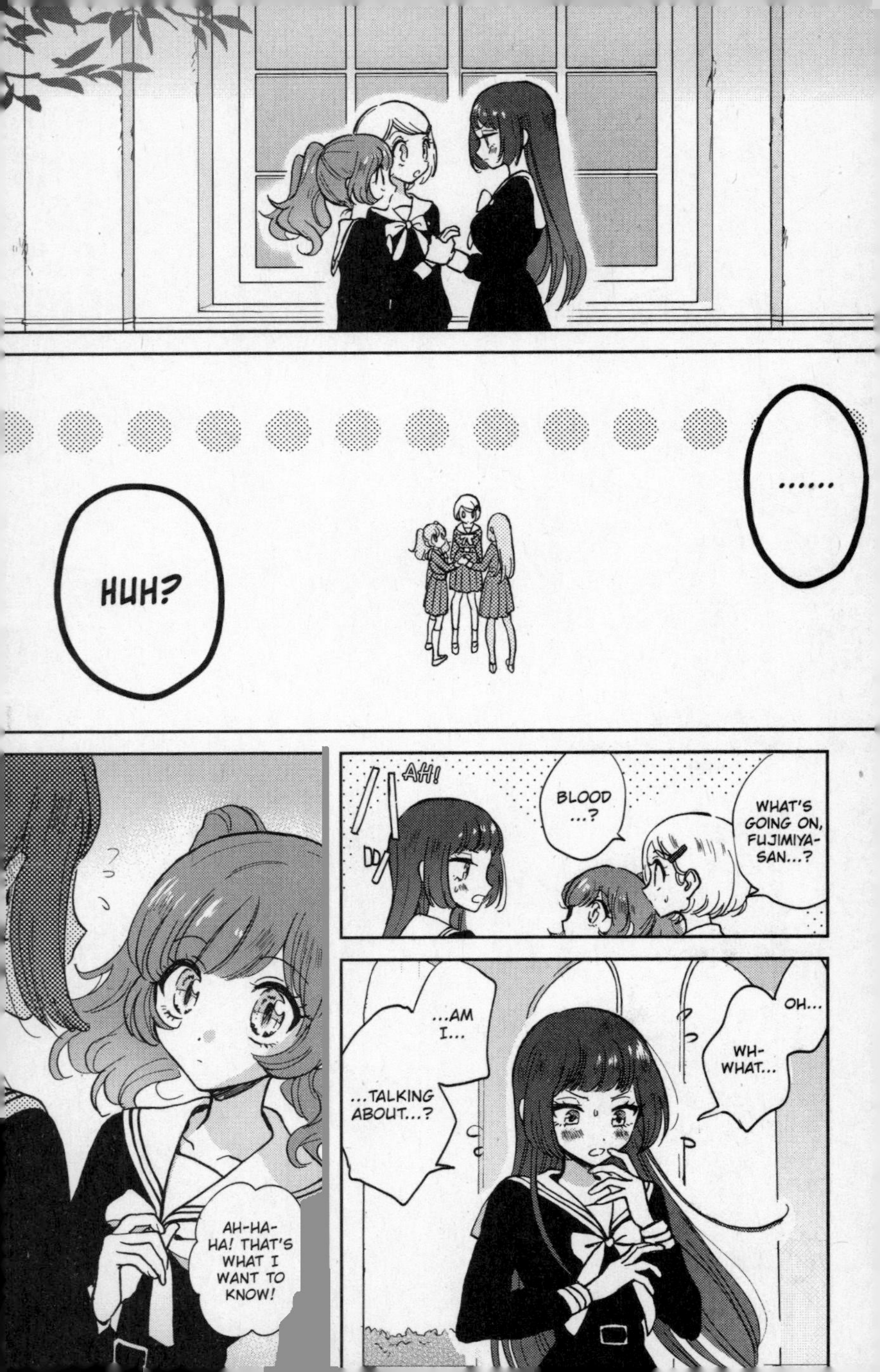
......
HUH?
WHAT'S GOING ON, FUJIMIYA-SAN...?
BLOOD ...?
AH!
OH...
WH-WHAT...
...AM I...
...TALKING ABOUT...?
AH-HA-HA! THAT'S WHAT I WANT TO KNOW!

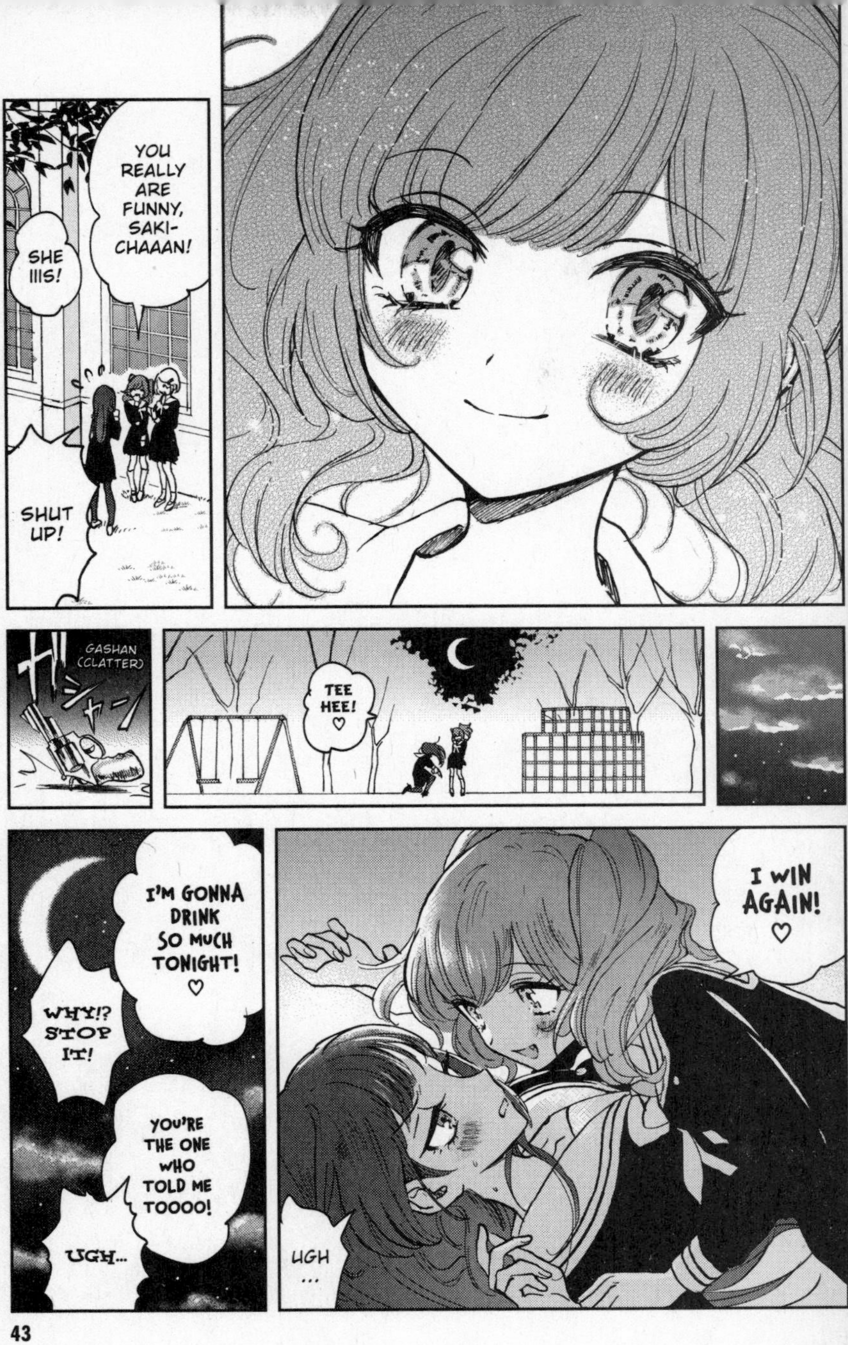

YOU REALLY ARE FUNNY, SAKI-CHAAAN!
SHE IIIS!
SHUT UP!
TEE HEE! ♡
GASHAN (CLATTER)
ガシャーン
I WIN AGAIN! ♡
UGH ...
I'M GONNA DRINK SO MUCH TONIGHT! ♡
WHY!? STOP IT!
YOU'RE THE ONE WHO TOLD ME TOOOO!
UGH...

Killing me!

1

Chapter 4

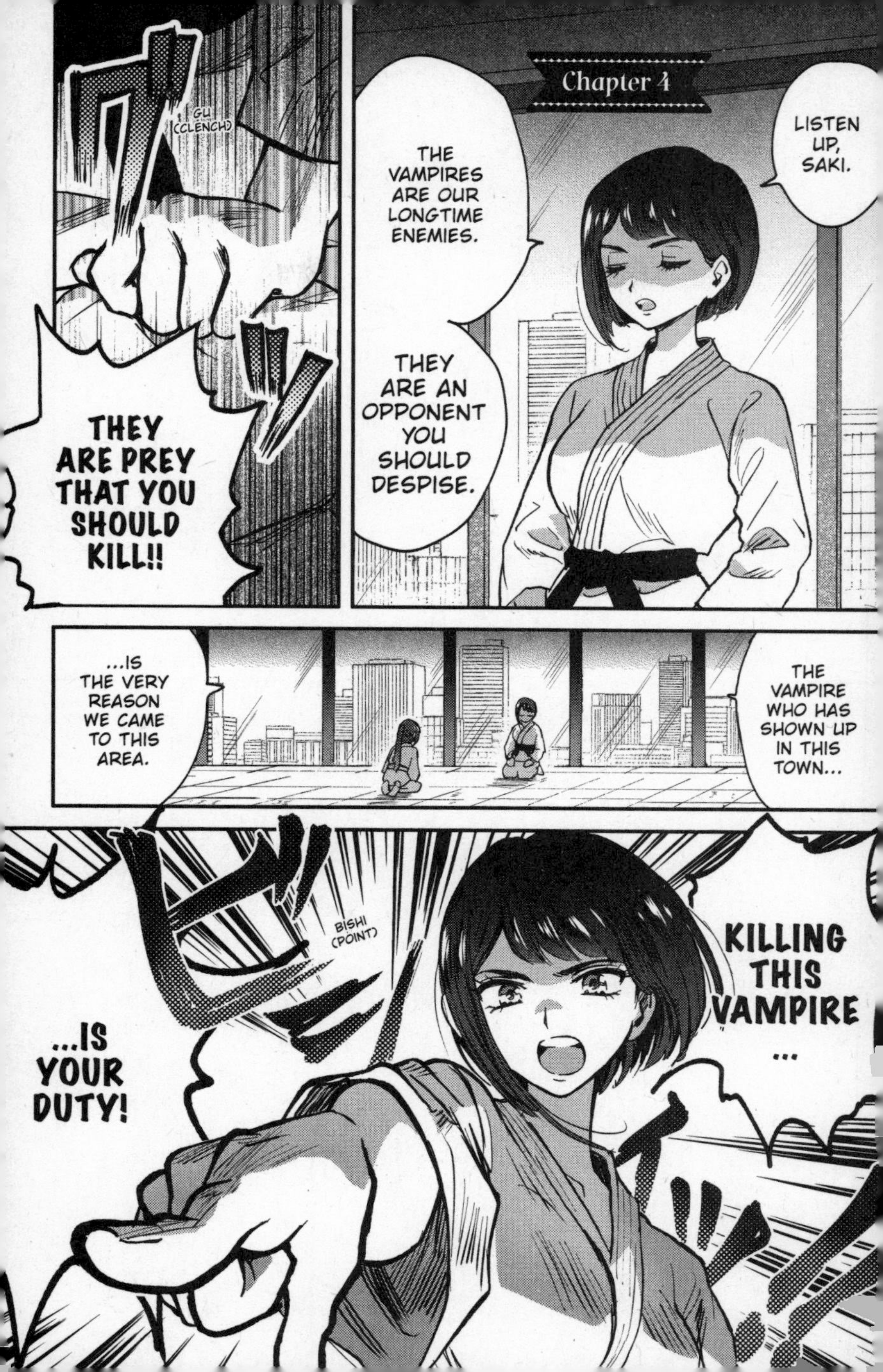
LISTEN UP, SAKI.
THE VAMPIRES ARE OUR LONGTIME ENEMIES.
THEY ARE AN OPPONENT YOU SHOULD DESPISE.
GU (CLENCH)
THEY ARE PREY THAT YOU SHOULD KILL!!
THE VAMPIRE WHO HAS SHOWN UP IN THIS TOWN...
...IS THE VERY REASON WE CAME TO THIS AREA.
KILLING THIS VAMPIRE...
BISHI (POINT)
...IS YOUR DUTY!

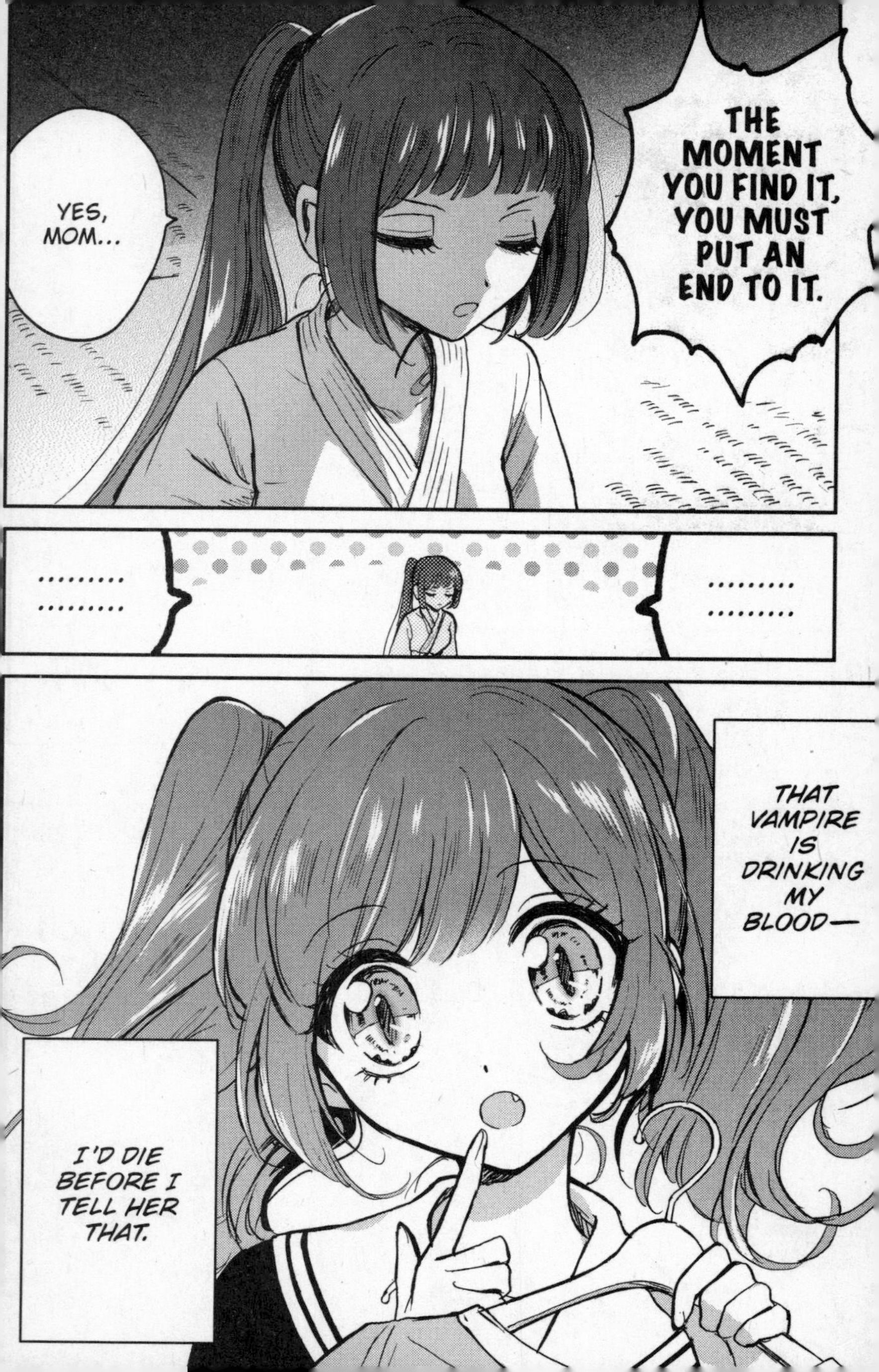
THE MOMENT YOU FIND IT, YOU MUST PUT AN END TO IT.
YES, MOM...
....
....
....
....
THAT VAMPIRE IS DRINKING MY BLOOD—
I'D DIE BEFORE I TELL HER THAT.

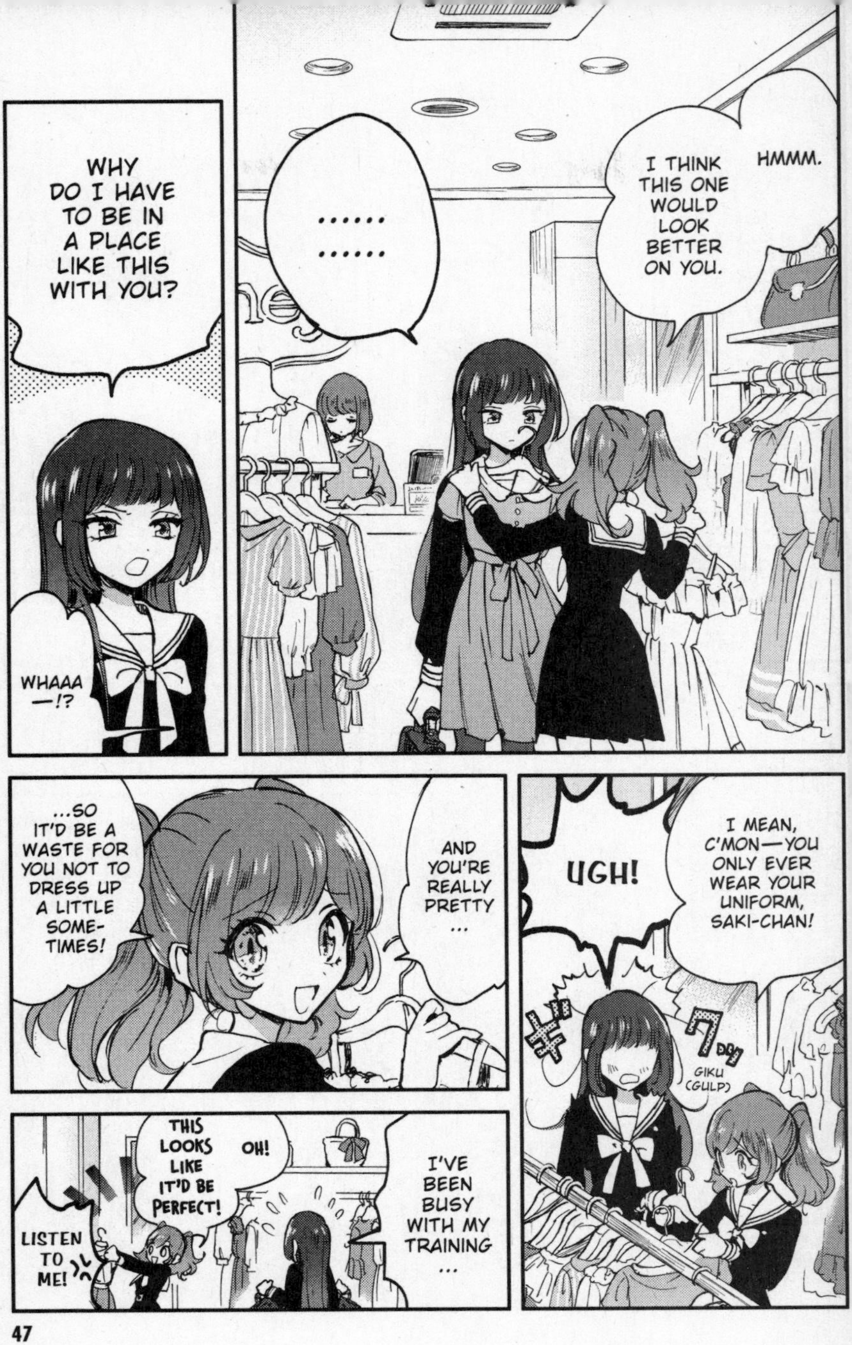
HMMM.
I THINK THIS ONE WOULD LOOK BETTER ON YOU.
......
......
WHY DO I HAVE TO BE IN A PLACE LIKE THIS WITH YOU?
WHAAA—!?
I MEAN, C'MON—YOU ONLY EVER WEAR YOUR UNIFORM, SAKI-CHAN!
UGH!
GIKU (GULP)
AND YOU'RE REALLY PRETTY ...
...SO IT'D BE A WASTE FOR YOU NOT TO DRESS UP A LITTLE SOME-TIMES!
I'VE BEEN BUSY WITH MY TRAINING ...
OH!
THIS LOOKS LIKE IT'D BE PERFECT!
LISTEN TO ME!

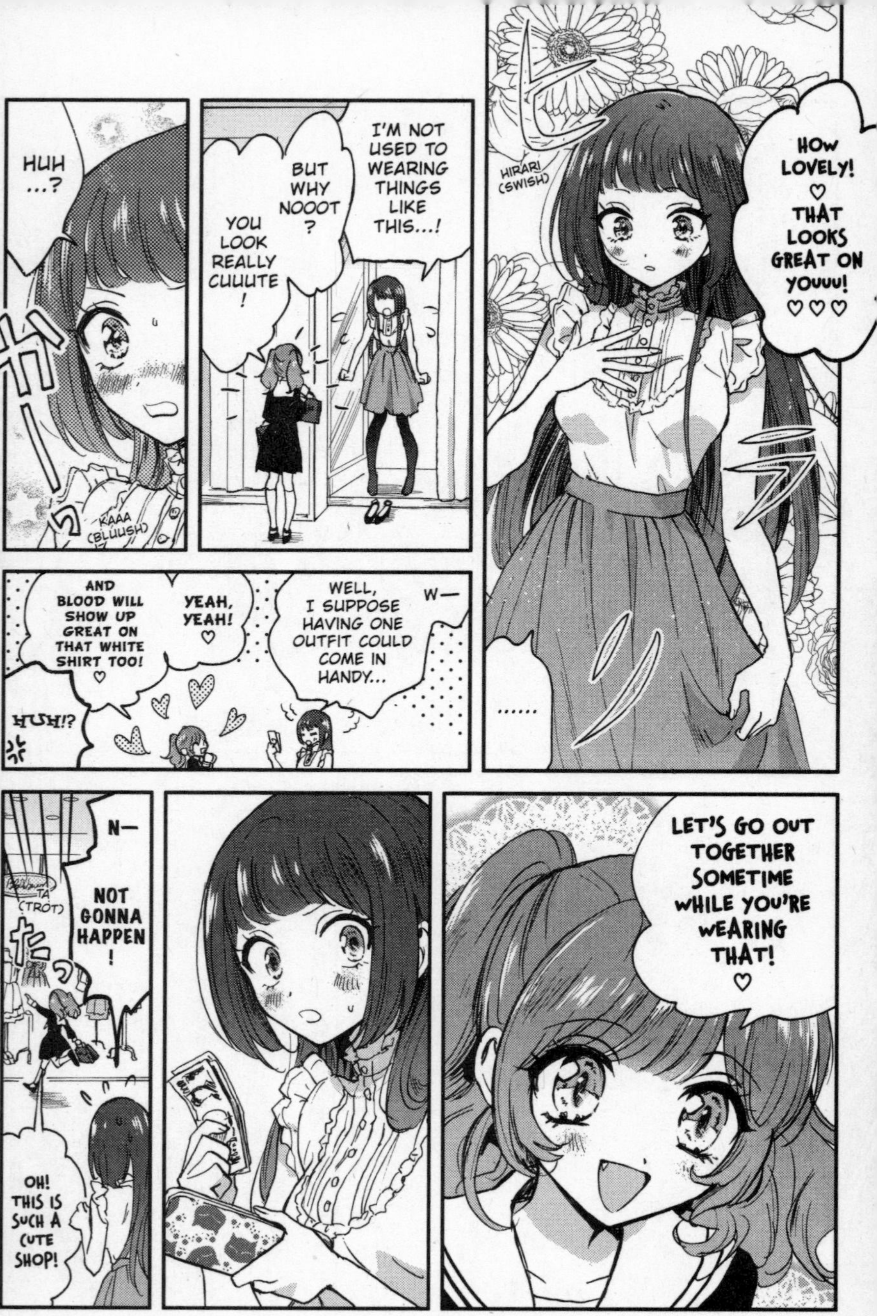
HOW LOVELY! ♡ THAT LOOKS GREAT ON YOUUU! ♡♡♡
HIRARI (SWISH)
......
I'M NOT USED TO WEARING THINGS LIKE THIS...!
BUT WHY NOOOT?
YOU LOOK REALLY CUUUTE!
HUH...?
KAAA (BLUUSH)
W—
WELL, I SUPPOSE HAVING ONE OUTFIT COULD COME IN HANDY...
YEAH, YEAH! ♡
AND BLOOD WILL SHOW UP GREAT ON THAT WHITE SHIRT TOO! ♡
HUH!?
LET'S GO OUT TOGETHER SOMETIME WHILE YOU'RE WEARING THAT! ♡
N—
NOT GONNA HAPPEN!
TA (TROT)
OH! THIS IS SUCH A CUTE SHOP!

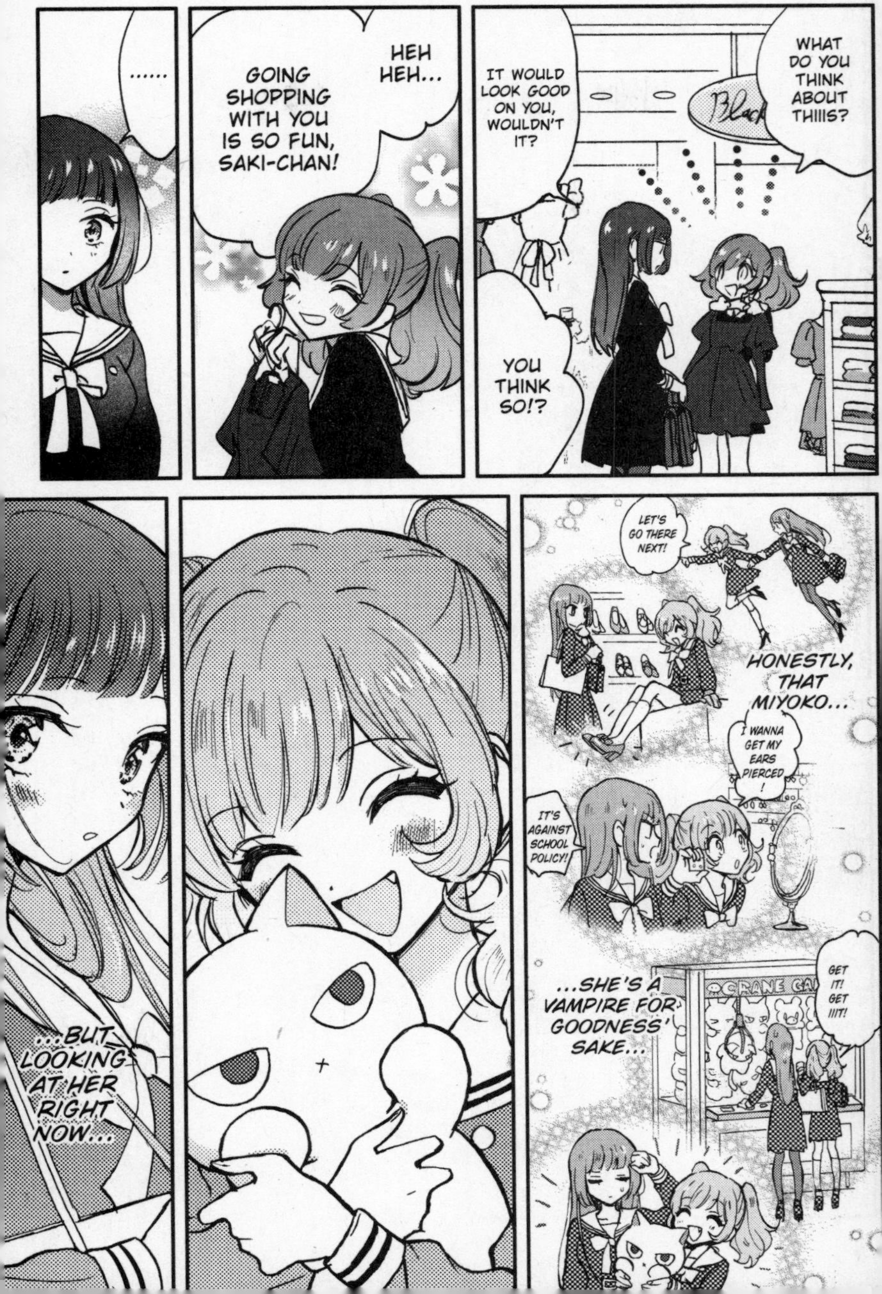
WHAT DO YOU THINK ABOUT THIIIS?
IT WOULD LOOK GOOD ON YOU, WOULDN'T IT?
YOU THINK SO!?
HEH HEH...
GOING SHOPPING WITH YOU IS SO FUN, SAKI-CHAN!
......
LET'S GO THERE NEXT!
HONESTLY, THAT MIYOKO...
I WANNA GET MY EARS PIERCED!
IT'S AGAINST SCHOOL POLICY!
...SHE'S A VAMPIRE FOR GOODNESS' SAKE...
GET IT! GET IIIT!
...BUT LOOKING AT HER RIGHT NOW...

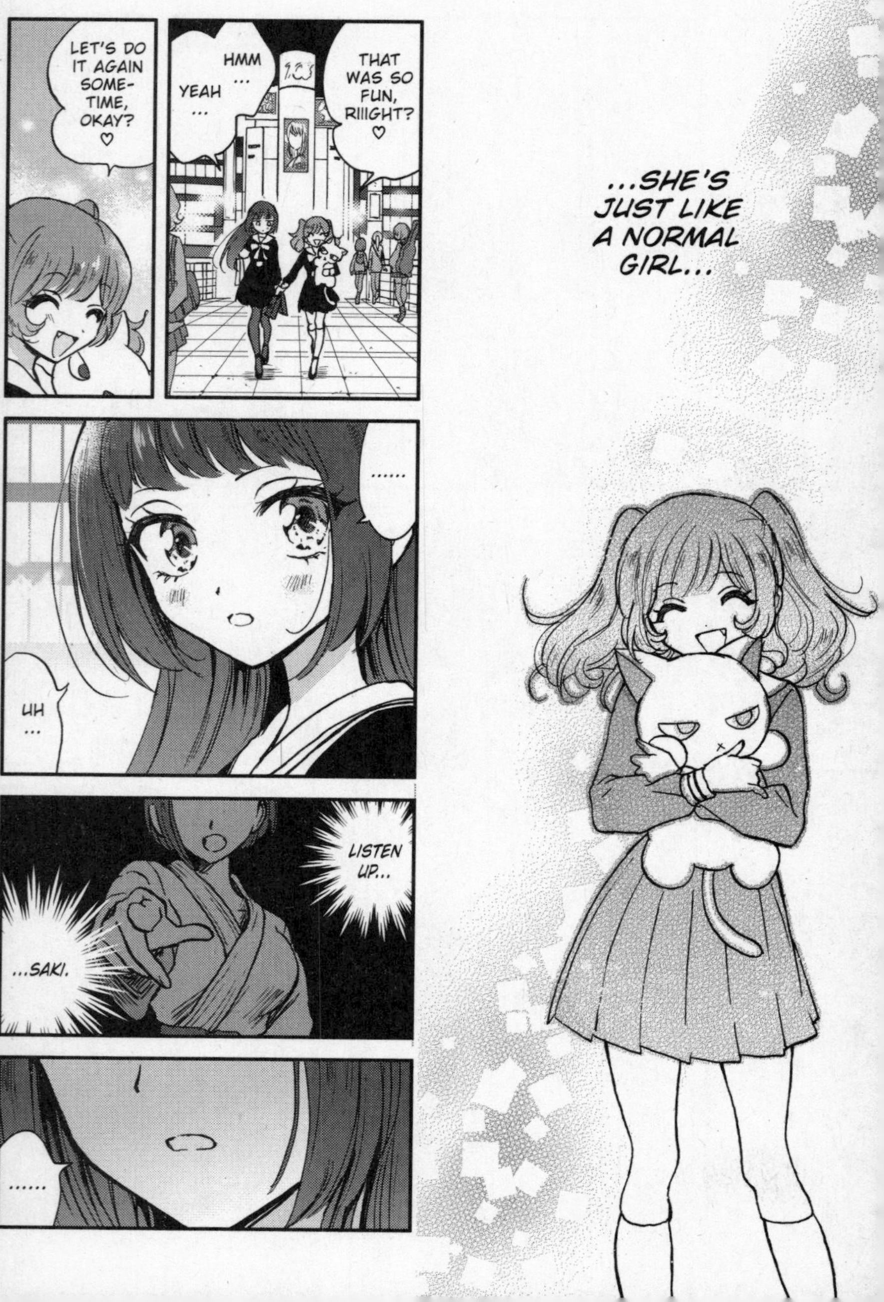
...SHE'S JUST LIKE A NORMAL GIRL...
THAT WAS SO FUN, RIIIGHT? ♡
HMM ... YEAH ...
LET'S DO IT AGAIN SOME-TIME, OKAY? ♡
......
UH ...
LISTEN UP...
...SAKI.
......

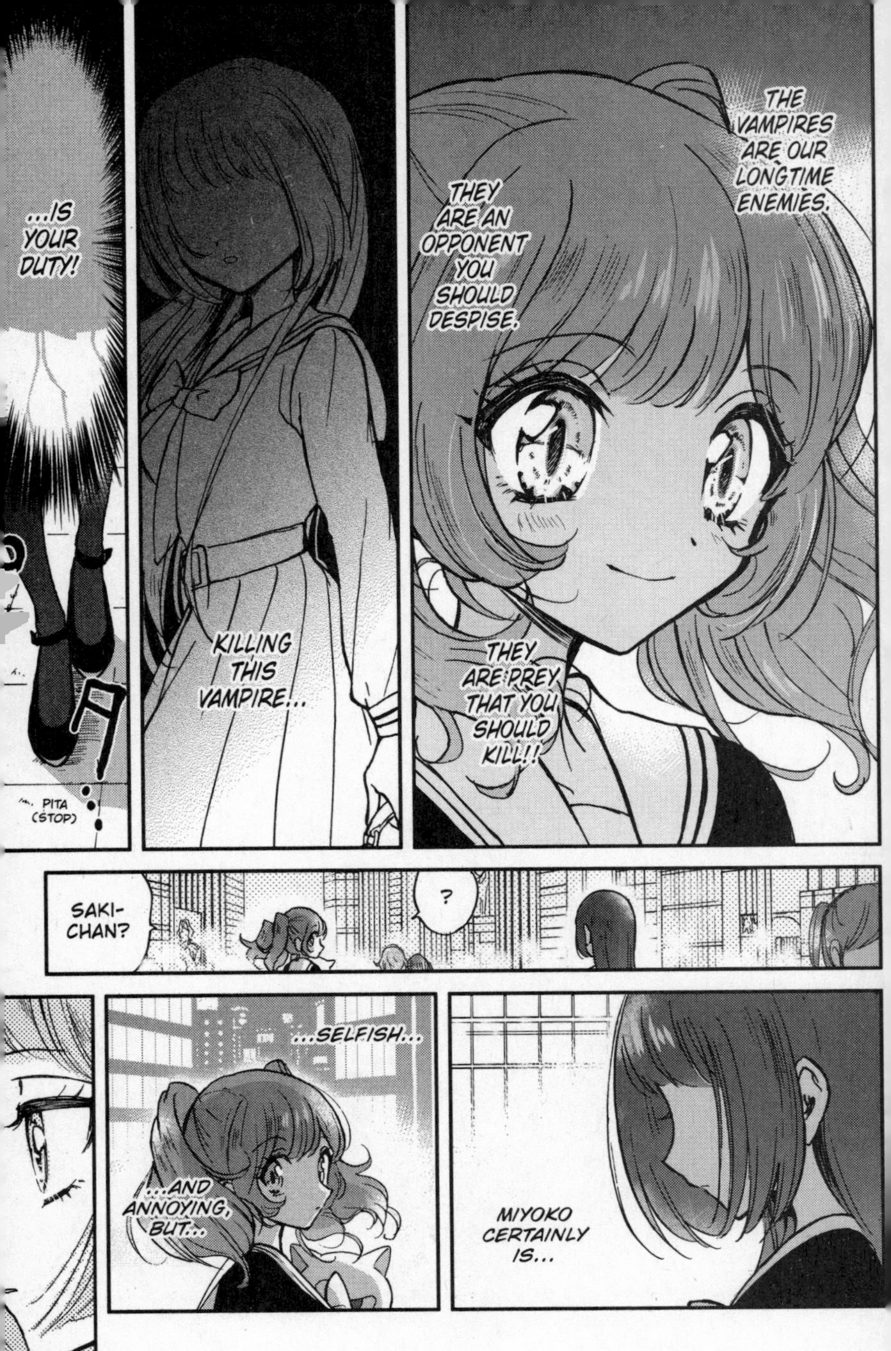
THE VAMPIRES ARE OUR LONGTIME ENEMIES.
THEY ARE AN OPPONENT YOU SHOULD DESPISE.
THEY ARE PREY THAT YOU SHOULD KILL!!
KILLING THIS VAMPIRE...
...IS YOUR DUTY!
PITA (STOP)
?
SAKI-CHAN?
MIYOKO CERTAINLY IS...
...SELFISH...
...AND ANNOYING, BUT...

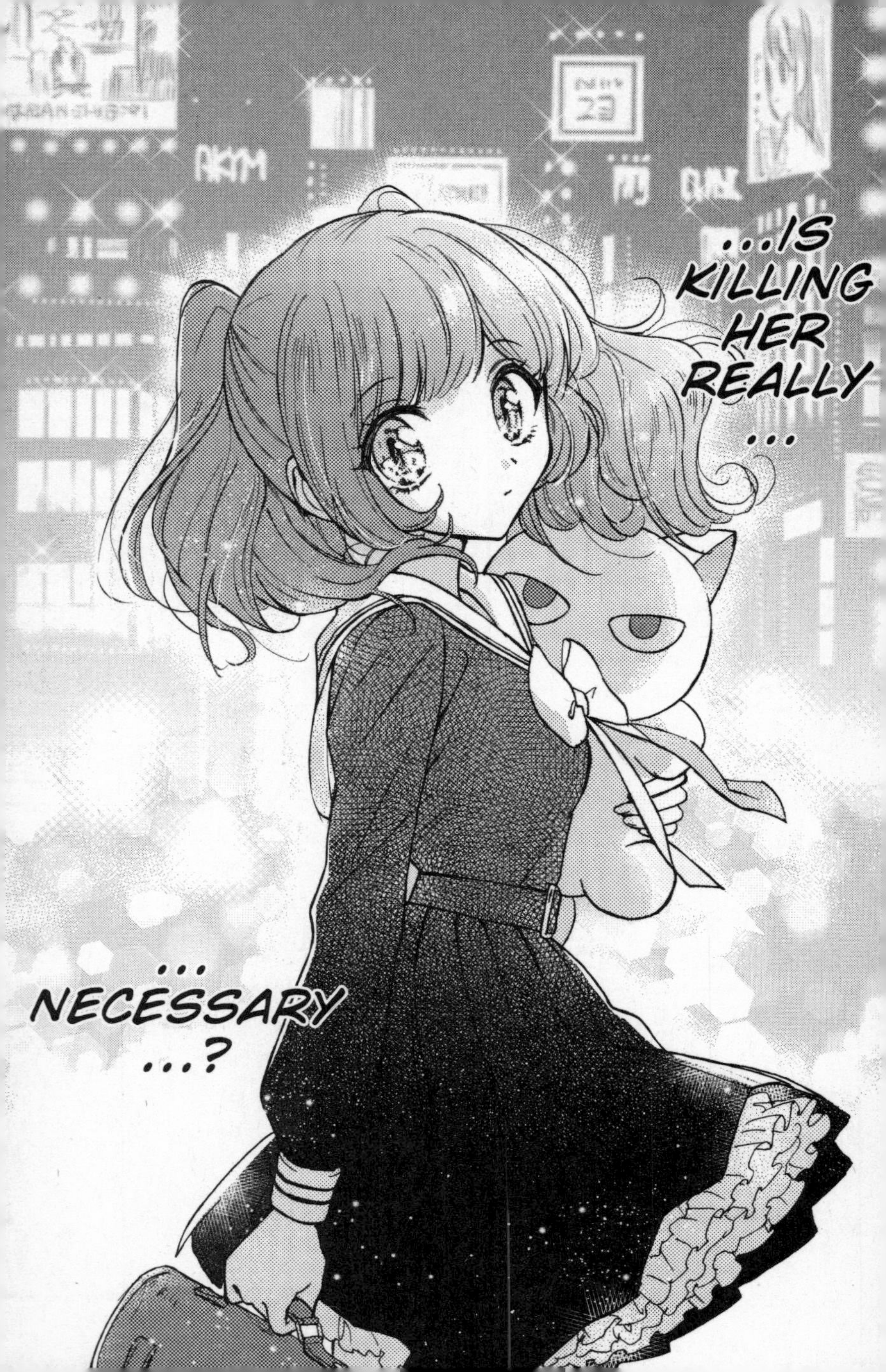
...IS KILLING HER REALLY ...
... NECESSARY ...?

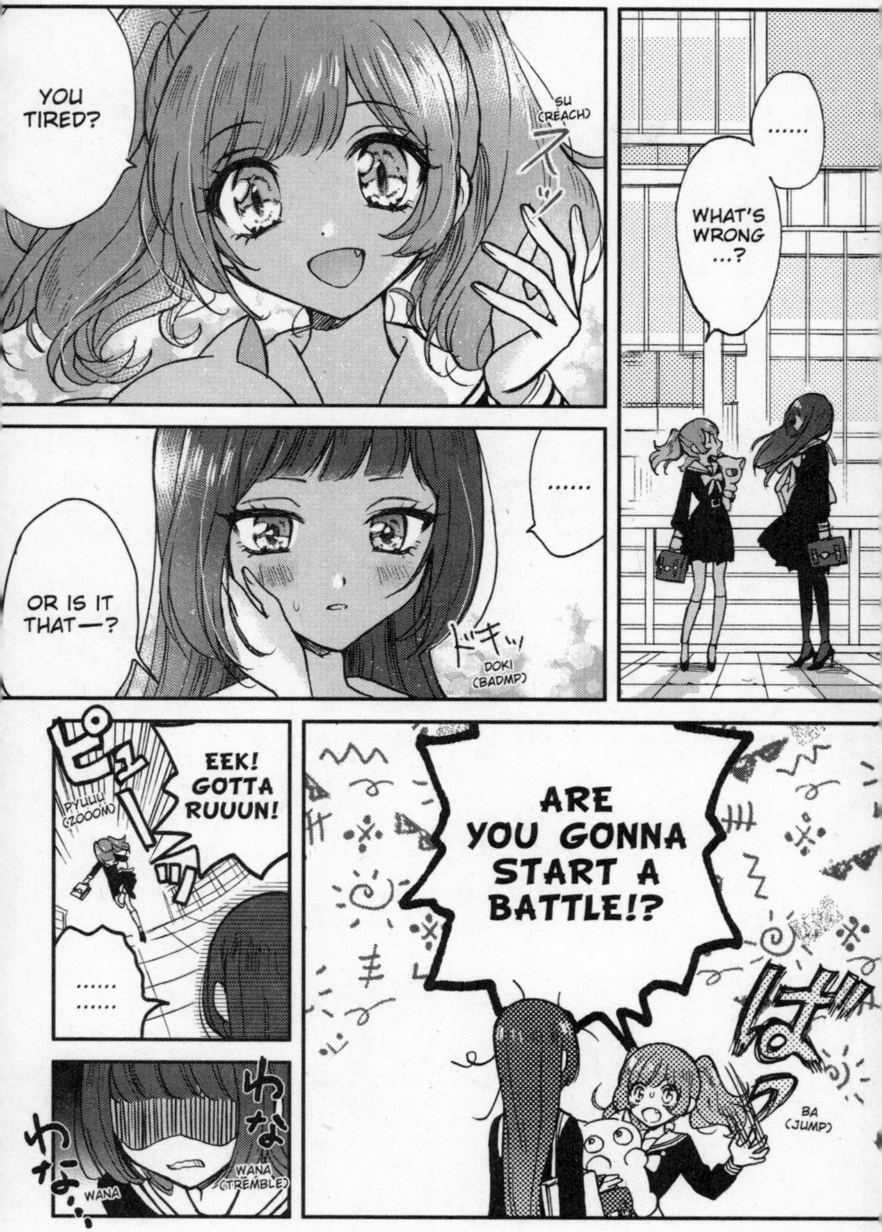
......
WHAT'S WRONG ...?
YOU TIRED?
SU (REACH)
......
OR IS IT THAT—?
DOKI (BADMP)
ARE YOU GONNA START A BATTLE!?
BA (JUMP)
EEK! GOTTA RUUUN!
PYUUU (ZOOOM)
....
WANA (TREMBLE)
WANA

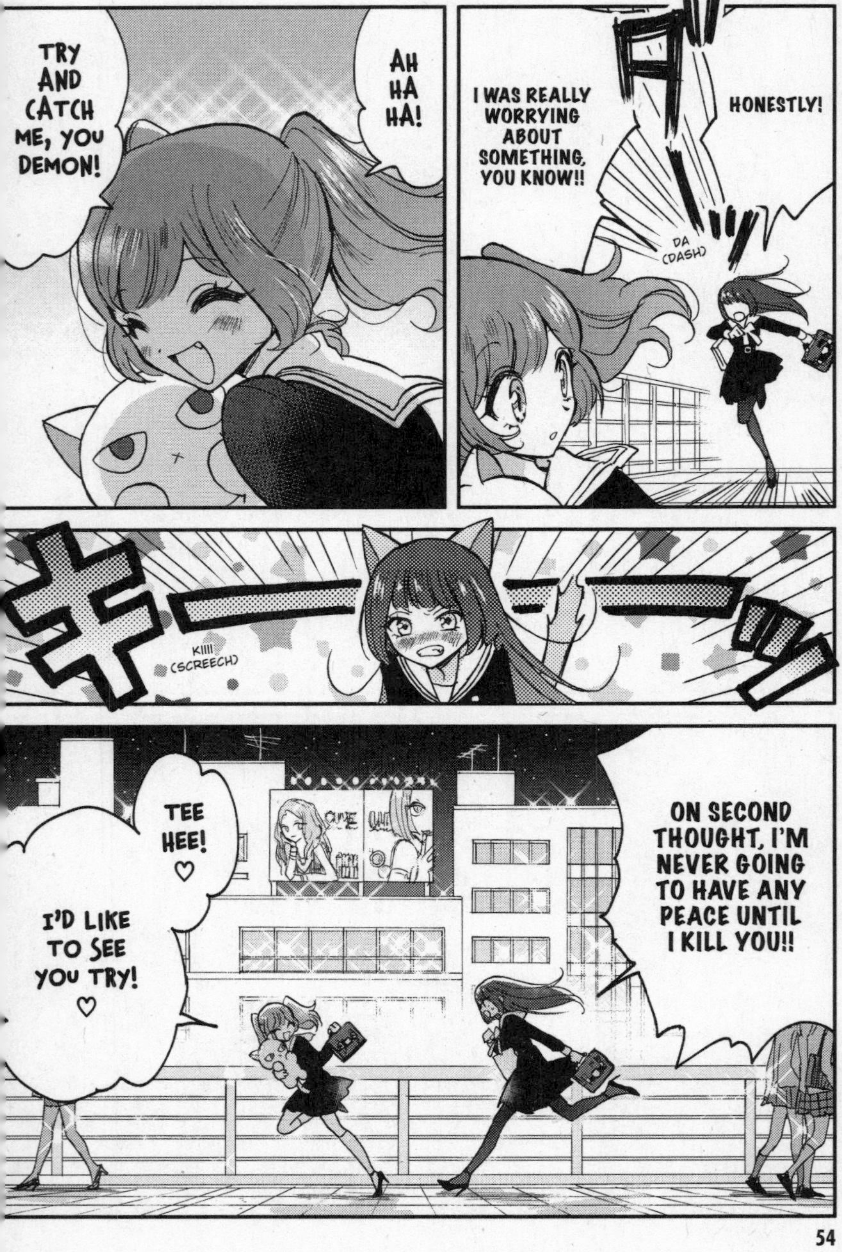
HONESTLY!
I WAS REALLY WORRYING ABOUT SOMETHING, YOU KNOW!!
DA (DASH)
AH HA HA!
TRY AND CATCH ME, YOU DEMON!
KIIII (SCREECH)
ON SECOND THOUGHT, I'M NEVER GOING TO HAVE ANY PEACE UNTIL I KILL YOU!!
TEE HEE! ♡
I'D LIKE TO SEE YOU TRY! ♡

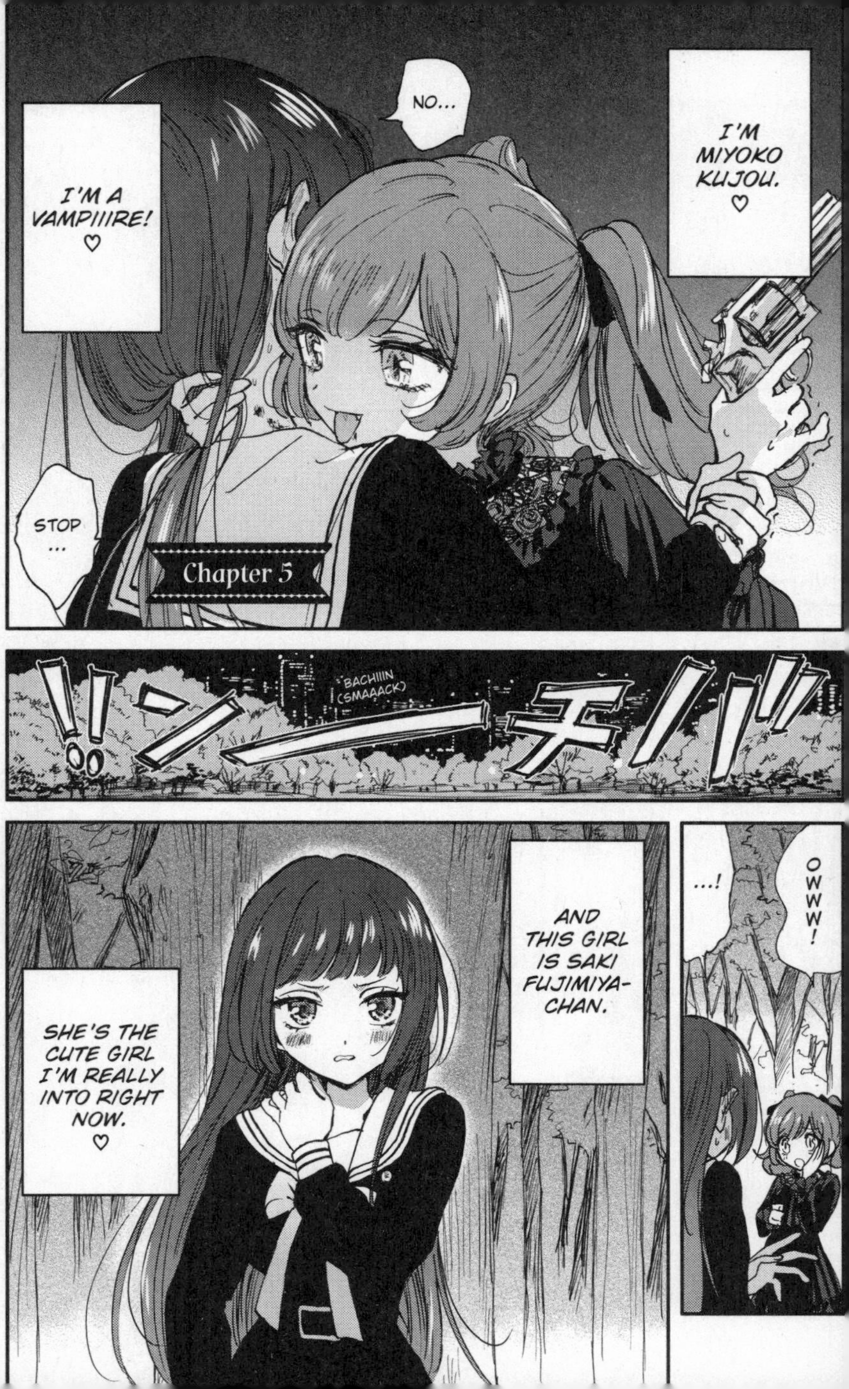
I'M MIYOKO KUJOU. ♡
NO...
I'M A VAMPIIIRE! ♡
STOP ...
Chapter 5
BACHIIIN (SMAAACK)
OWWW!
...!
AND THIS GIRL IS SAKI FUJIMIYA-CHAN.
SHE'S THE CUTE GIRL I'M REALLY INTO RIGHT NOW. ♡

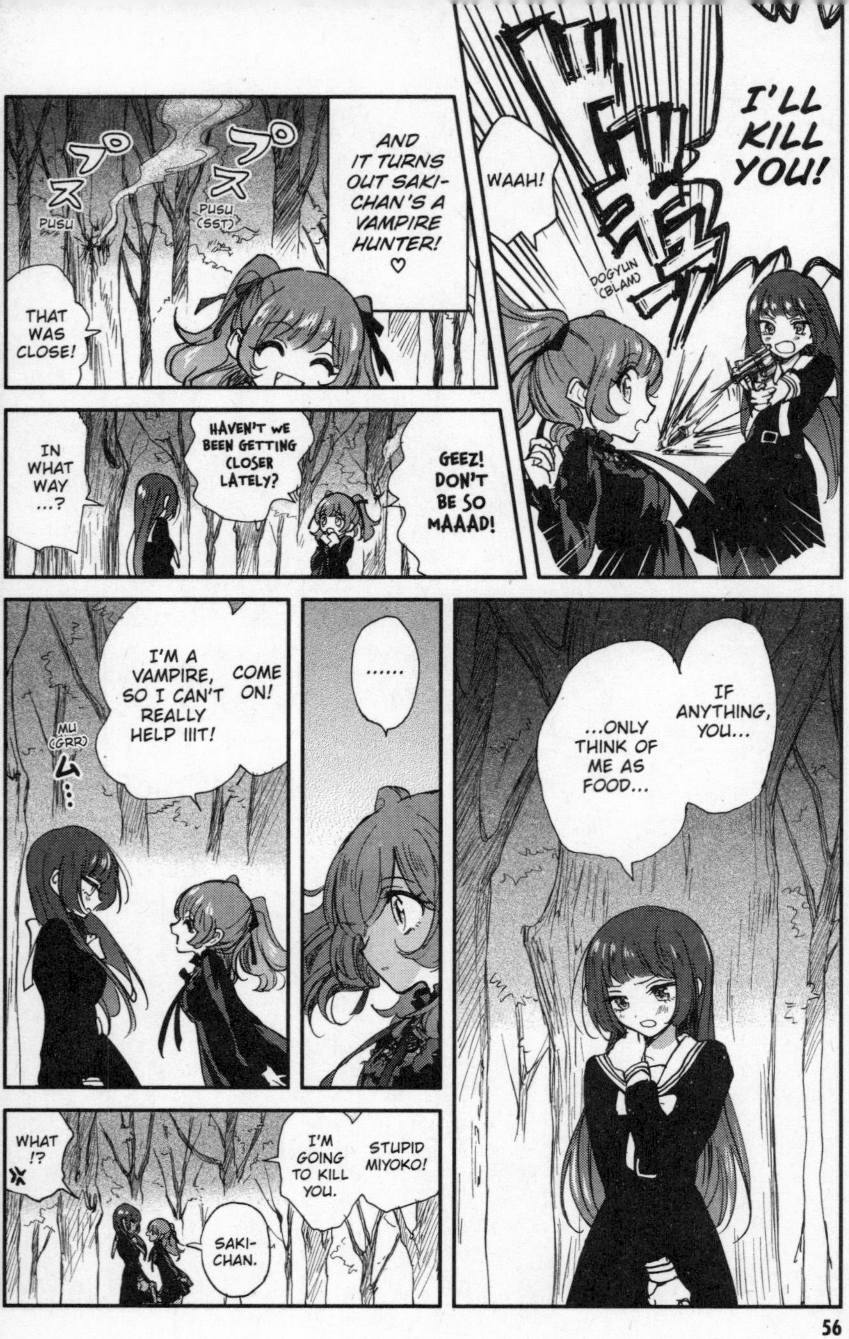
I'LL KILL YOU!
WAAH!
DOGYUN (BLAM)
AND IT TURNS OUT SAKI-CHAN'S A VAMPIRE HUNTER! ♡
プス
PUSU (SST)
プス
PUSU
THAT WAS CLOSE!
GEEZ! DON'T BE SO MAAAD!
HAVEN'T WE BEEN GETTING CLOSER LATELY?
IN WHAT WAY ...?
IF ANYTHING, YOU...
...ONLY THINK OF ME AS FOOD...
......
COME ON!
I'M A VAMPIRE, SO I CAN'T REALLY HELP IIIT!
MU (GRR)
ム…
STUPID MIYOKO!
I'M GOING TO KILL YOU.
SAKI-CHAN.
WHAT !?

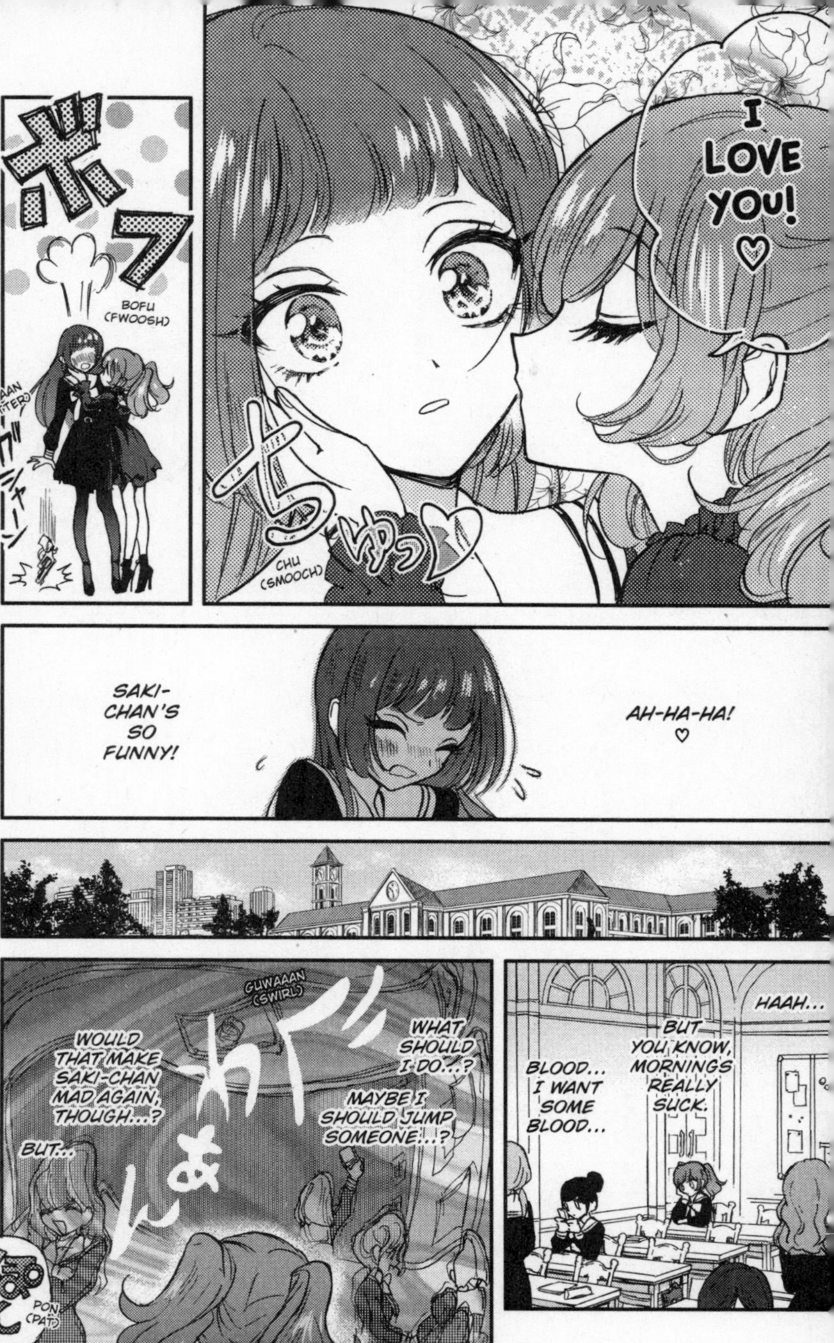
I LOVE YOU! ♡
ちゅっ♡
CHU (SMOOCH)
ボフ
BOFU (FWOOSH)
GASHAAN (CLATTER)
ガシャーン
AH-HA-HA! ♡
SAKI-CHAN'S SO FUNNY!
HAAH...
BUT YOU KNOW, MORNINGS REALLY SUCK.
BLOOD... I WANT SOME BLOOD...
GUWAAAN (SWIRL)
WHAT SHOULD I DO...?
MAYBE I SHOULD JUMP SOMEONE...?
WOULD THAT MAKE SAKI-CHAN MAD AGAIN, THOUGH...?
BUT...
PON (PAT)

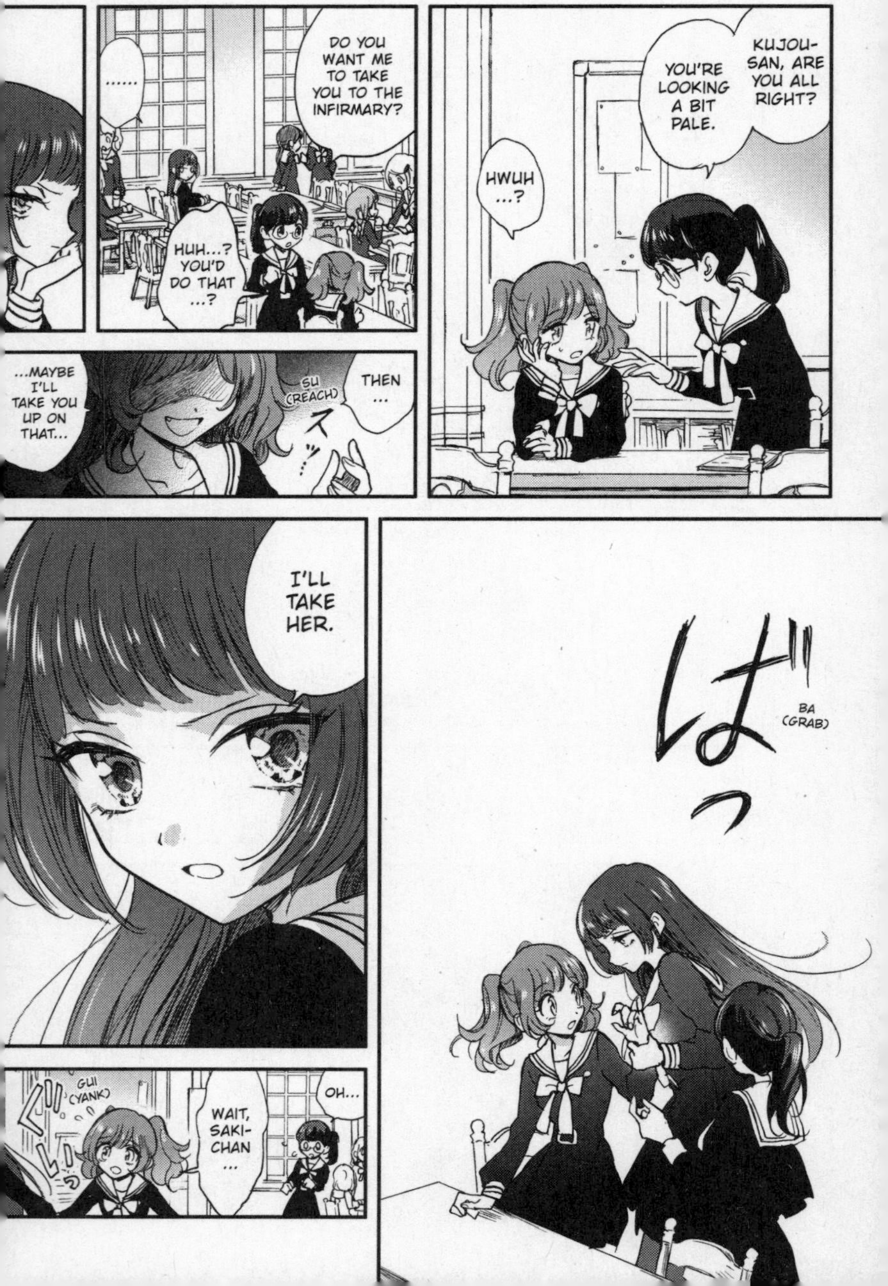
KUJOU-SAN, ARE YOU ALL RIGHT?
YOU'RE LOOKING A BIT PALE.
HWUH ...?
DO YOU WANT ME TO TAKE YOU TO THE INFIRMARY?
HUH...? YOU'D DO THAT ...?
......
THEN ...
SU (REACH)
...MAYBE I'LL TAKE YOU UP ON THAT...
BA (GRAB)
I'LL TAKE HER.
OH...
WAIT, SAKI-CHAN ...
GUI (YANK)

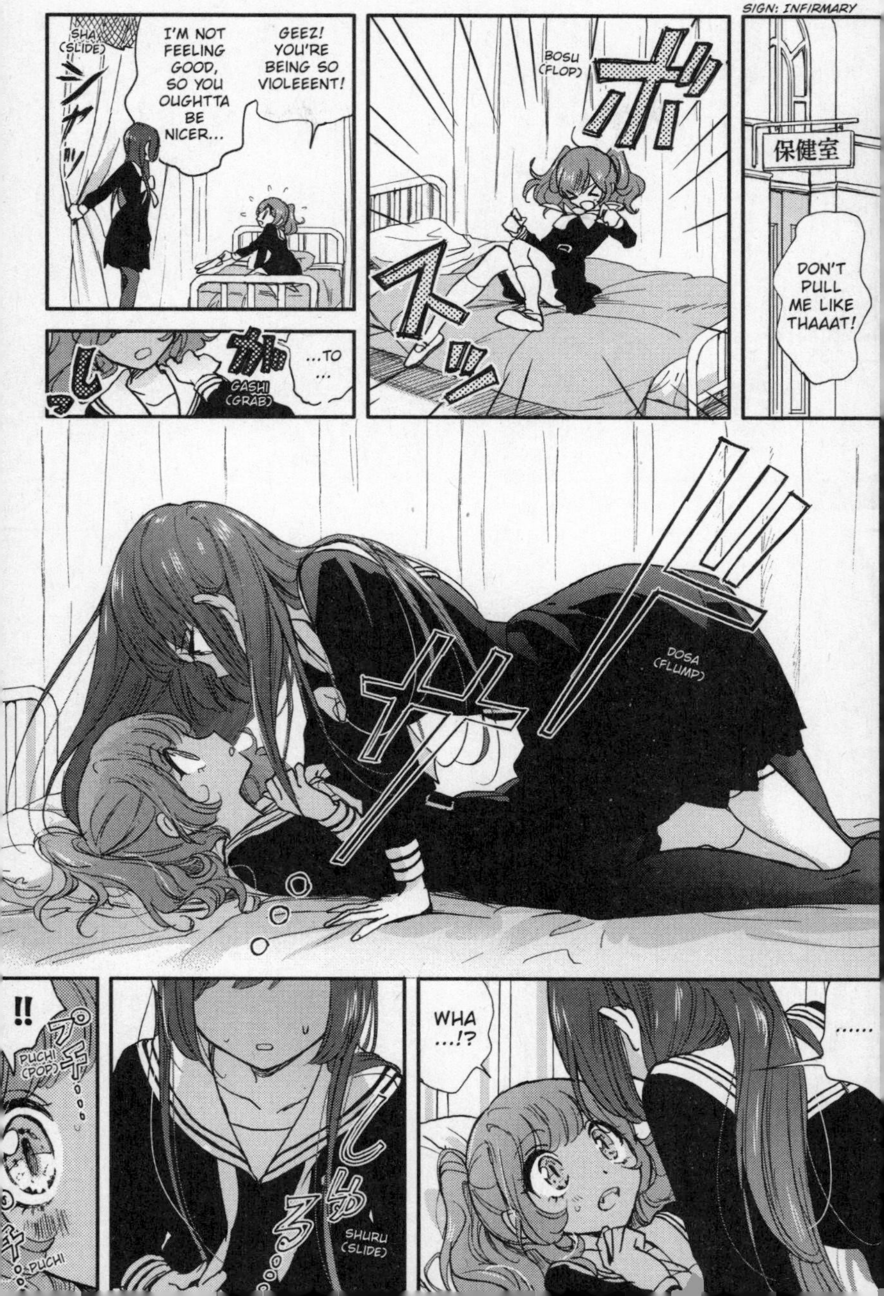
SIGN: INFIRMARY
保健室
DON'T PULL ME LIKE THAAAT!
BOSU (FLOP)
GEEZ! YOU'RE BEING SO VIOLEEENT!
I'M NOT FEELING GOOD, SO YOU OUGHTTA BE NICER...
SHA (SLIDE)
...TO ...
GASHI (GRAB)
DOSA (FLUMP)
......
WHA ...!?
SHURU (SLIDE)
!!
PUCHI (POP)
PUCHI

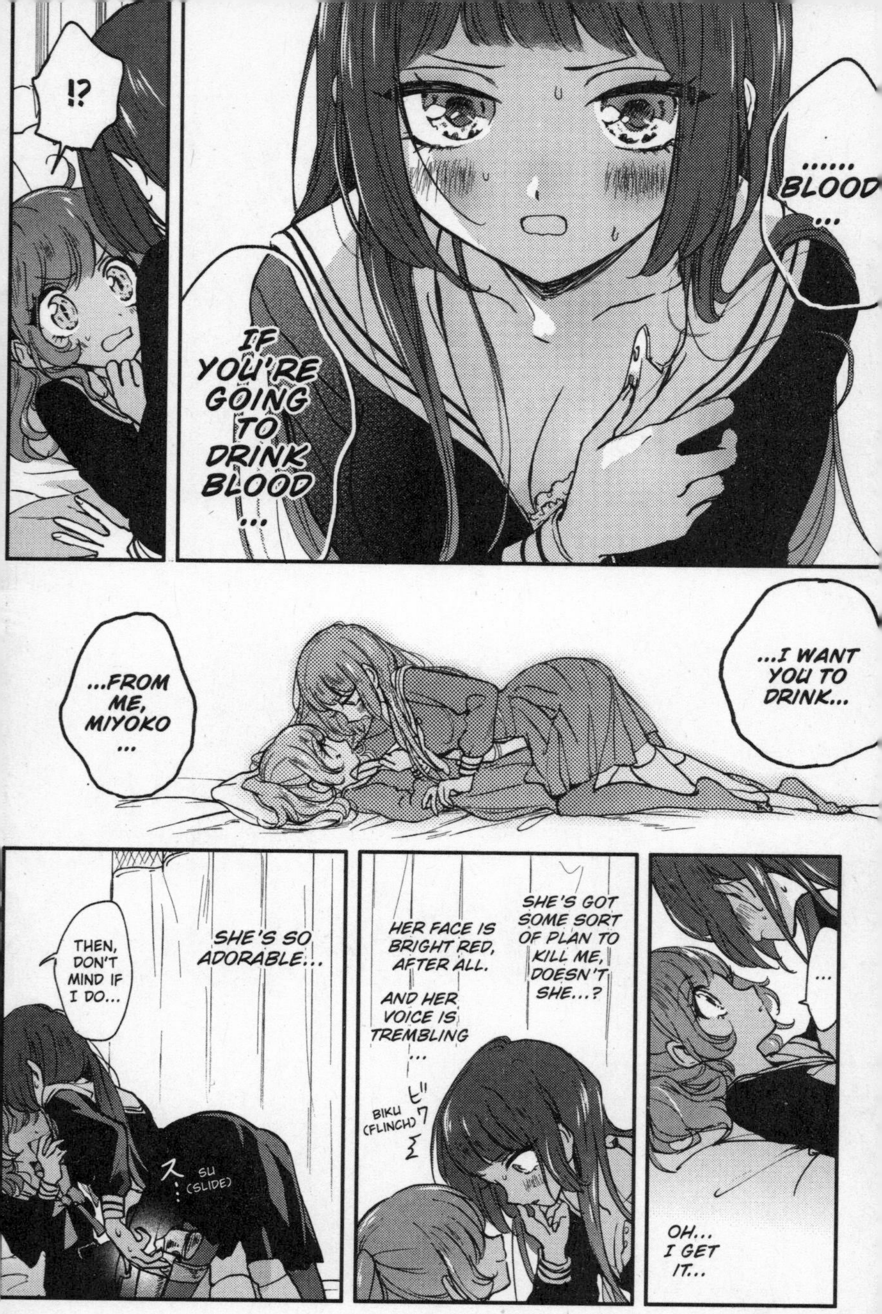
......BLOOD...
IF YOU'RE GOING TO DRINK BLOOD...
!?
...I WANT YOU TO DRINK...
...FROM ME, MIYOKO...
...
OH... I GET IT...
SHE'S GOT SOME SORT OF PLAN TO KILL ME, DOESN'T SHE...?
HER FACE IS BRIGHT RED, AFTER ALL.
AND HER VOICE IS TREMBLING...
ビク
BIKU (FLINCH)
SHE'S SO ADORABLE...
THEN, DON'T MIND IF I DO...
ス
SU (SLIDE)

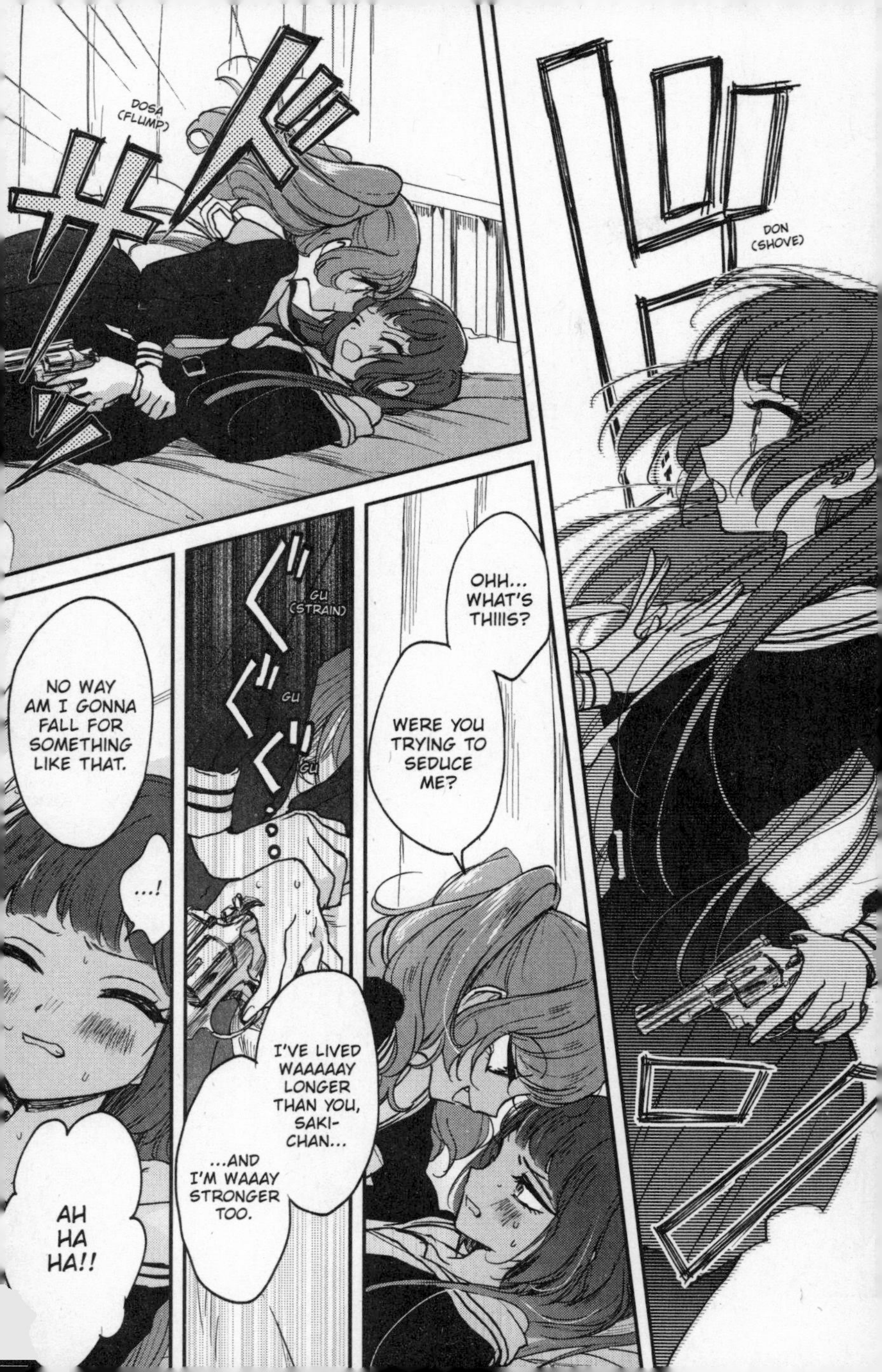
DON (SHOVE)
DOSA (FLUMP)
OHH... WHAT'S THIIIS?
WERE YOU TRYING TO SEDUCE ME?
I'VE LIVED WAAAAAY LONGER THAN YOU, SAKI-CHAN...
...AND I'M WAAAY STRONGER TOO.
GU (STRAIN)
GU
GU
NO WAY AM I GONNA FALL FOR SOMETHING LIKE THAT.
...!
AH HA HA!!

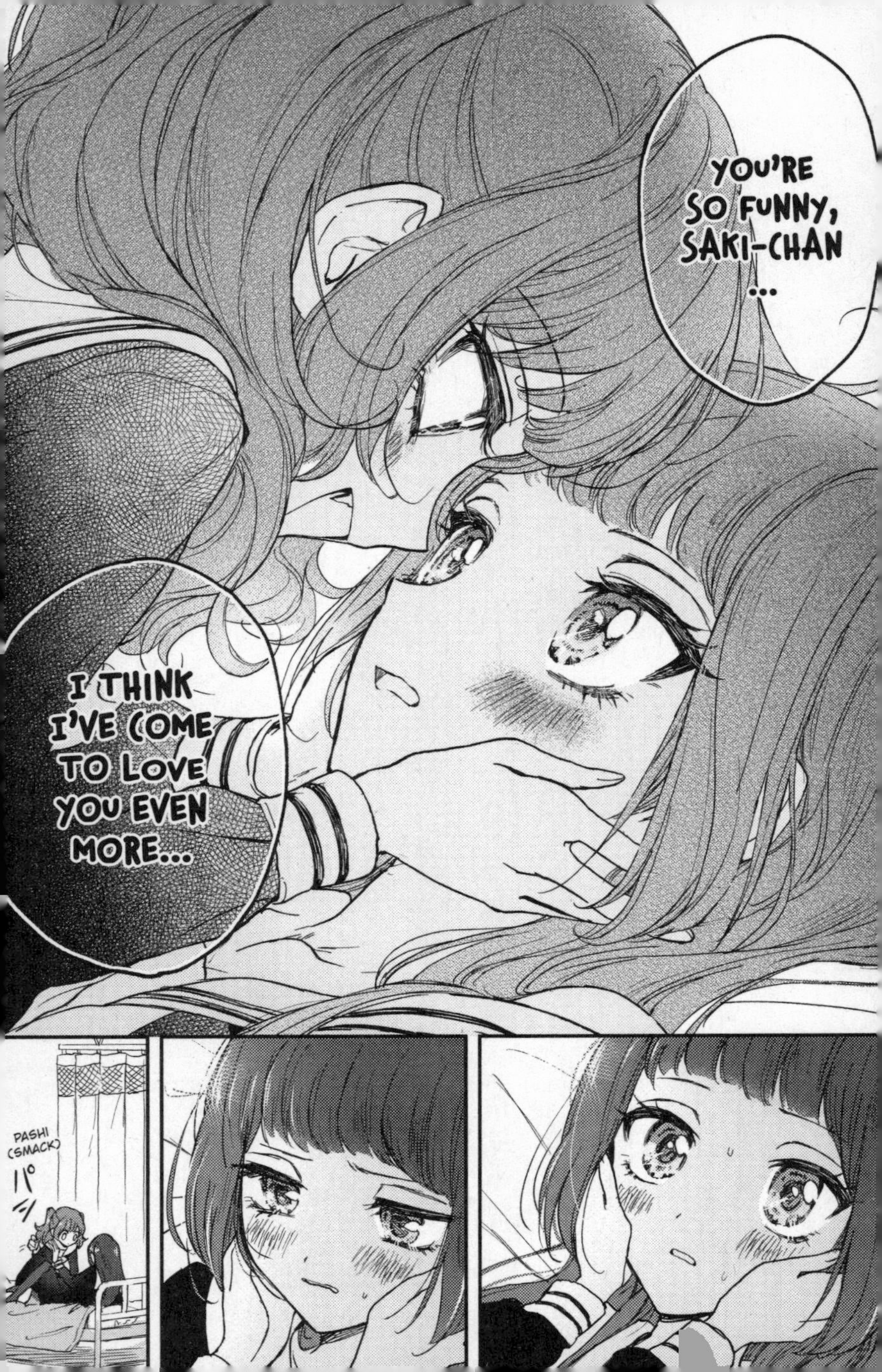
YOU'RE SO FUNNY, SAKI-CHAN ...
I THINK I'VE COME TO LOVE YOU EVEN MORE...
PASHI (SMACK)

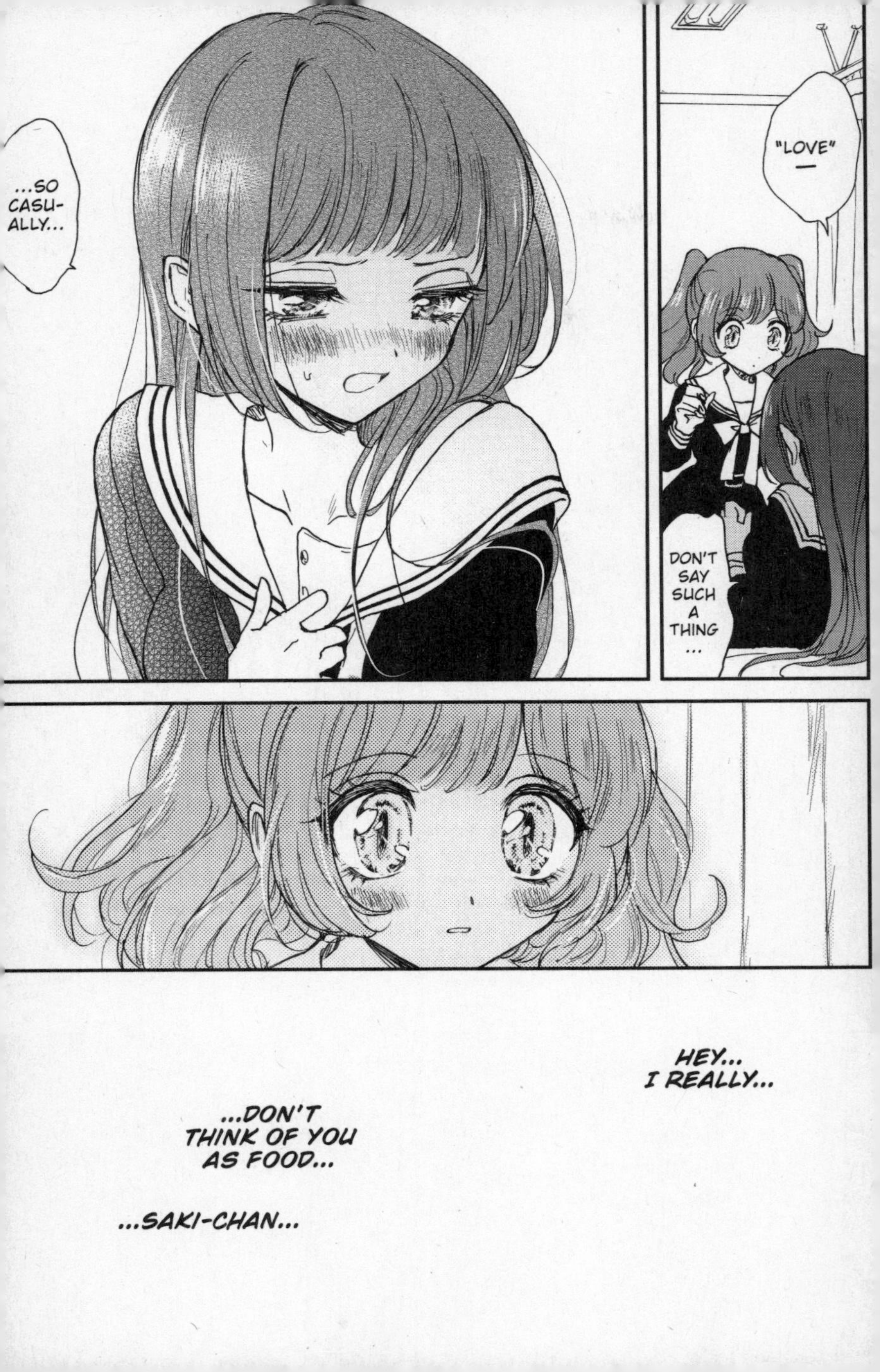
"LOVE" —
DON'T SAY SUCH A THING ...
...SO CASU-ALLY...
HEY... I REALLY...
...DON'T THINK OF YOU AS FOOD...
...SAKI-CHAN...

Killing me!
1

Chapter 6

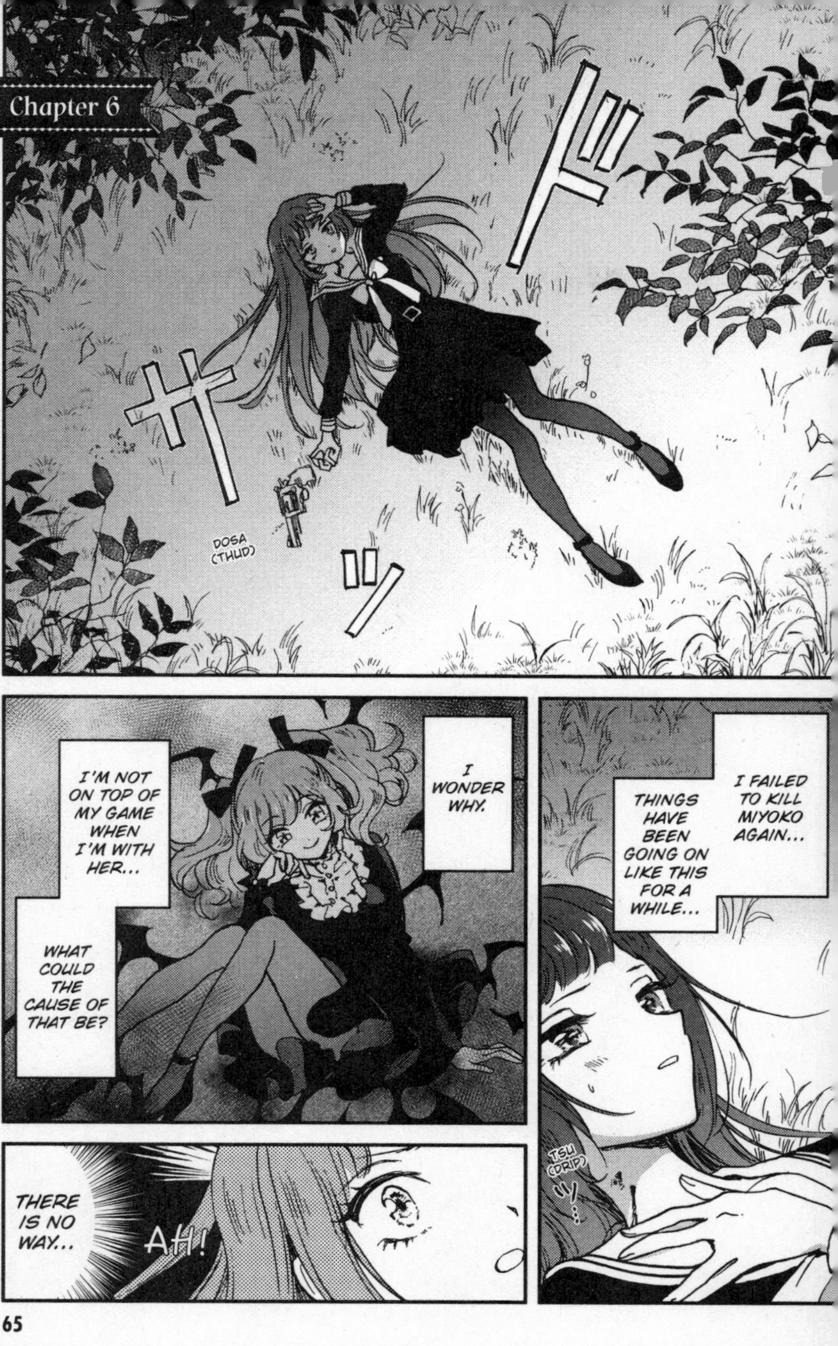

DOSA (THUD)
I FAILED TO KILL MIYOKO AGAIN...
THINGS HAVE BEEN GOING ON LIKE THIS FOR A WHILE...
TSU (DRIP)
I WONDER WHY.
I'M NOT ON TOP OF MY GAME WHEN I'M WITH HER...
WHAT COULD THE CAUSE OF THAT BE?
AH!
THERE IS NO WAY...

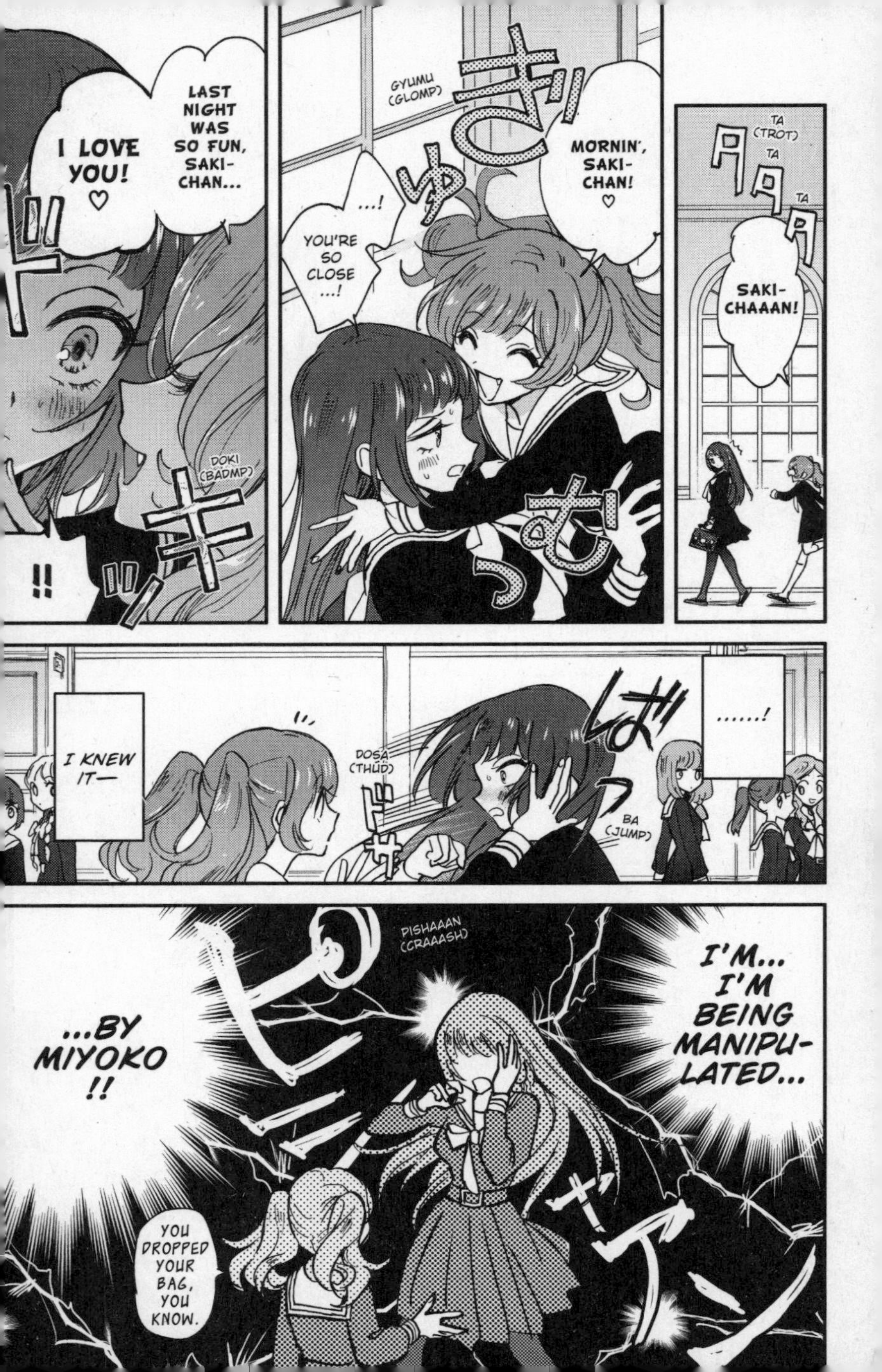

TA (TROT) TA TA
SAKI-CHAAAN!
GYUMU (GLOMP)
MORNIN', SAKI-CHAN! ♡
...!
YOU'RE SO CLOSE ...!
LAST NIGHT WAS SO FUN, SAKI-CHAN...
I LOVE YOU! ♡
DOKI (BADMP)
!!
......!
BA (JUMP)
DOSA (THUD)
I KNEW IT—
PISHAAAN (CRAAASH)
I'M... I'M BEING MANIPU-LATED...
...BY MIYOKO !!
YOU DROPPED YOUR BAG, YOU KNOW.

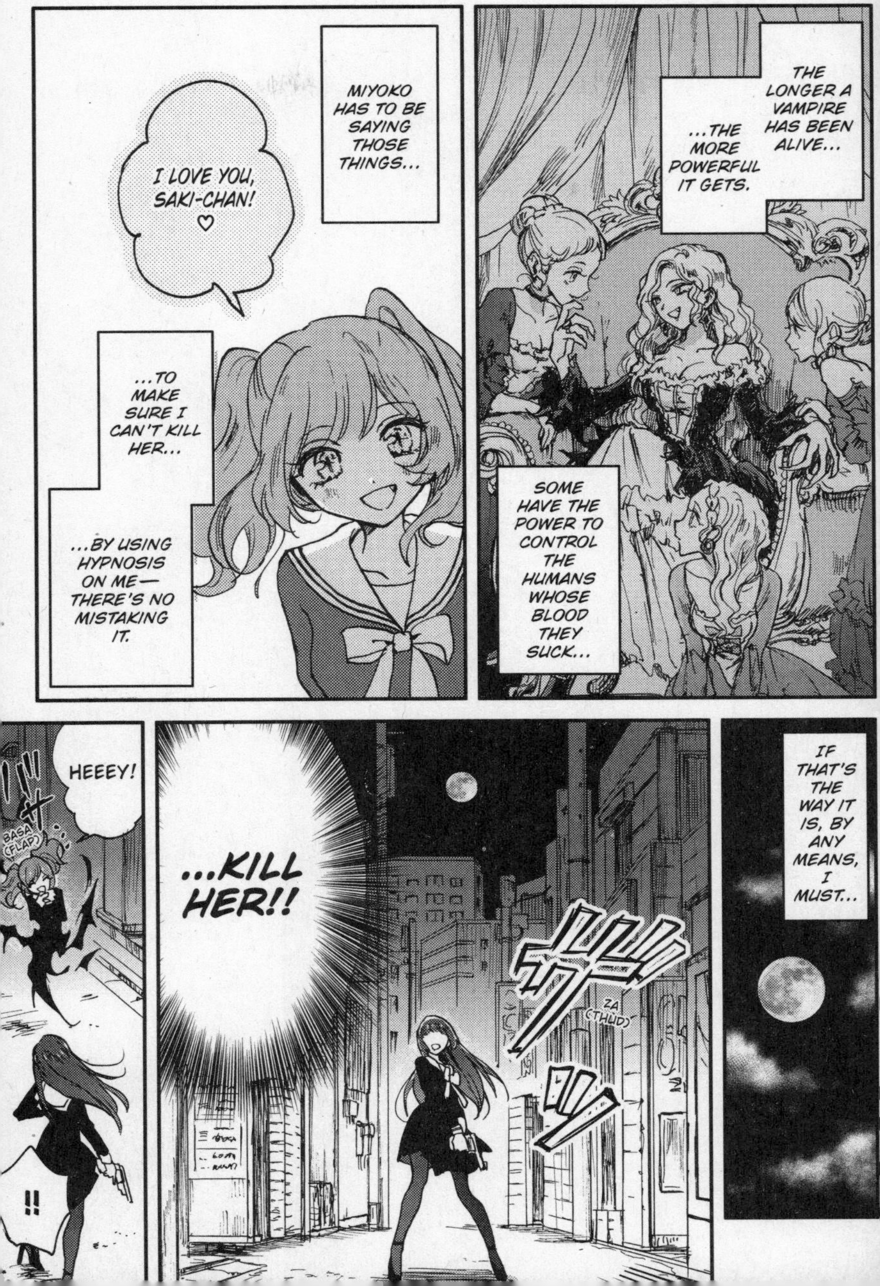
THE LONGER A VAMPIRE HAS BEEN ALIVE...
...THE MORE POWERFUL IT GETS.
SOME HAVE THE POWER TO CONTROL THE HUMANS WHOSE BLOOD THEY SUCK...
MIYOKO HAS TO BE SAYING THOSE THINGS...
I LOVE YOU, SAKI-CHAN! ♡
...TO MAKE SURE I CAN'T KILL HER...
...BY USING HYPNOSIS ON ME—THERE'S NO MISTAKING IT.
IF THAT'S THE WAY IT IS, BY ANY MEANS, I MUST...
...KILL HER!!
ZA (THUD)
HEEEY!
BASA (FLAP)
!!

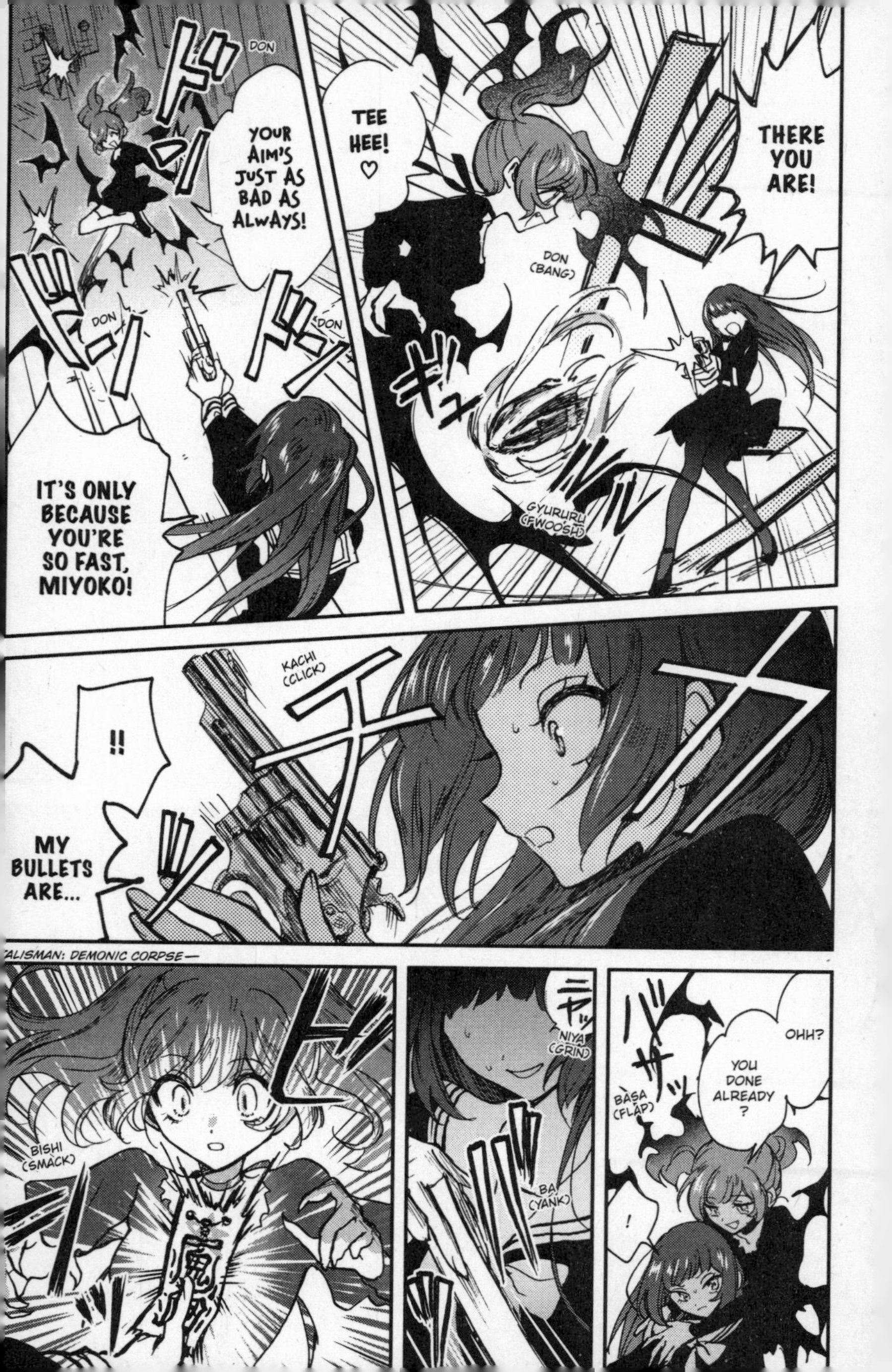
THERE YOU ARE!
TEE HEE! ♡
DON (BANG)
GYURURU (FWOOSH)
DON
YOUR AIM'S JUST AS BAD AS ALWAYS!
DON
DON
IT'S ONLY BECAUSE YOU'RE SO FAST, MIYOKO!
KACHI (CLICK)
!!
MY BULLETS ARE...
TALISMAN: DEMONIC CORPSE—
OHH?
YOU DONE ALREADY ?
BASA (FLAP)
!
NIYA (GRIN)
BA (YANK)
BISHI (SMACK)

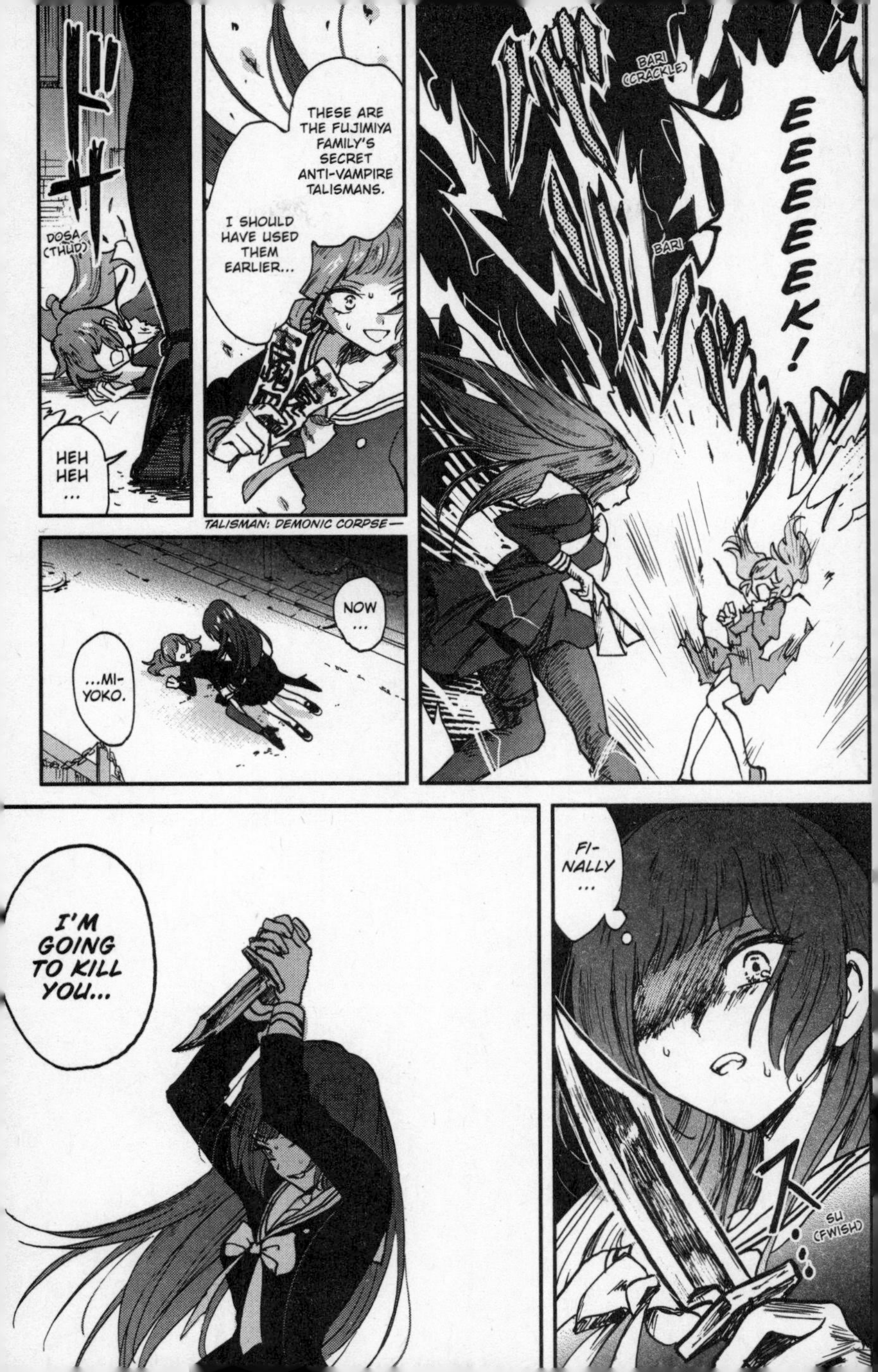
BARI (CRACKLE)
EEEEEEK!
BARI
THESE ARE THE FUJIMIYA FAMILY'S SECRET ANTI-VAMPIRE TALISMANS.
I SHOULD HAVE USED THEM EARLIER...
DOSA (THUD)
HEH HEH ...
TALISMAN: DEMONIC CORPSE—
NOW ...
...MI-YOKO.
FI-NALLY ...
SU (FWISH)
I'M GOING TO KILL YOU...

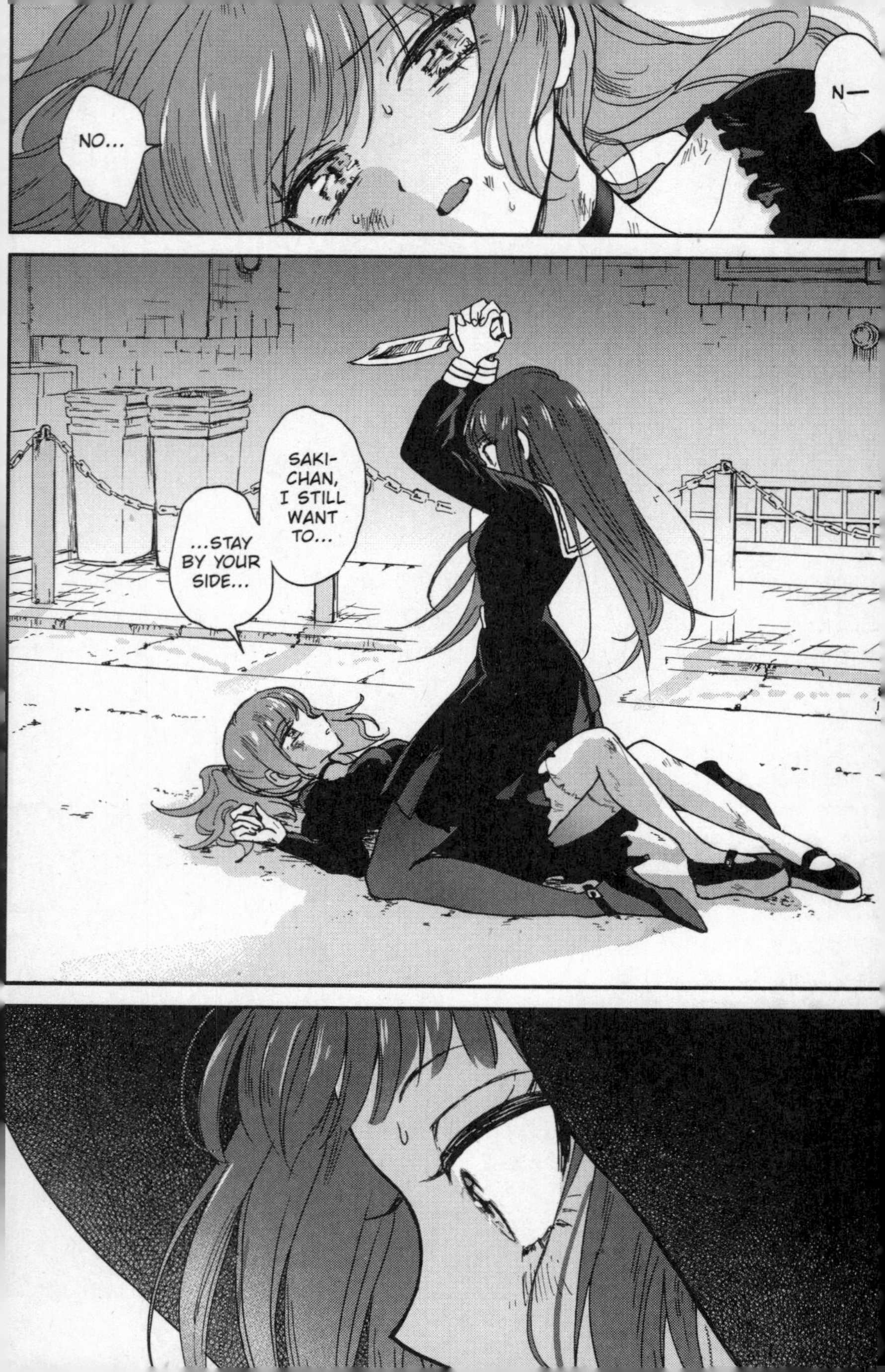
N—
NO...
SAKI-CHAN, I STILL WANT TO...
...STAY BY YOUR SIDE...

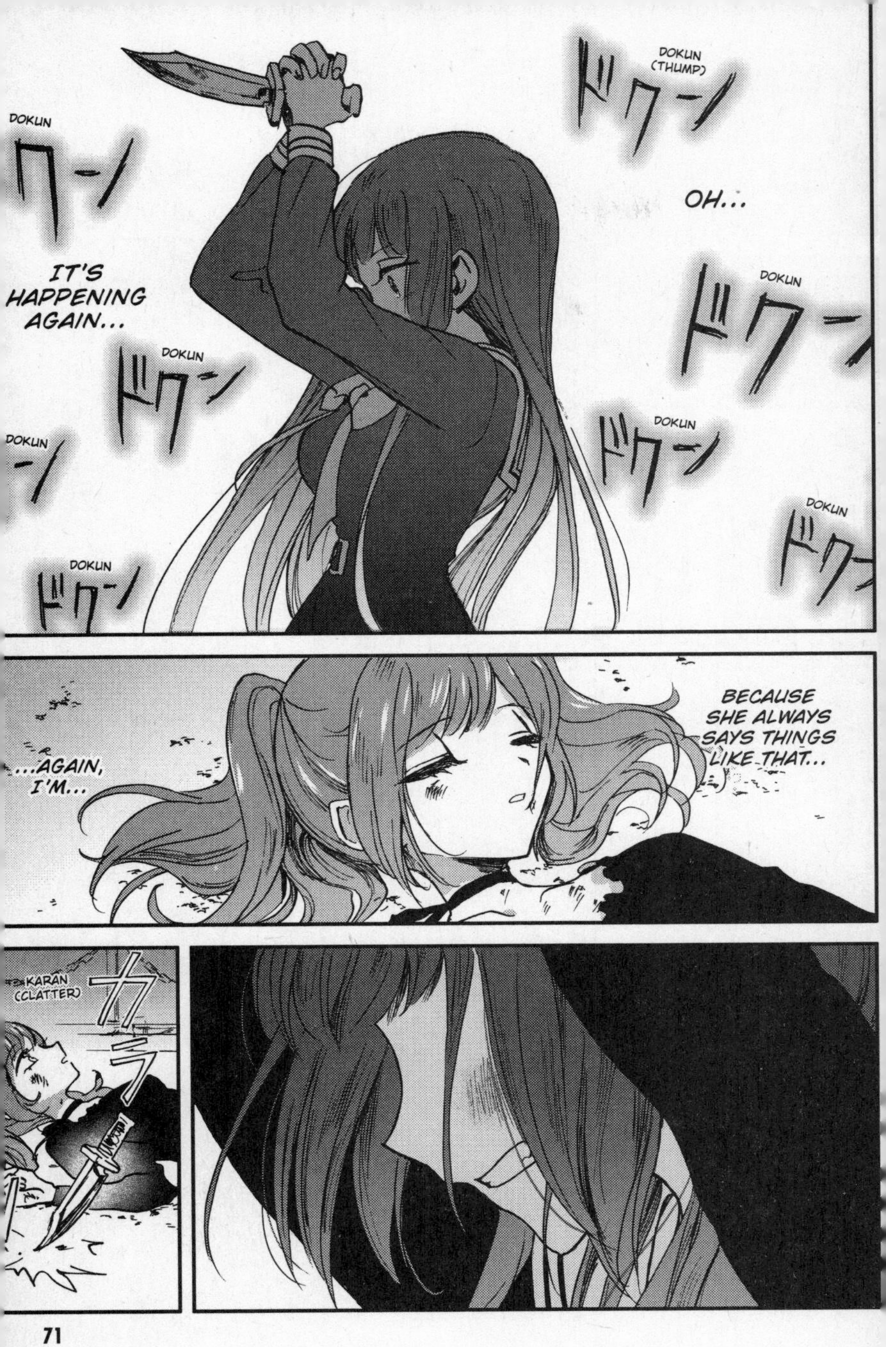
DOKUN
(THUMP)
OH...
DOKUN
DOKUN
DOKUN
DOKUN
IT'S HAPPENING AGAIN...
DOKUN
DOKUN
DOKUN
BECAUSE SHE ALWAYS SAYS THINGS LIKE THAT...
...AGAIN, I'M...
KARAN
(CLATTER)

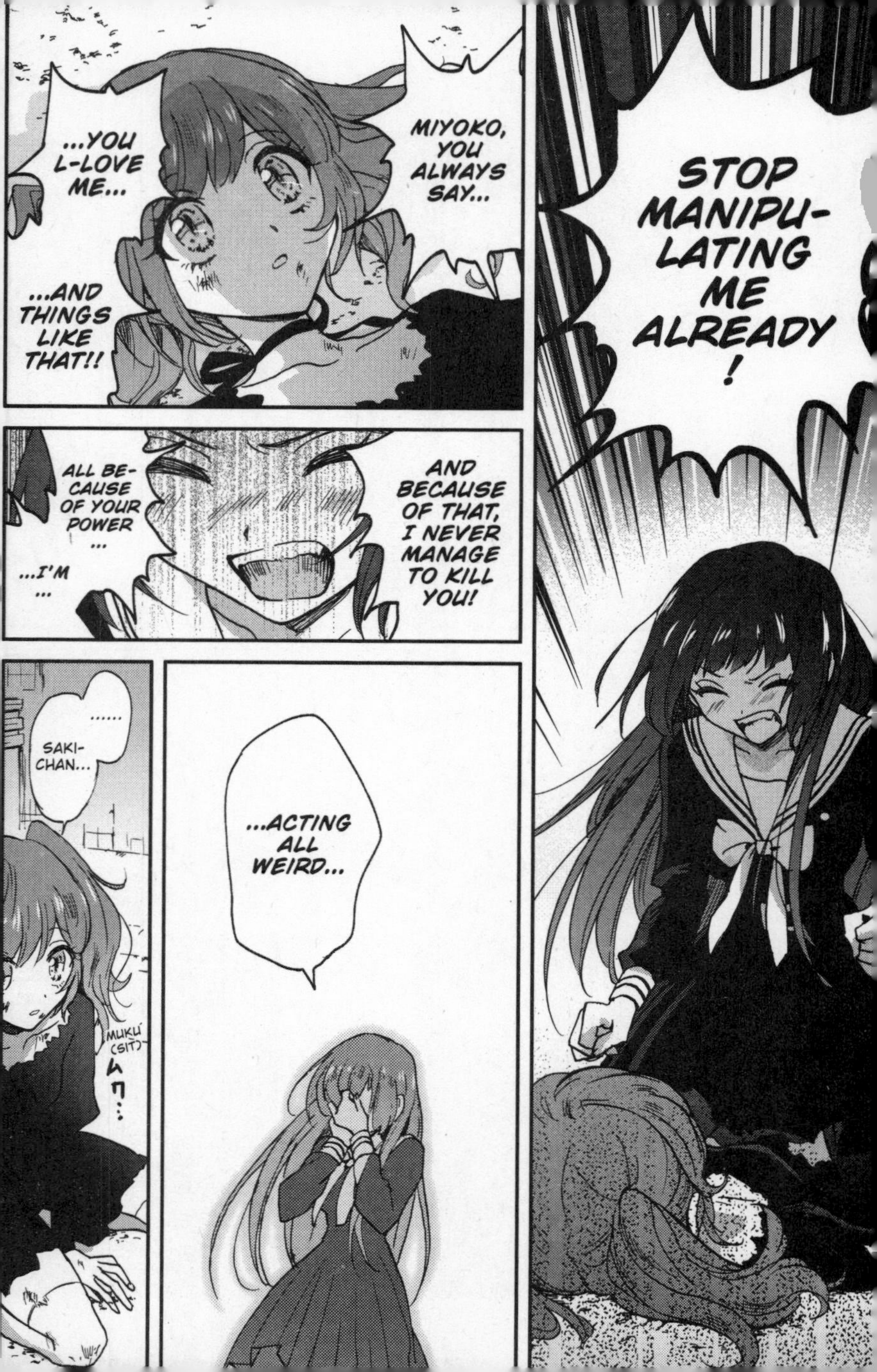
STOP MANIPU-LATING ME ALREADY!
MIYOKO, YOU ALWAYS SAY...
...YOU L-LOVE ME...
...AND THINGS LIKE THAT!!
AND BECAUSE OF THAT, I NEVER MANAGE TO KILL YOU!
ALL BE-CAUSE OF YOUR POWER...
...I'M ...
...ACTING ALL WEIRD...
......
SAKI-CHAN...
MUKU (SIT)
ムク...

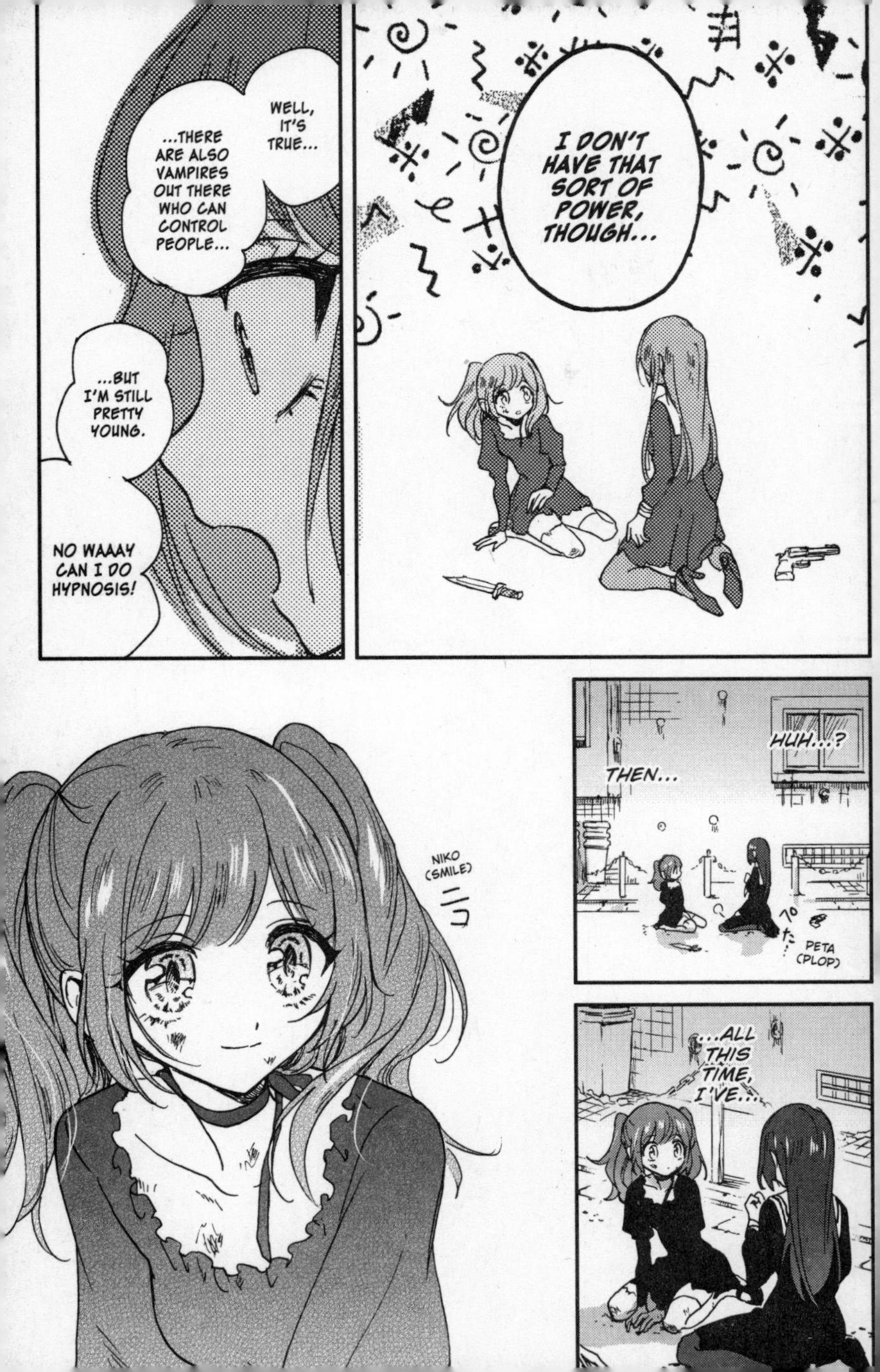
I DON'T HAVE THAT SORT OF POWER, THOUGH...
WELL, IT'S TRUE...
...THERE ARE ALSO VAMPIRES OUT THERE WHO CAN CONTROL PEOPLE...
...BUT I'M STILL PRETTY YOUNG.
NO WAAAY CAN I DO HYPNOSIS!
HUH...?
THEN...
PETA (PLOP)
...ALL THIS TIME, I'VE...
NIKO (SMILE)

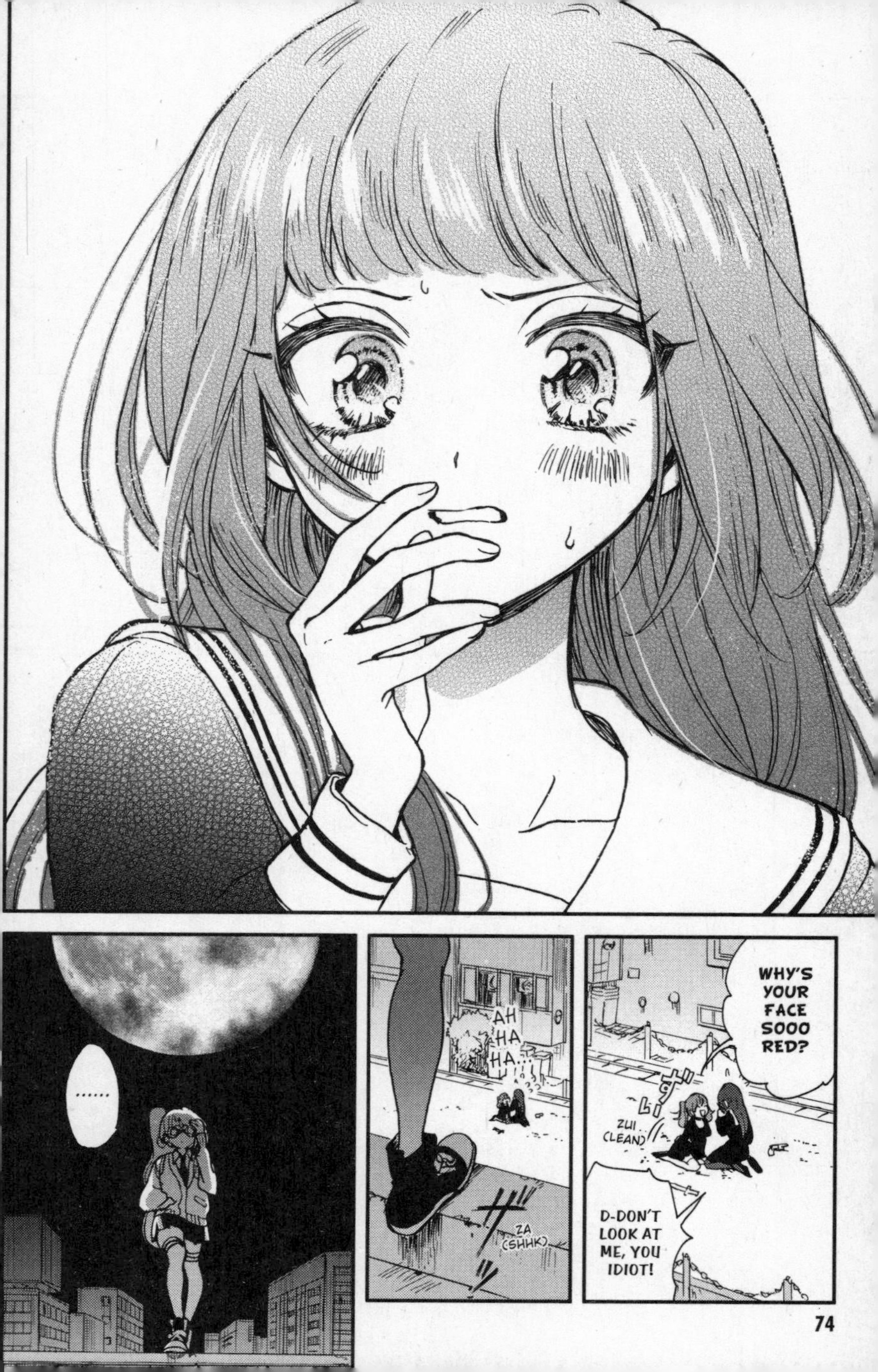
WHY'S YOUR FACE SOOO RED?
ZUI (CLEAN)
D-DON'T LOOK AT ME, YOU IDIOT!
AH HA HA...
ZA (SHHK)
......

Chapter 7

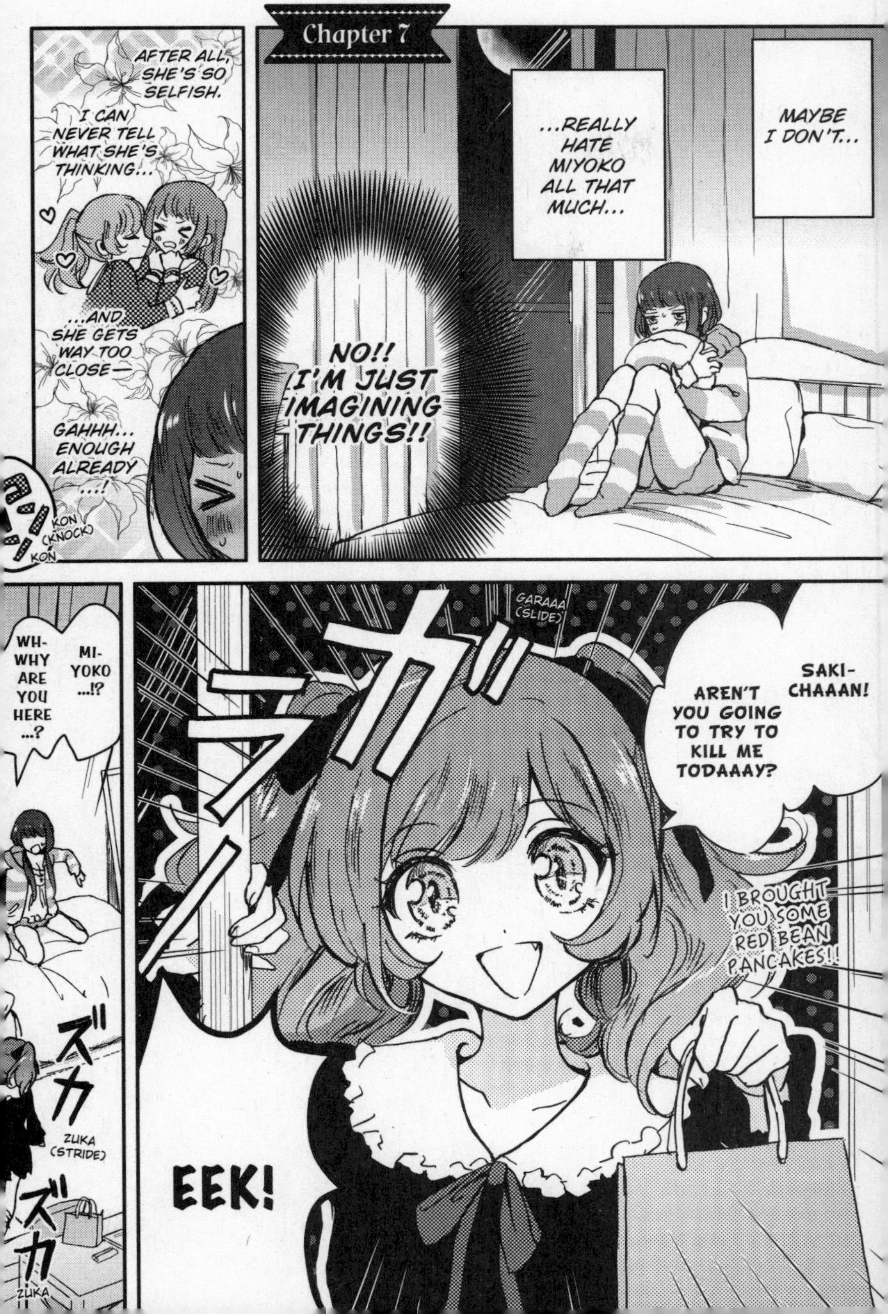
MAYBE I DON'T...
...REALLY HATE MIYOKO ALL THAT MUCH...
NO!! I'M JUST IMAGINING THINGS!!
AFTER ALL, SHE'S SO SELFISH.
I CAN NEVER TELL WHAT SHE'S THINKING...
...AND SHE GETS WAY TOO CLOSE—
GAHHH... ENOUGH ALREADY...!
KON (KNOCK) KON
GARAAA (SLIDE)
SAKI-CHAAAN!
AREN'T YOU GOING TO TRY TO KILL ME TODAAAY?
I BROUGHT YOU SOME RED BEAN PANCAKES!!
EEK!
MI-YOKO...!?
WH-WHY ARE YOU HERE...?
ZUKA (STRIDE)
ZUKA

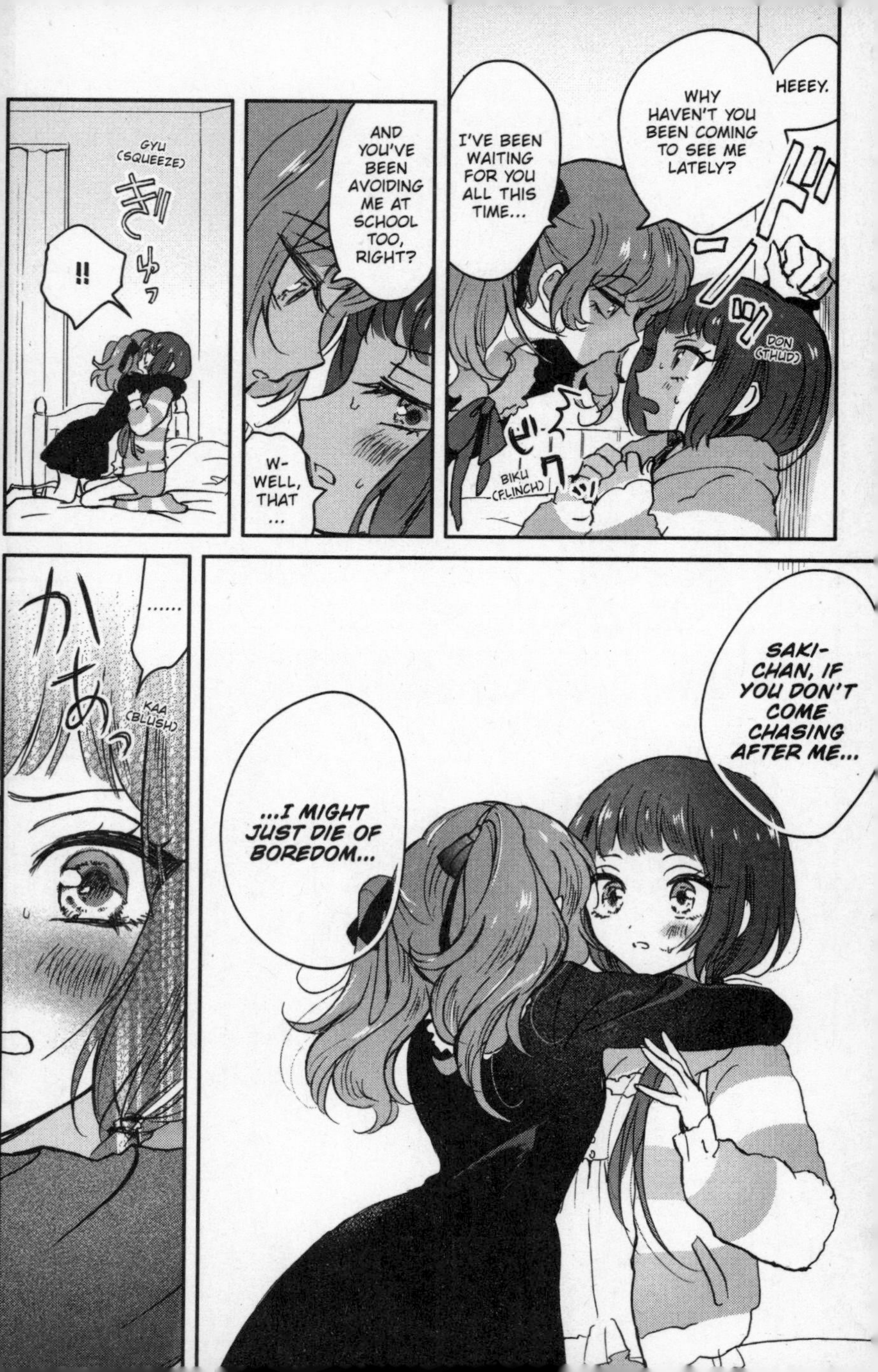

HEEEY.
WHY HAVEN'T YOU BEEN COMING TO SEE ME LATELY?
DON (THUD)
I'VE BEEN WAITING FOR YOU ALL THIS TIME...
BIKU (FLINCH)
AND YOU'VE BEEN AVOIDING ME AT SCHOOL TOO, RIGHT?
W-WELL, THAT ...
GYU (SQUEEZE)
!!
SAKI-CHAN, IF YOU DON'T COME CHASING AFTER ME...
...I MIGHT JUST DIE OF BOREDOM...
......
KAA (BLUSH)

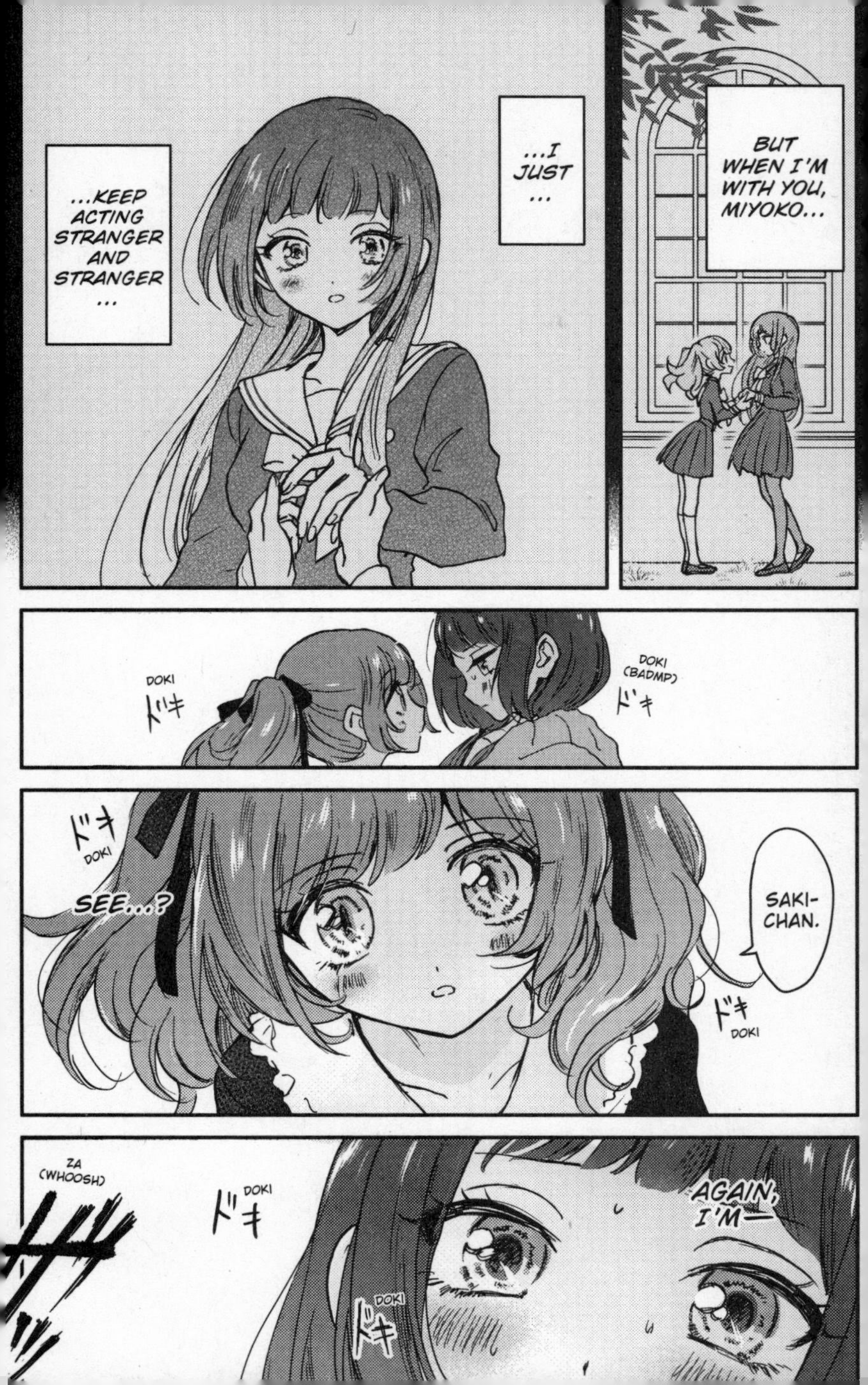
BUT WHEN I'M WITH YOU, MIYOKO...
...I JUST ...
...KEEP ACTING STRANGER AND STRANGER ...
DOKI (BADMP)
ドキ
DOKI
ドキ
SAKI-CHAN.
ドキ
DOKI
ドキ
DOKI
SEE...?
AGAIN, I'M—
DOKI
ドキ
ZA (WHOOSH)
DOKI
ドキ

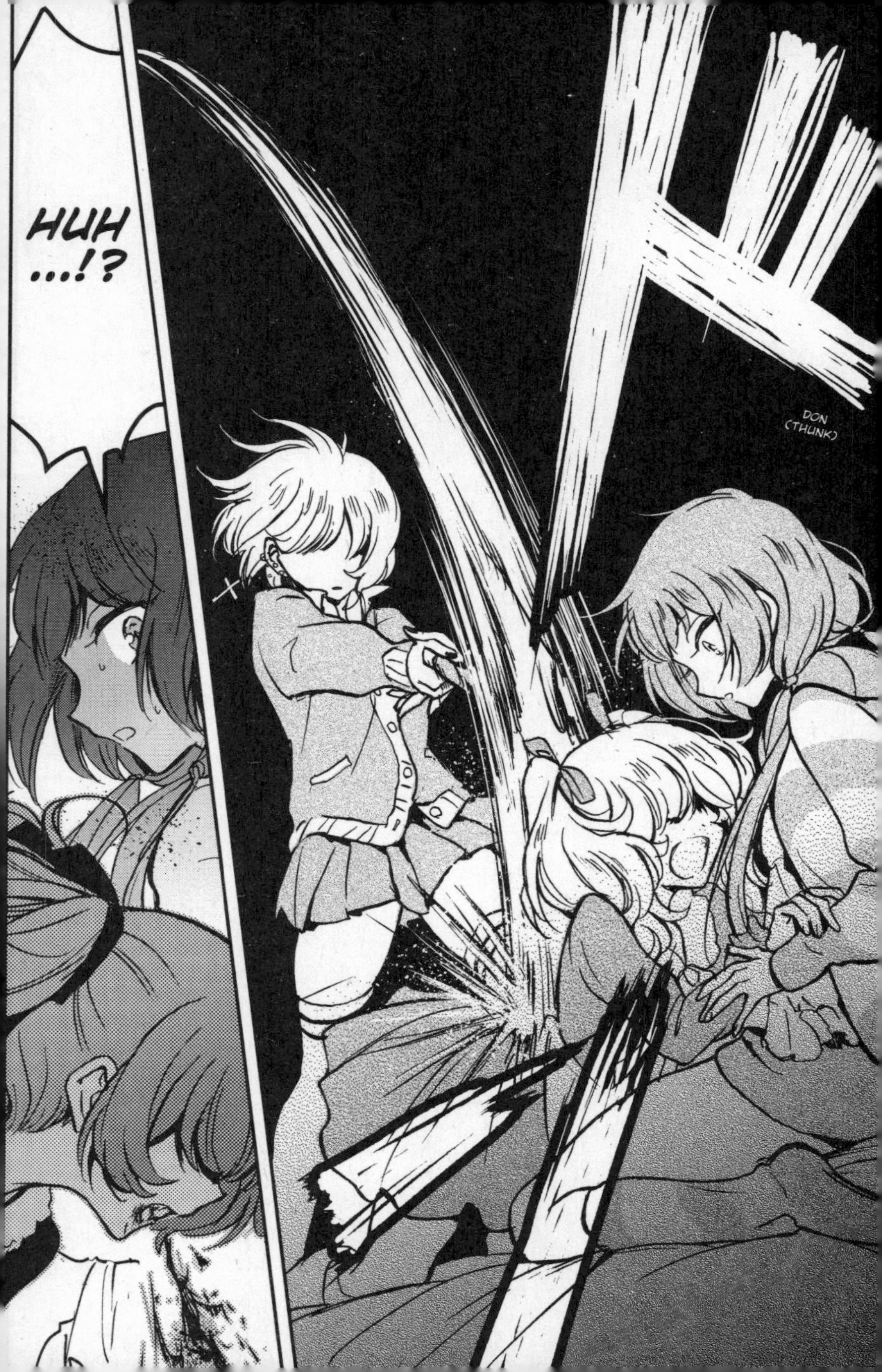
DON
(THUNK)
HUH
...!?

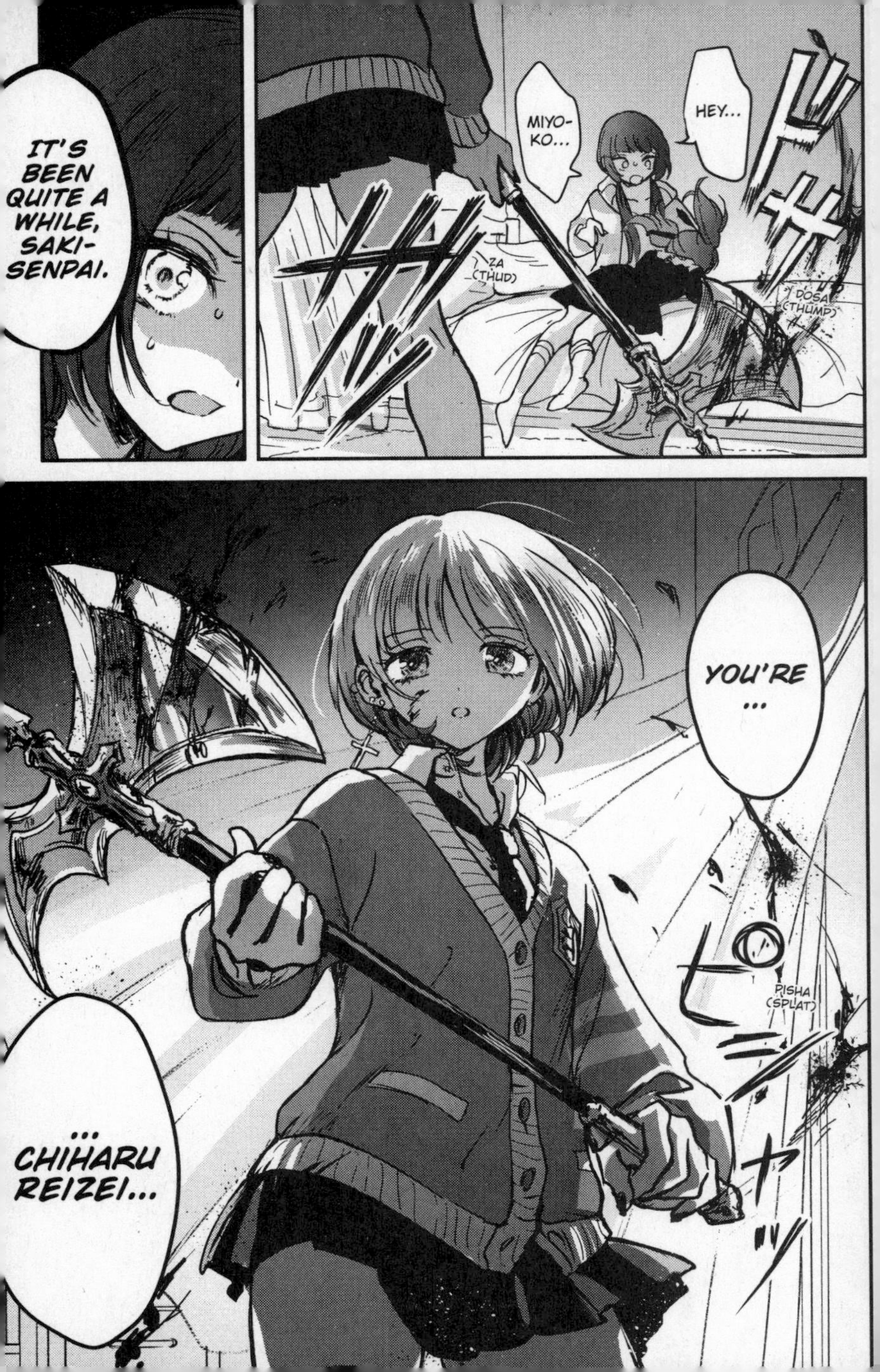
HEY...
MIYO-KO...
DOSA (THUMP)
ZA (THUD)
IT'S BEEN QUITE A WHILE, SAKI-SENPAI.
YOU'RE ...
... CHIHARU REIZEI...
PISHA (SPLAT)

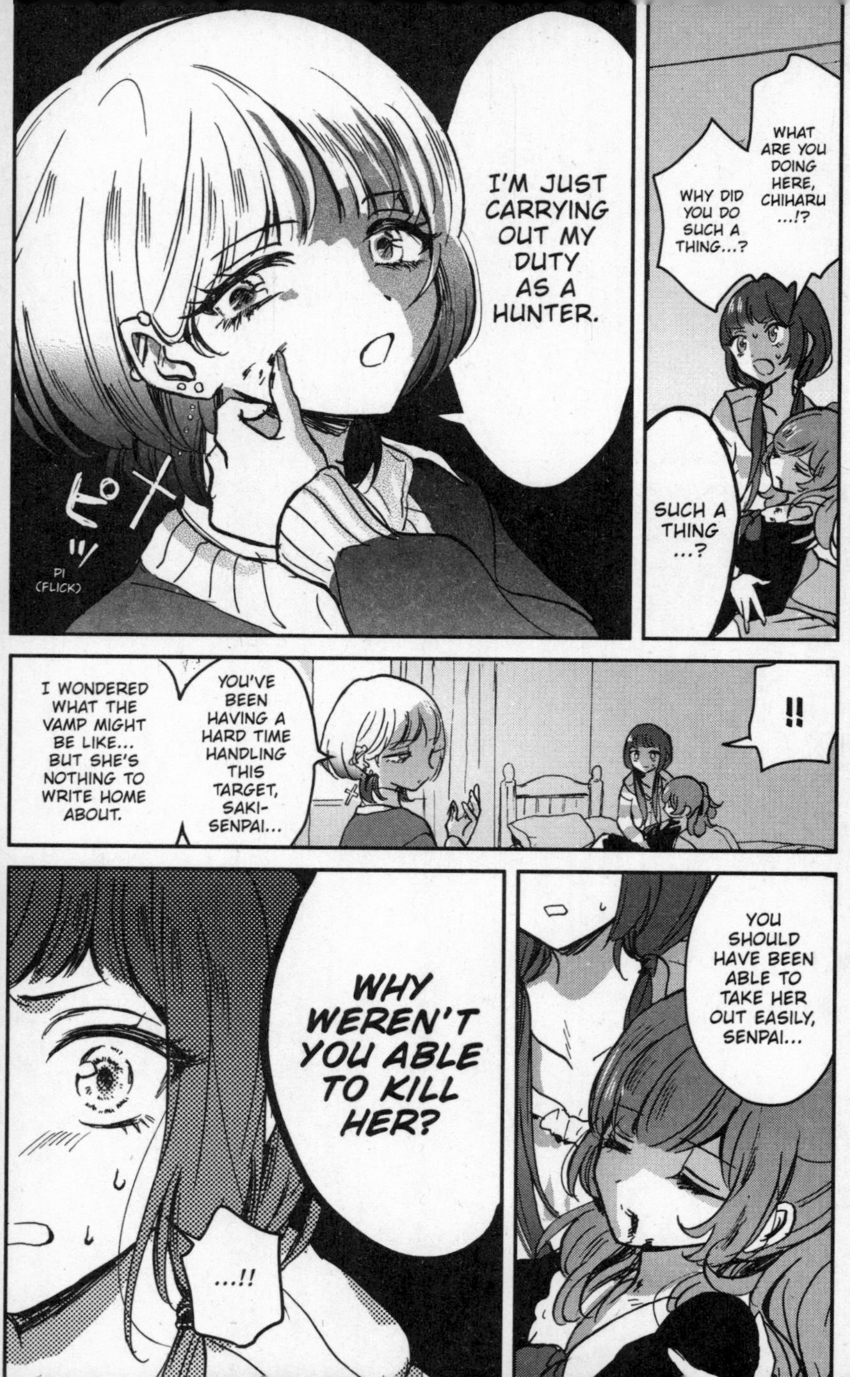
WHAT ARE YOU DOING HERE, CHIHARU ...!?
WHY DID YOU DO SUCH A THING...?
SUCH A THING ...?
I'M JUST CARRYING OUT MY DUTY AS A HUNTER.
PI (FLICK)
!!
YOU'VE BEEN HAVING A HARD TIME HANDLING THIS TARGET, SAKI-SENPAI...
I WONDERED WHAT THE VAMP MIGHT BE LIKE... BUT SHE'S NOTHING TO WRITE HOME ABOUT.
YOU SHOULD HAVE BEEN ABLE TO TAKE HER OUT EASILY, SENPAI...
WHY WEREN'T YOU ABLE TO KILL HER?
...!!

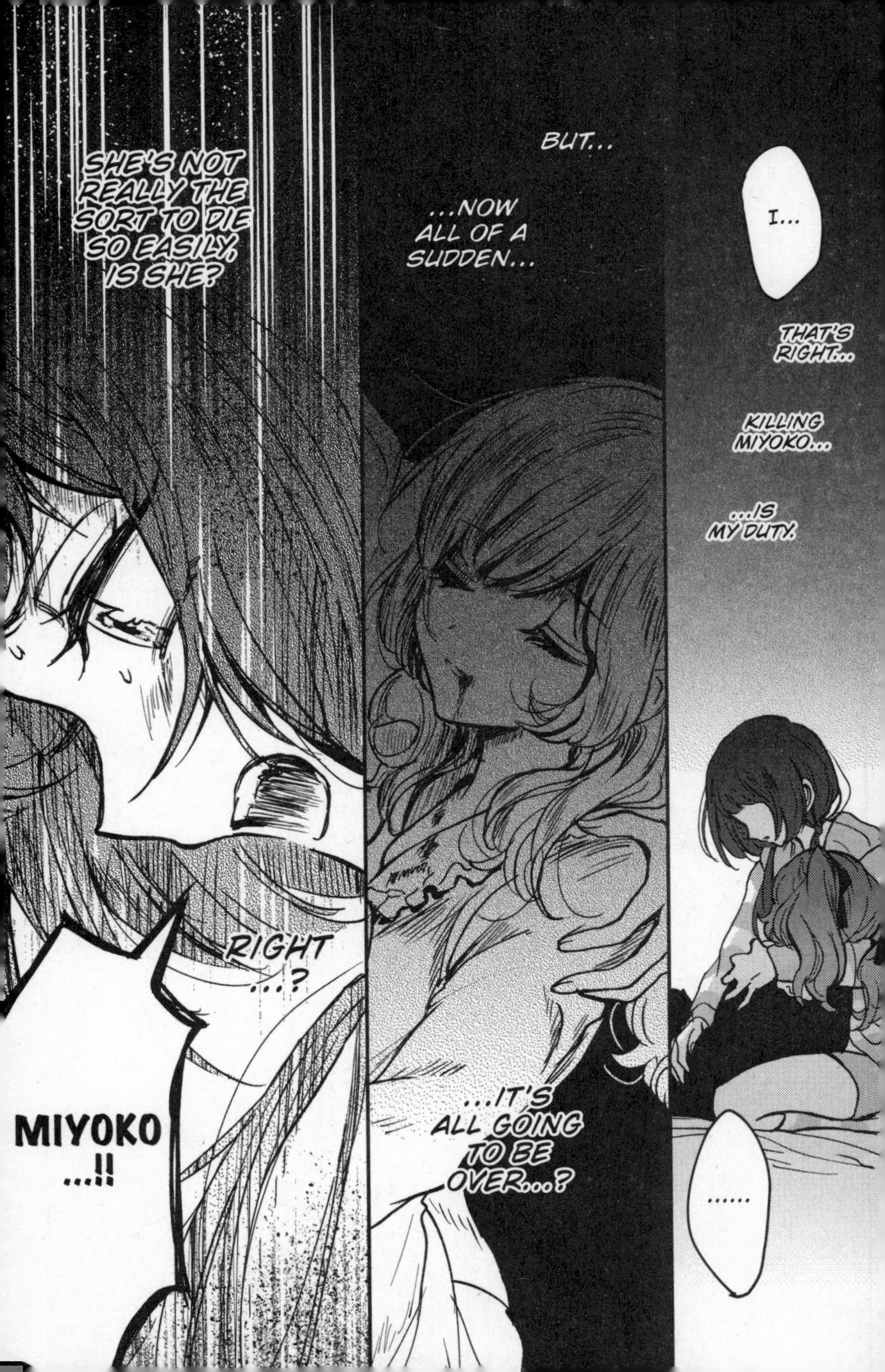
I...
THAT'S RIGHT...
KILLING MIYOKO...
...IS MY DUTY.
......
BUT...
...NOW ALL OF A SUDDEN...
...IT'S ALL GOING TO BE OVER...?
SHE'S NOT REALLY THE SORT TO DIE SO EASILY, IS SHE?
RIGHT ...?
MIYOKO ...!!

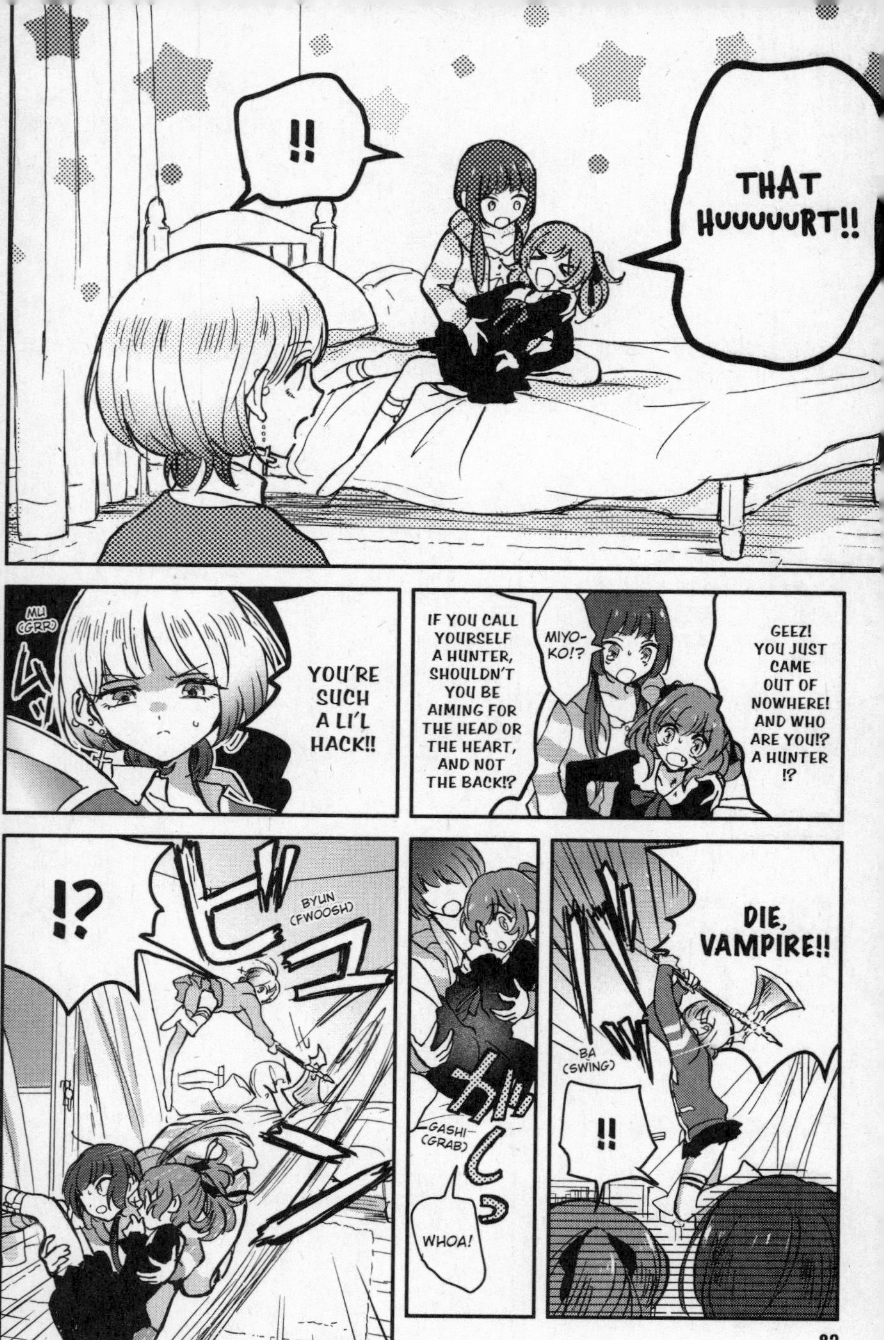
THAT HUUUUURT!!
!!
GEEZ! YOU JUST CAME OUT OF NOWHERE! AND WHO ARE YOU!? A HUNTER !?
MIYO-KO!?
IF YOU CALL YOURSELF A HUNTER, SHOULDN'T YOU BE AIMING FOR THE HEAD OR THE HEART, AND NOT THE BACK!?
YOU'RE SUCH A LI'L HACK!!
MU (GRR)
DIE, VAMPIRE!!
BA (SWING)
!!
GASHI (GRAB)
WHOA!
BYUN (FWOOSH)
!?

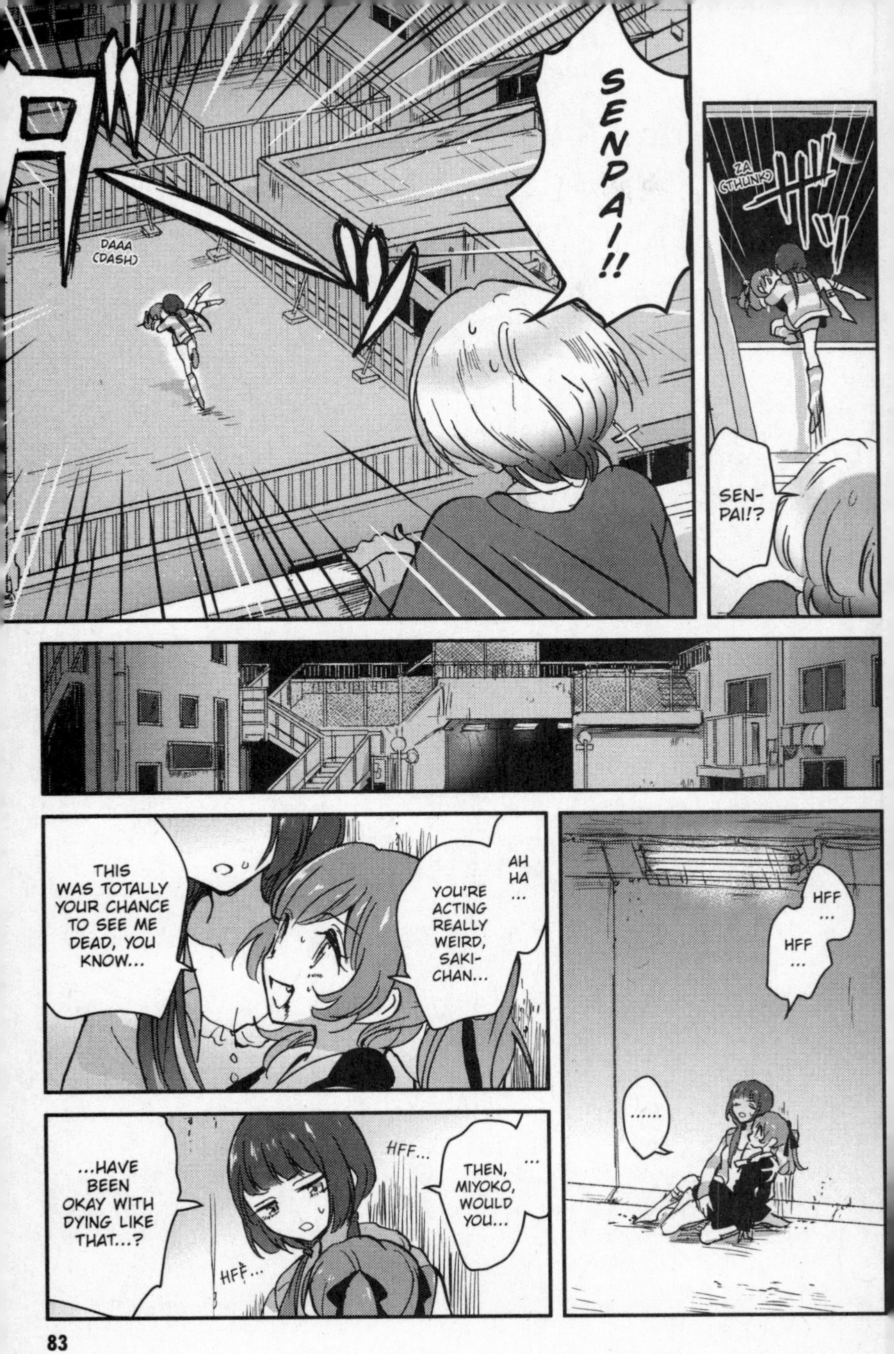
ZA (THUNK)
SEN-PAI!?
SENPAI!!
DAAA (DASH)
HFF... HFF...
......
AH HA...
YOU'RE ACTING REALLY WEIRD, SAKI-CHAN...
THIS WAS TOTALLY YOUR CHANCE TO SEE ME DEAD, YOU KNOW...
HFF...
...
THEN, MIYOKO, WOULD YOU...
...HAVE BEEN OKAY WITH DYING LIKE THAT...?
HFF...

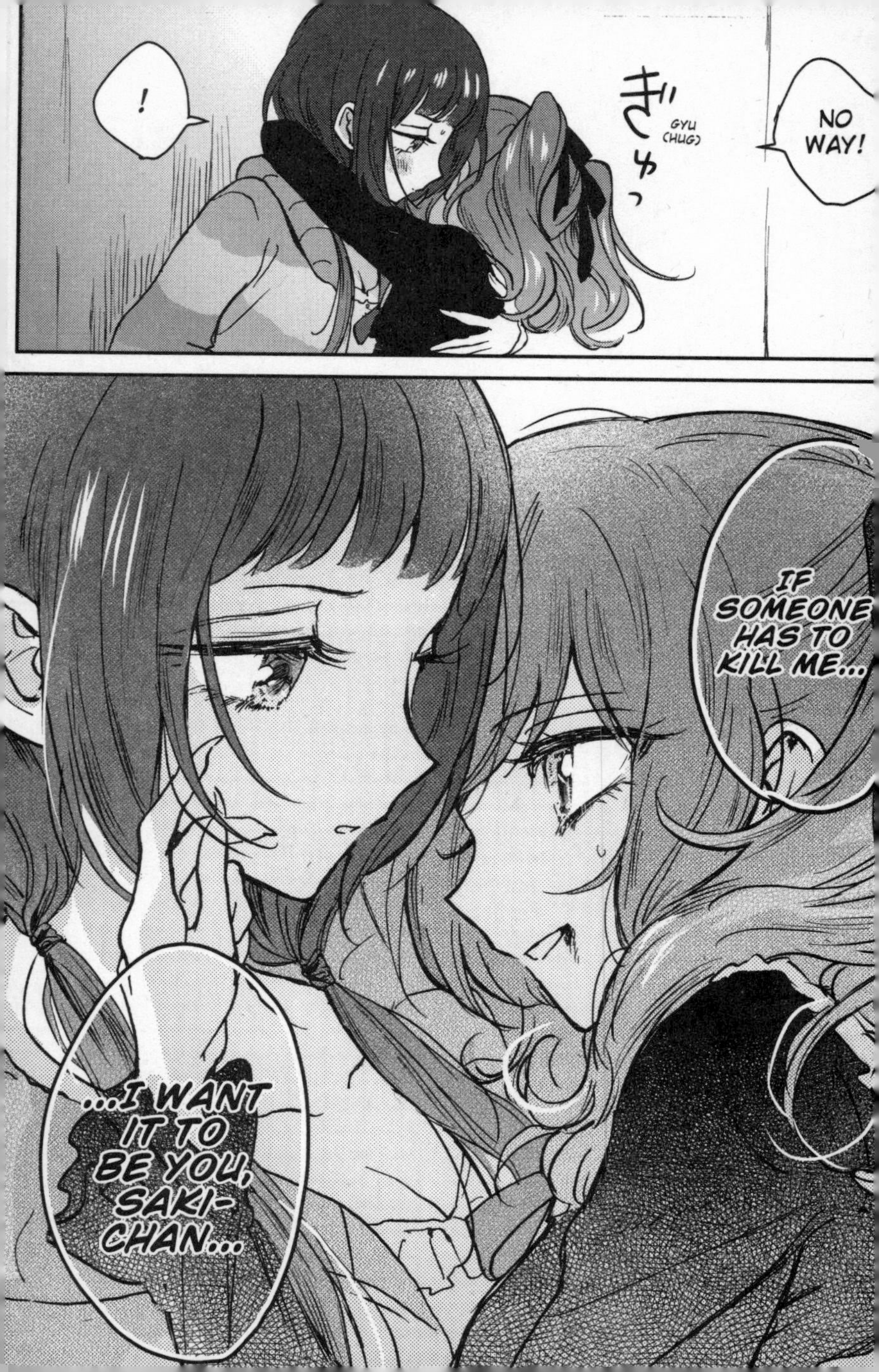
NO WAY!
ぎゅっ
GYU (HUG)
!
IF SOMEONE HAS TO KILL ME...
...I WANT IT TO BE YOU, SAKI-CHAN...

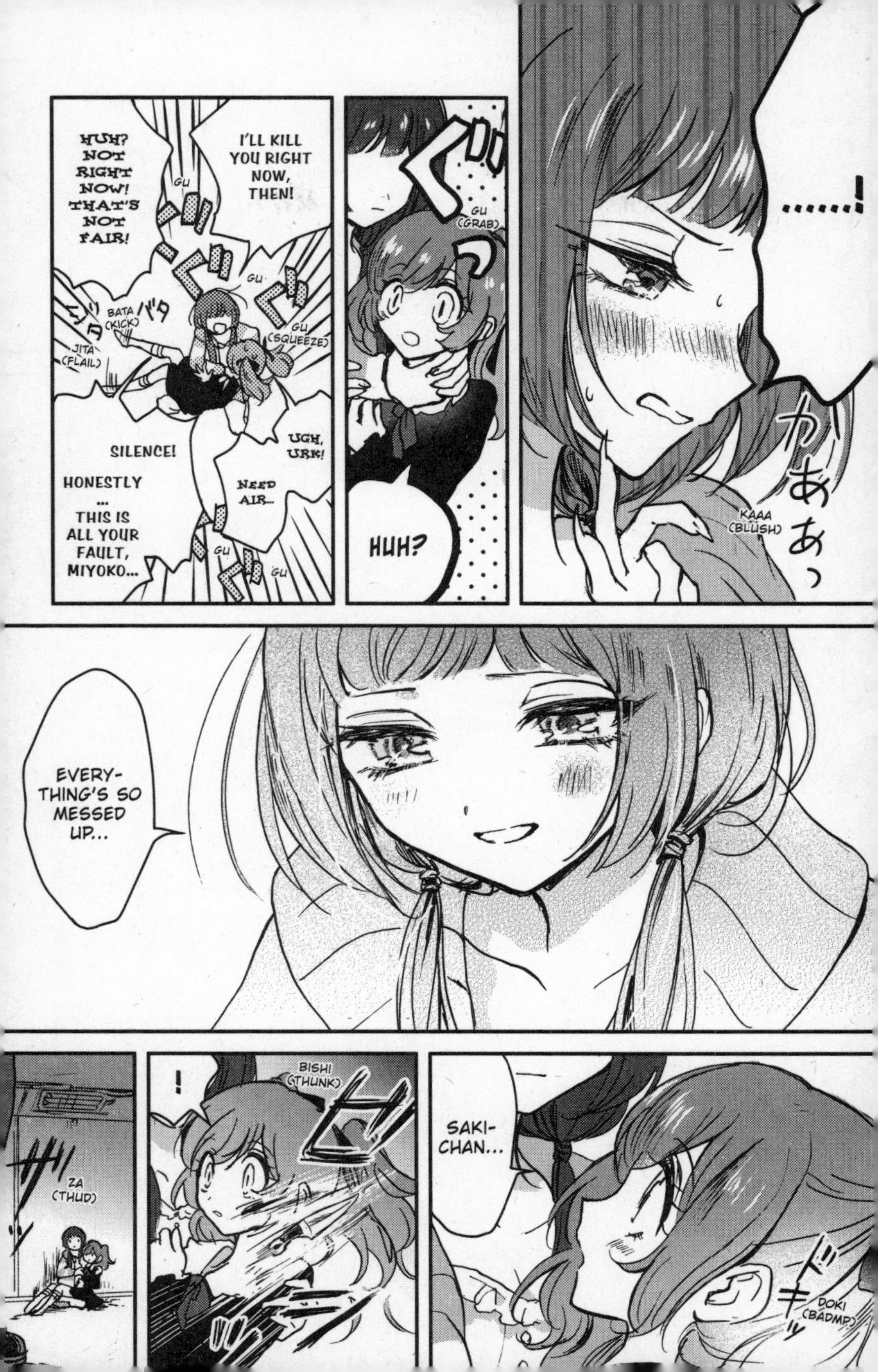
......!
KAAA (BLUSH)
GU (GRAB)
HUH?
I'LL KILL YOU RIGHT NOW, THEN!
HUH? NOT RIGHT NOW! THAT'S NOT FAIR!
GU
GU
BATA (KICK)
JITA (FLAIL)
GU (SQUEEZE)
UGH, URK!
NEED AIR...
SILENCE!
HONESTLY ... THIS IS ALL YOUR FAULT, MIYOKO...
GU
GU
EVERY-THING'S SO MESSED UP...
SAKI-CHAN...
DOKI (BADMP)
!
BISHI (THUNK)
ZA (THUD)

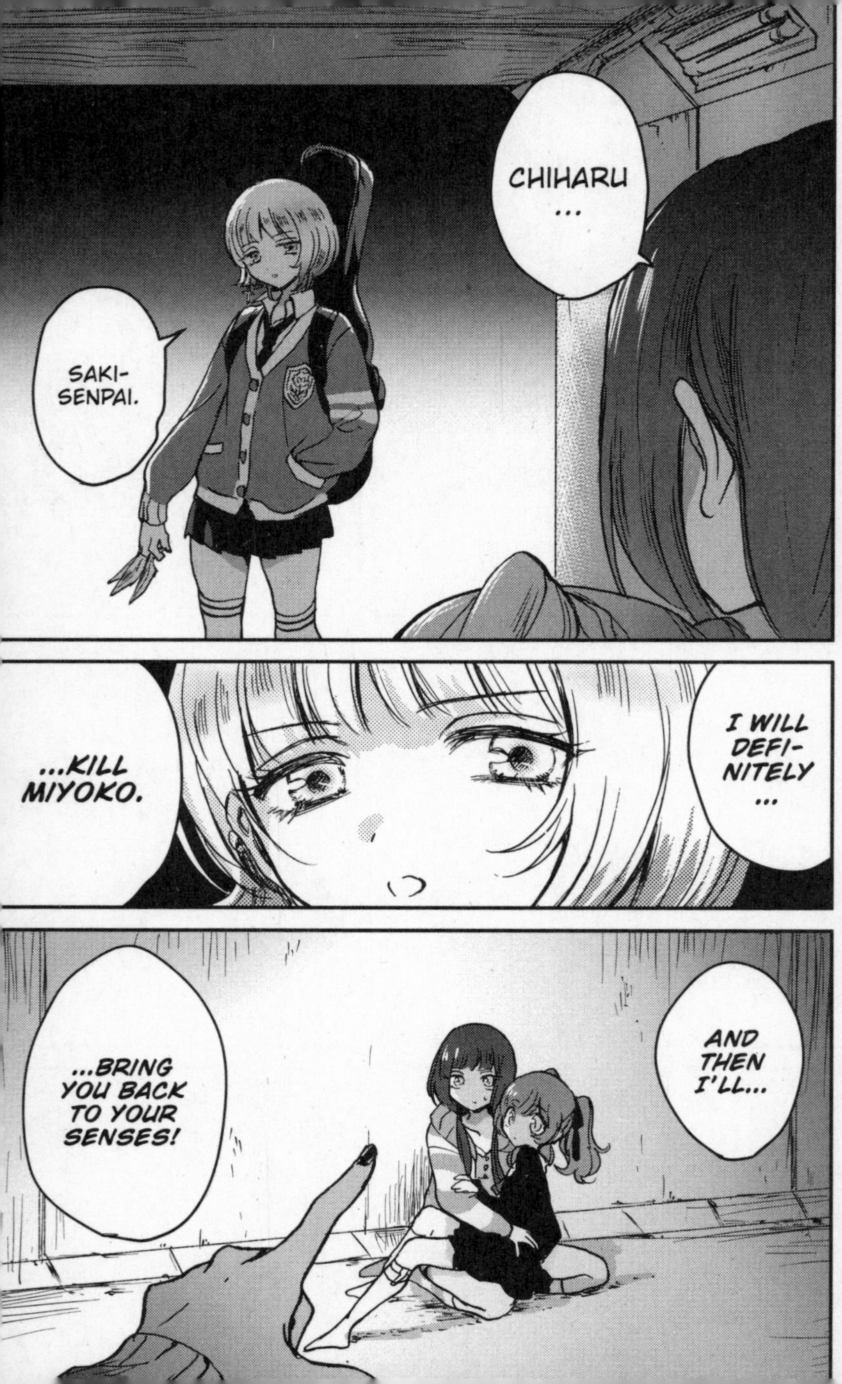
CHIHARU ...
SAKI-SENPAI.
I WILL DEFINITELY ...
...KILL MIYOKO.
AND THEN I'LL...
...BRING YOU BACK TO YOUR SENSES!

Killing me!
①

Killing me!
1

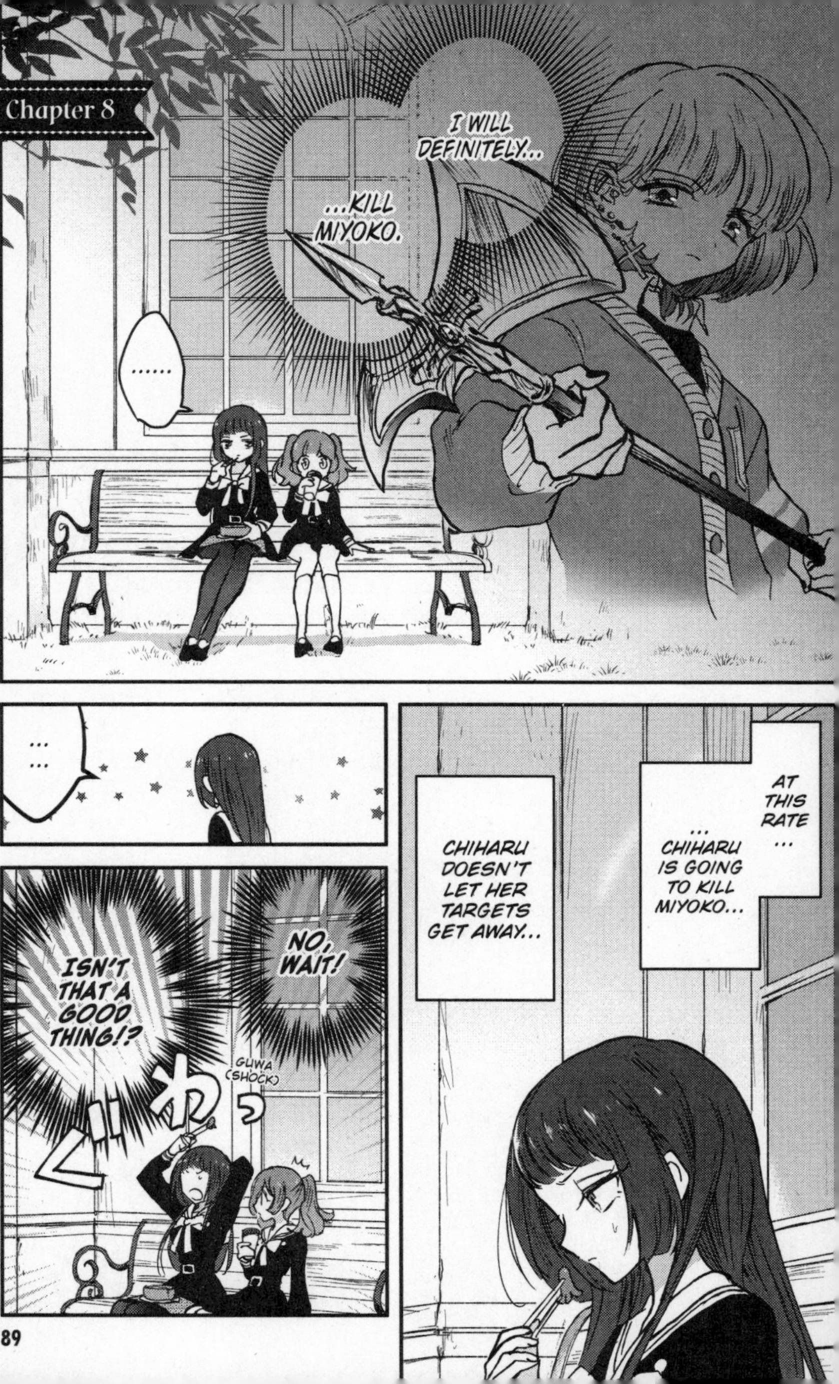

Chapter 8
I WILL DEFINITELY...
...KILL MIYOKO.
......
AT THIS RATE...
...CHIHARU IS GOING TO KILL MIYOKO...
CHIHARU DOESN'T LET HER TARGETS GET AWAY...
...
...
NO, WAIT!
ISN'T THAT A GOOD THING!?
GUWA (SHOCK)

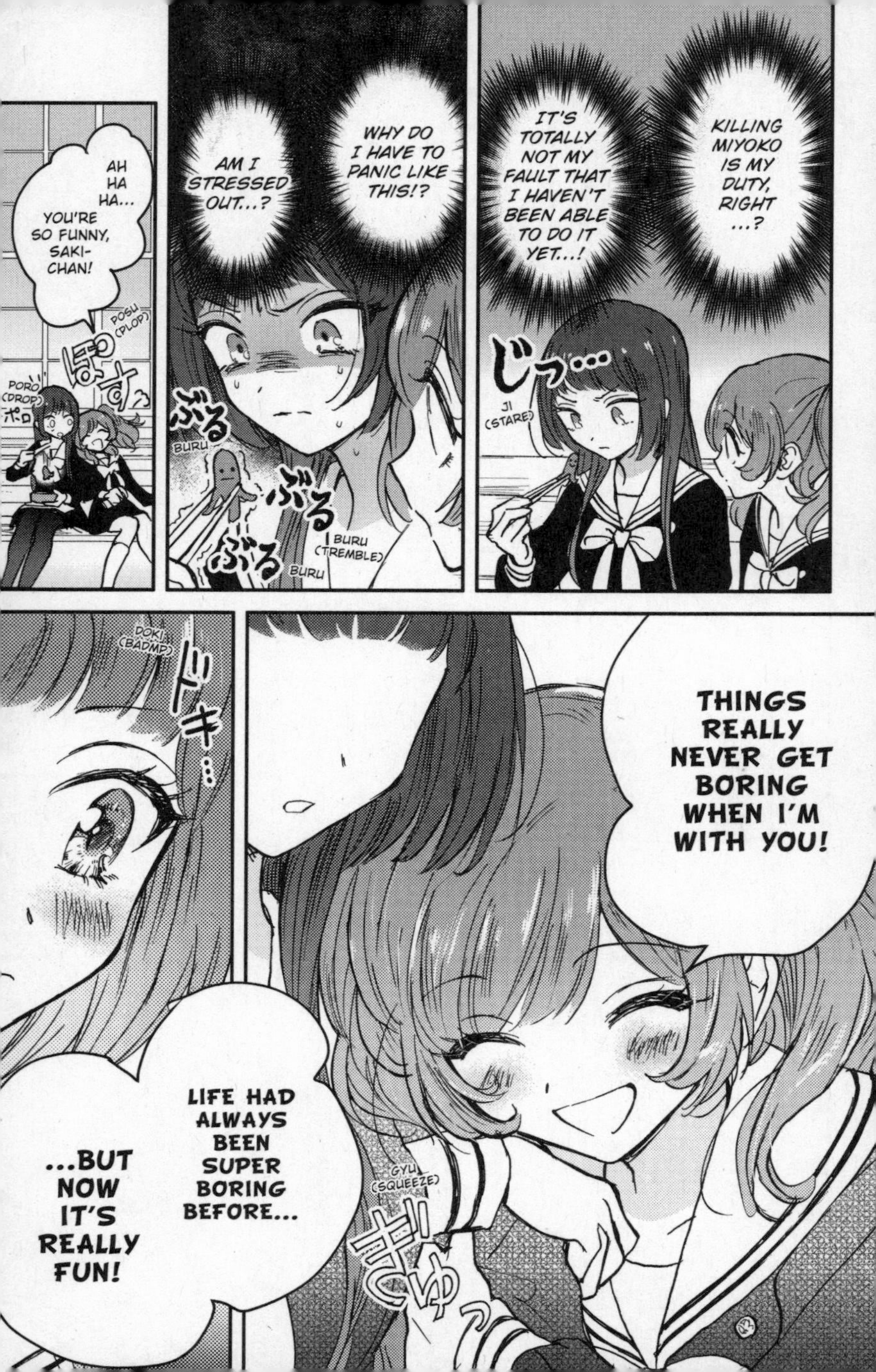

KILLING MIYOKO IS MY DUTY, RIGHT...?
IT'S TOTALLY NOT MY FAULT THAT I HAVEN'T BEEN ABLE TO DO IT YET...!
じっ…
JI (STARE)
WHY DO I HAVE TO PANIC LIKE THIS!?
AM I STRESSED OUT...?
ぶる
BURU
ぶる
BURU (TREMBLE)
ぶる
BURU
ぽす
POSU (PLOP)
AH HA HA... YOU'RE SO FUNNY, SAKI-CHAN!
POROポロ (DROP)
ポロ
THINGS REALLY NEVER GET BORING WHEN I'M WITH YOU!
LIFE HAD ALWAYS BEEN SUPER BORING BEFORE...
...BUT NOW IT'S REALLY FUN!
ぎゅっ
GYU (SQUEEZE)
ドキ…
DOKI (BADMP)

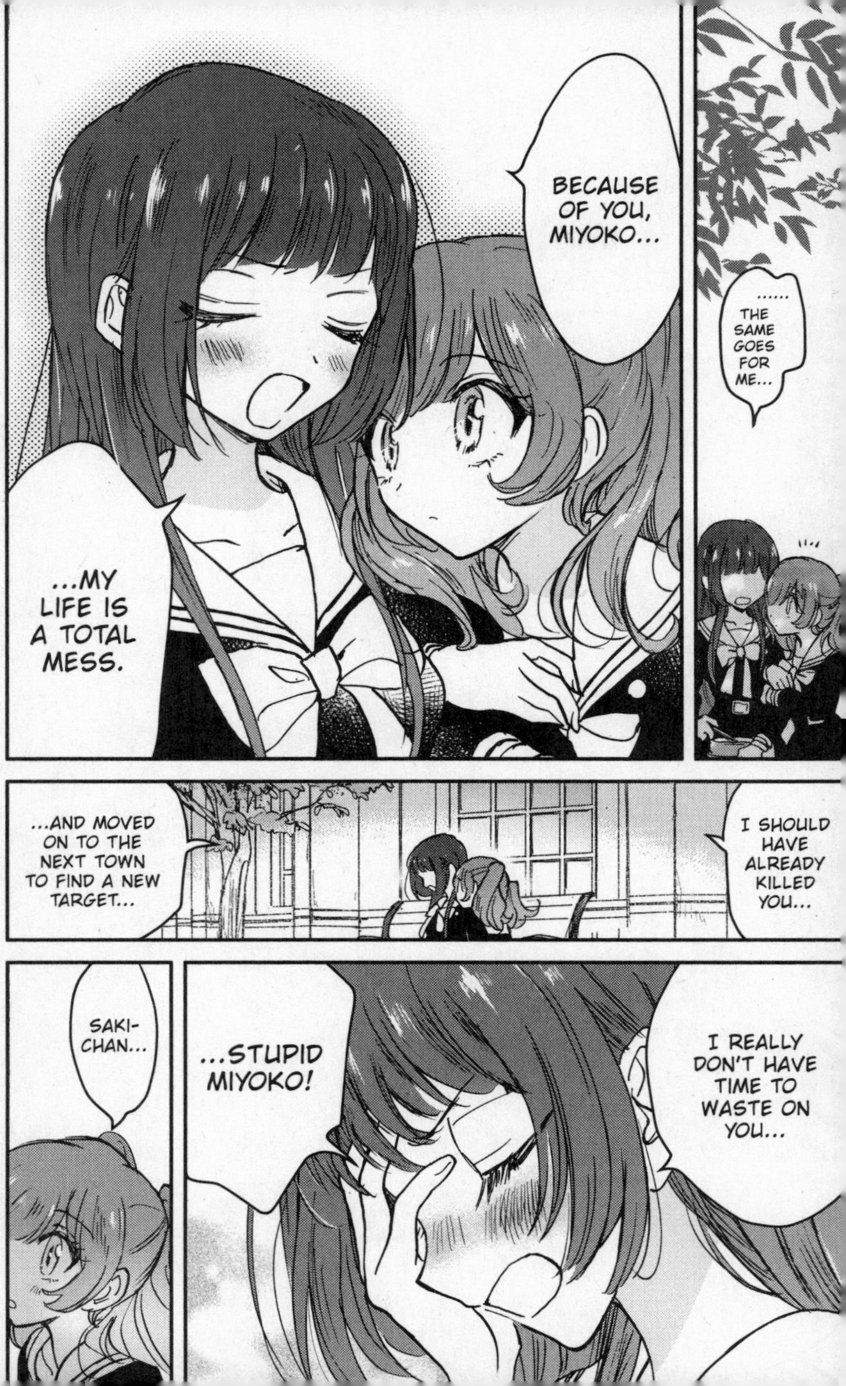
...... THE SAME GOES FOR ME...
BECAUSE OF YOU, MIYOKO...
...MY LIFE IS A TOTAL MESS.
I SHOULD HAVE ALREADY KILLED YOU...
...AND MOVED ON TO THE NEXT TOWN TO FIND A NEW TARGET...
I REALLY DON'T HAVE TIME TO WASTE ON YOU...
...STUPID MIYOKO!
SAKI-CHAN...

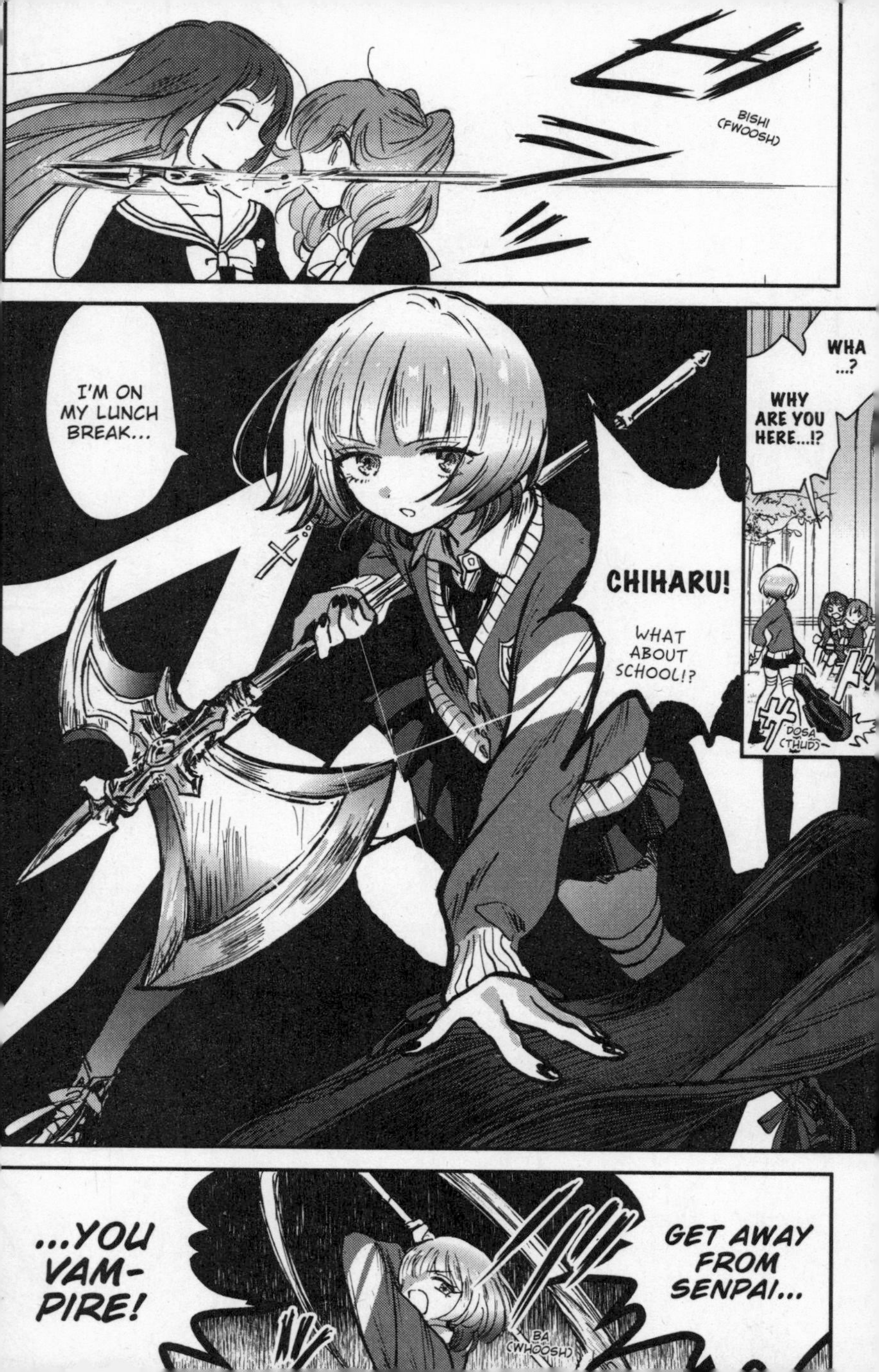
BISHI (FWOOSH)
WHA ...?
WHY ARE YOU HERE...!?
DOSA (THUD)
CHIHARU!
WHAT ABOUT SCHOOL!?
I'M ON MY LUNCH BREAK...
GET AWAY FROM SENPAI...
BA (WHOOSH)
...YOU VAM-PIRE!

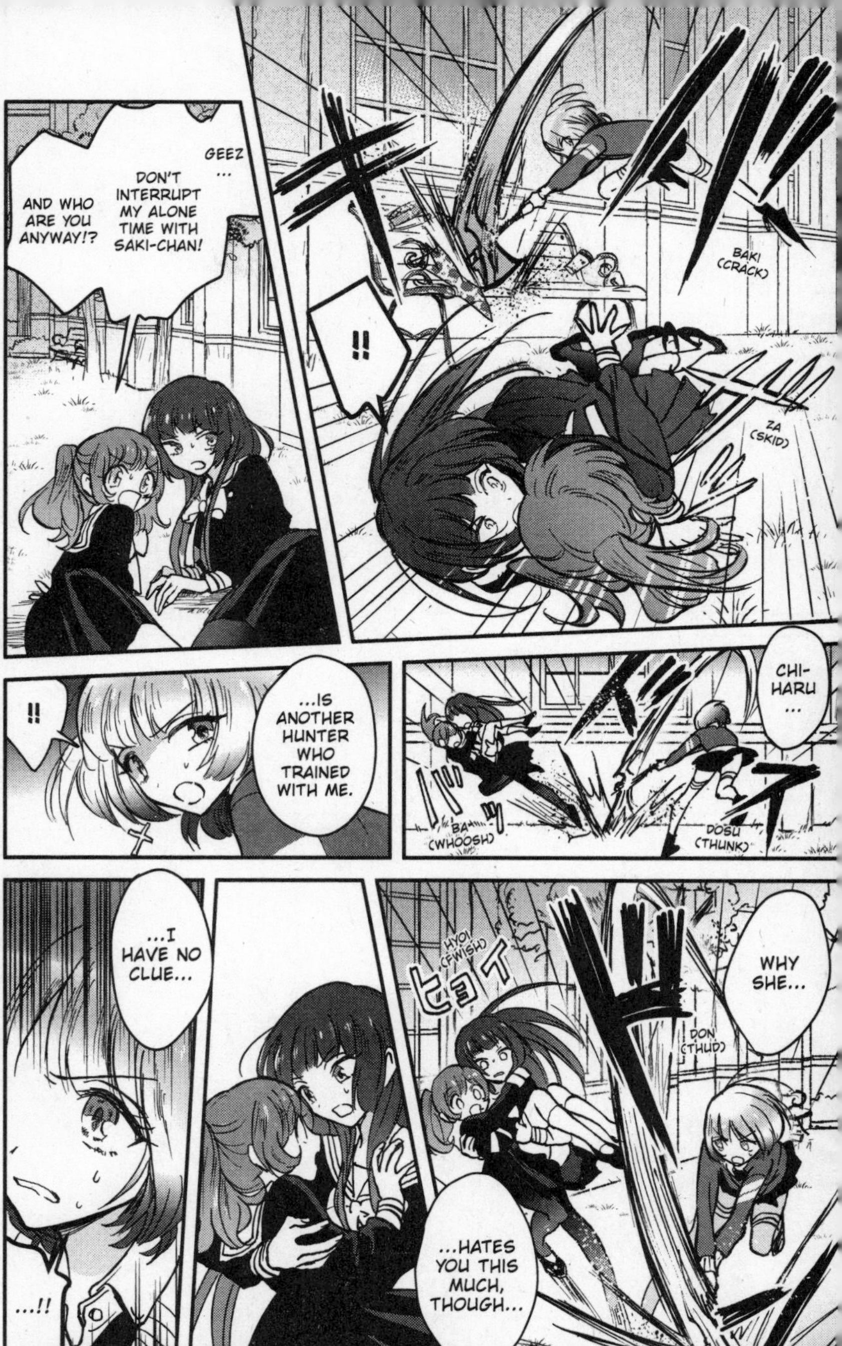
BAKI (CRACK)
!!
ZA (SKID)
GEEZ ...
DON'T INTERRUPT MY ALONE TIME WITH SAKI-CHAN!
AND WHO ARE YOU ANYWAY!?
CHI-HARU ...
DOSU (THUNK)
BA (WHOOSH)
...IS ANOTHER HUNTER WHO TRAINED WITH ME.
!!
WHY SHE...
HYOI (FWISH)
DON (THUD)
...HATES YOU THIS MUCH, THOUGH...
...I HAVE NO CLUE...
...!!

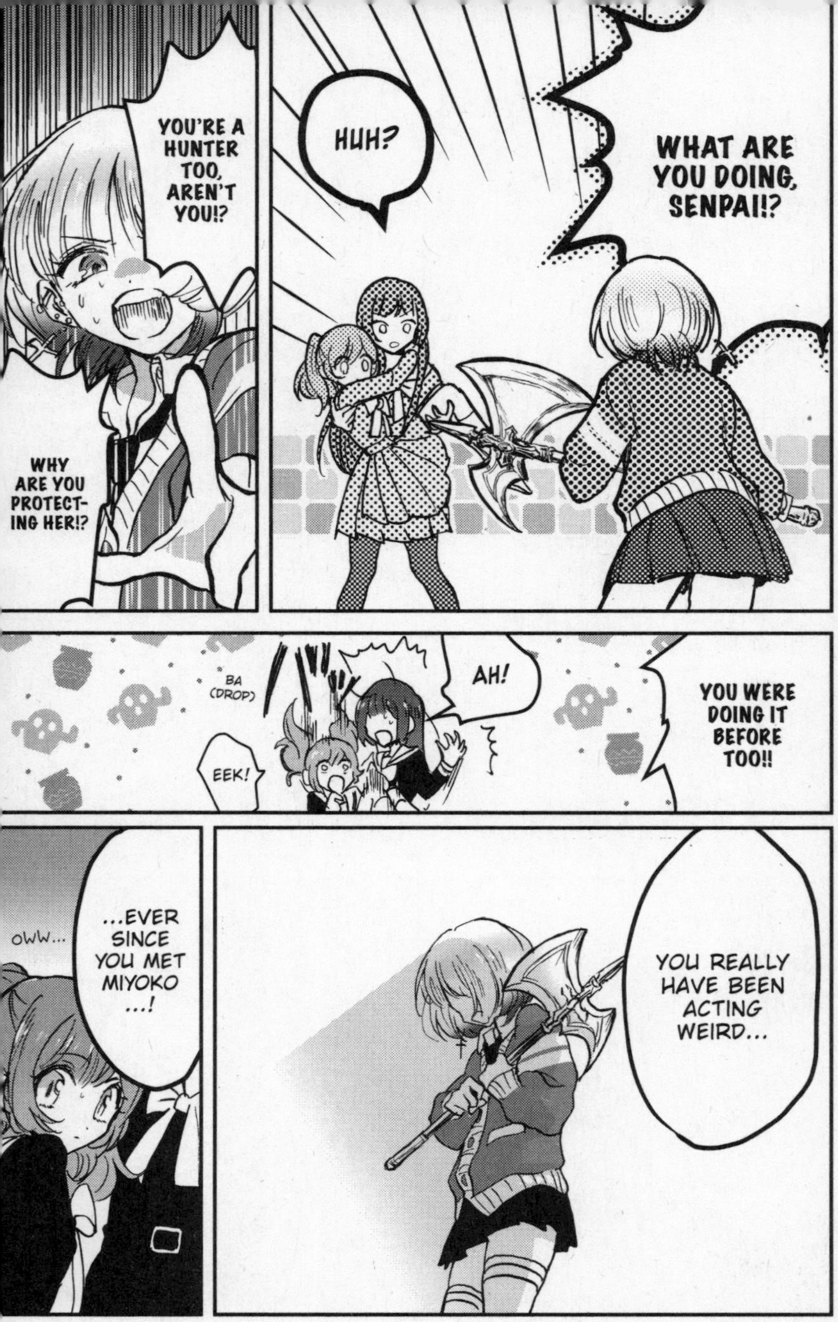
WHAT ARE YOU DOING, SENPAI!?
HUH?
YOU'RE A HUNTER TOO, AREN'T YOU!?
WHY ARE YOU PROTECTING HER!?
YOU WERE DOING IT BEFORE TOO!!
AH!
BA (DROP)
EEK!
YOU REALLY HAVE BEEN ACTING WEIRD...
...EVER SINCE YOU MET MIYOKO ...!
OWW...

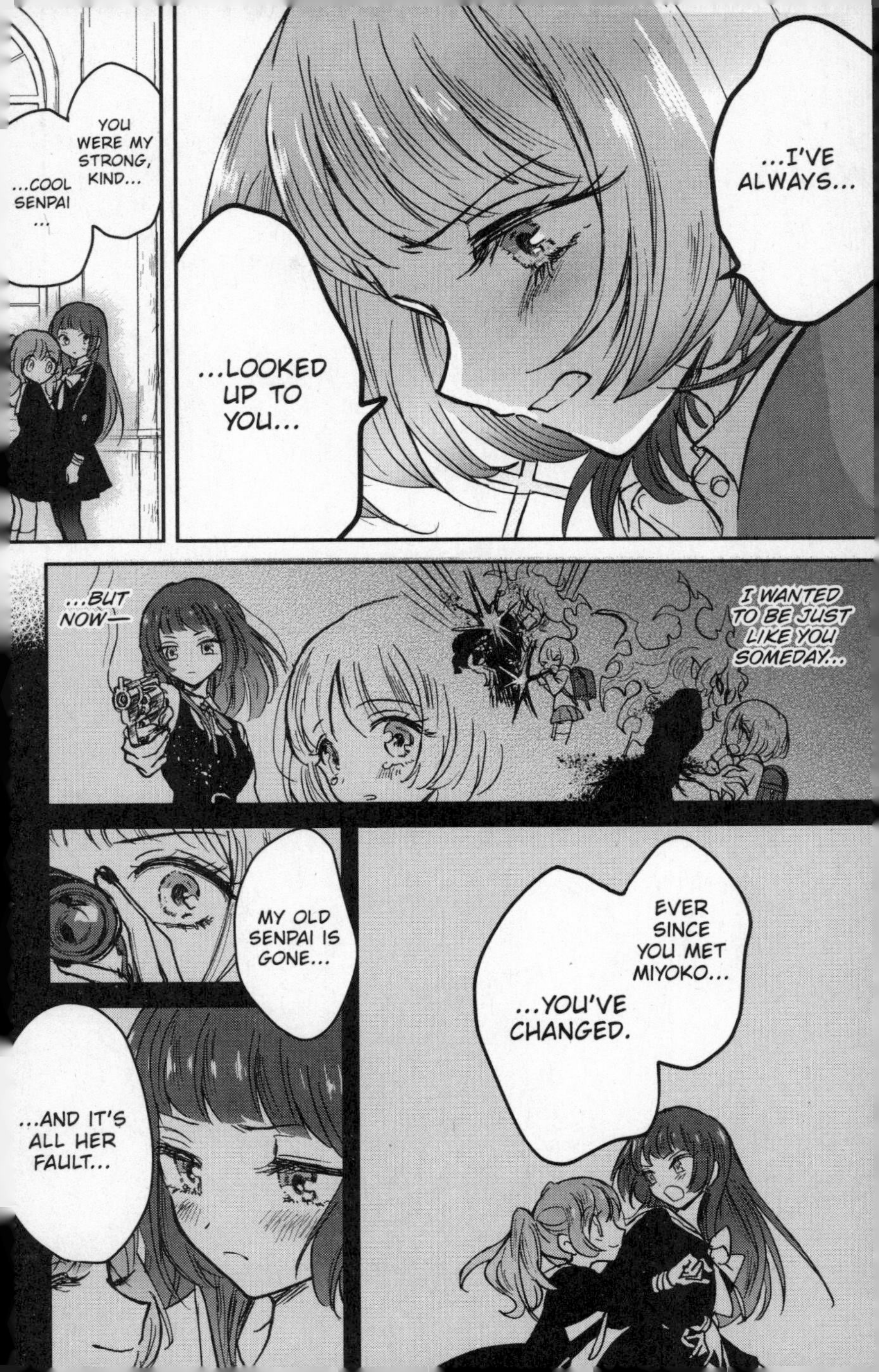
...I'VE ALWAYS...
...LOOKED UP TO YOU...
YOU WERE MY STRONG, KIND...
...COOL SENPAI ...
I WANTED TO BE JUST LIKE YOU SOMEDAY...
...BUT NOW—
EVER SINCE YOU MET MIYOKO...
...YOU'VE CHANGED.
MY OLD SENPAI IS GONE...
...AND IT'S ALL HER FAULT...

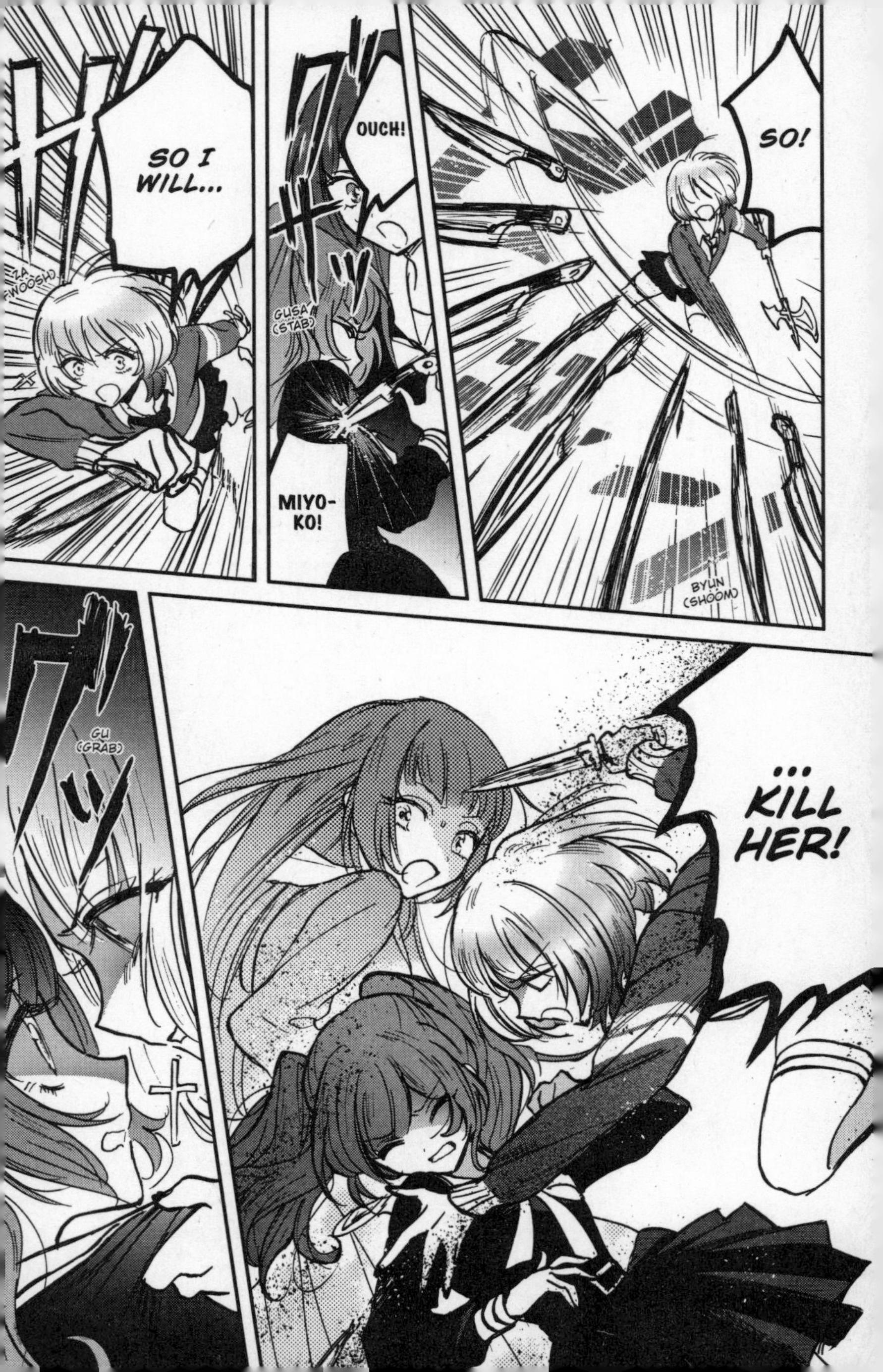
SO!
BYUN (SHOOM)
OUCH!
GUSA (STAB)
MIYO-KO!
SO I WILL...
ZA (WOOSH)
...KILL HER!
GU (GRAB)

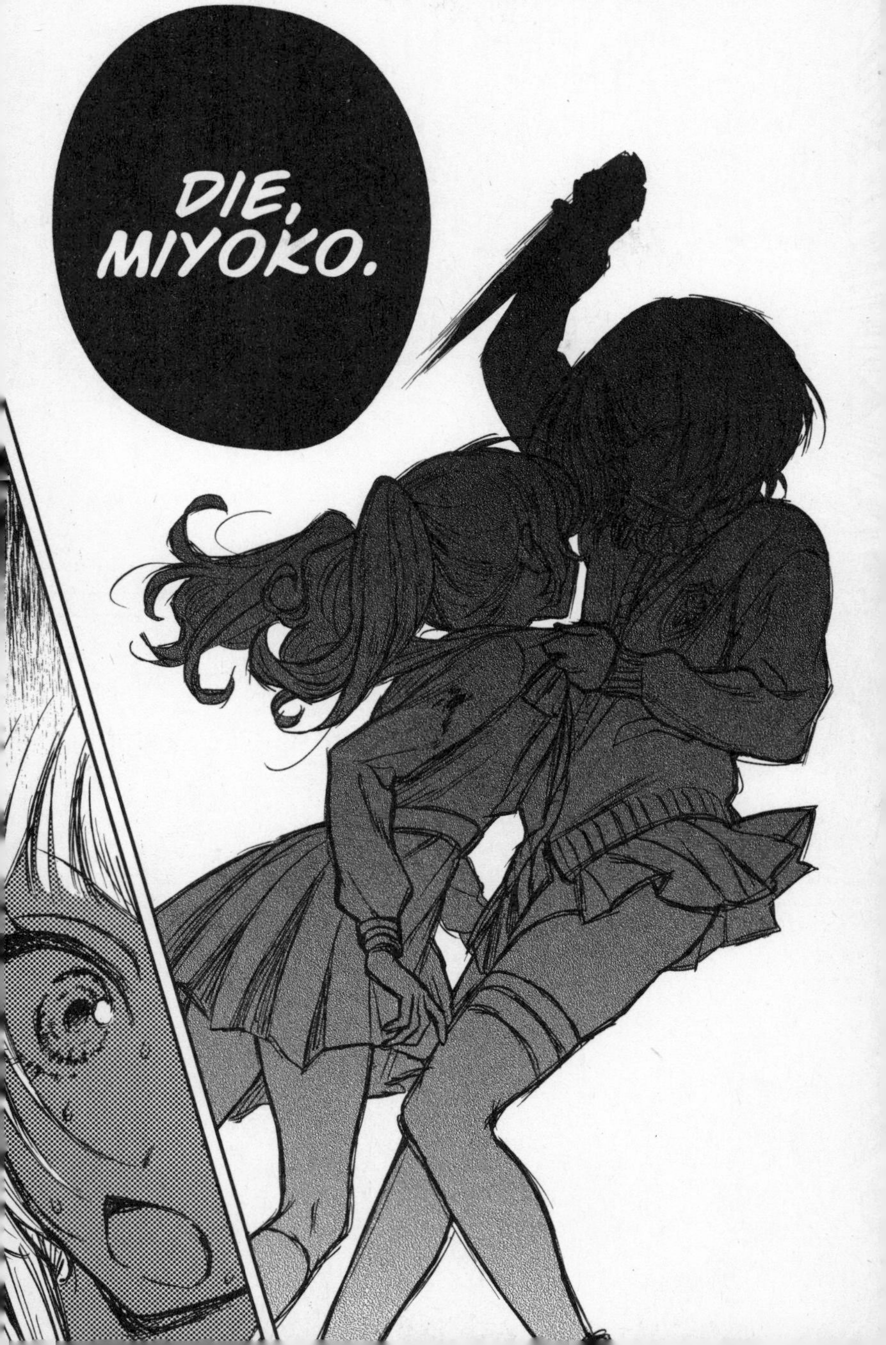
DIE, MIYOKO.

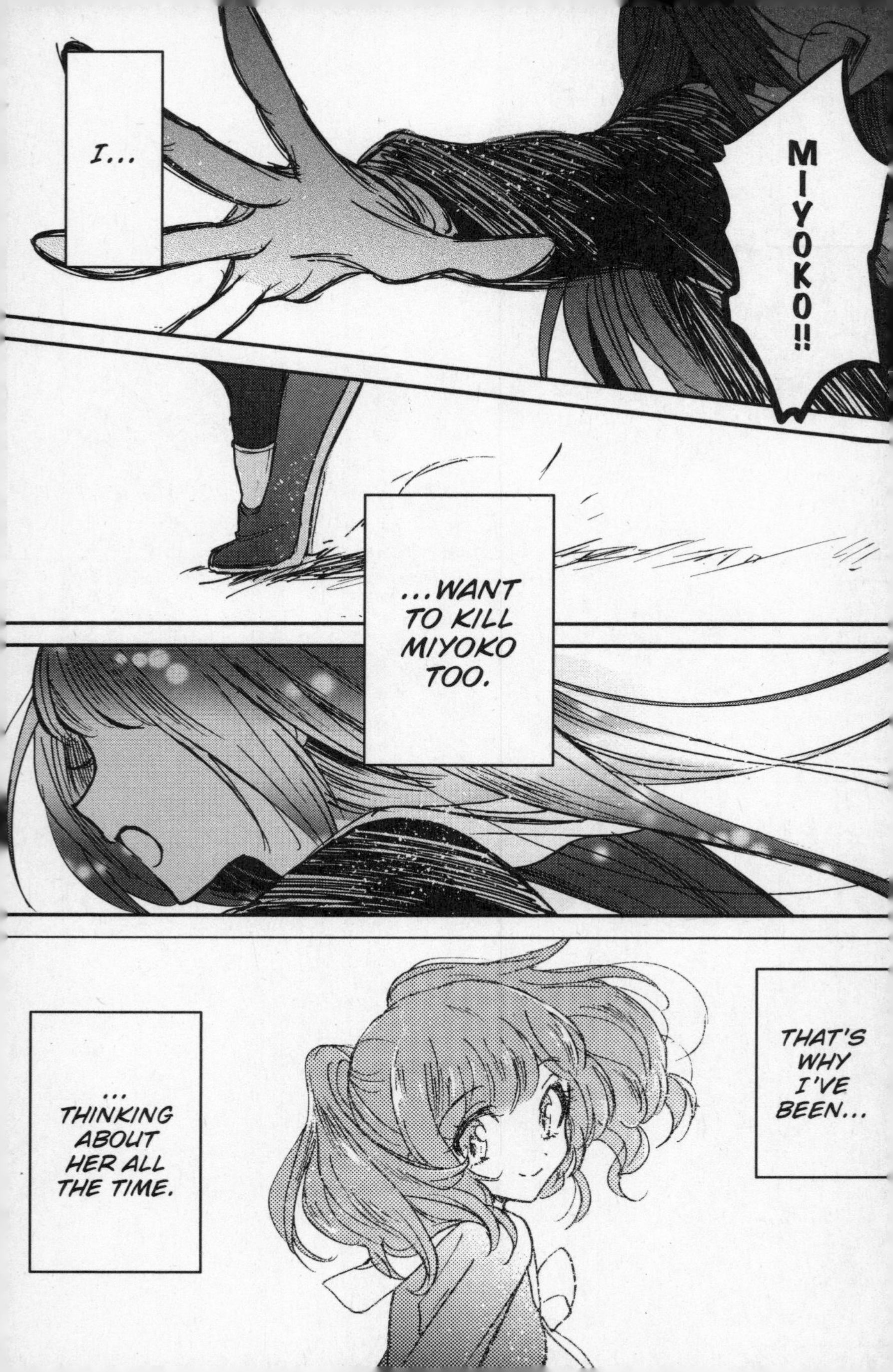
MIYOKO!!
I...
...WANT TO KILL MIYOKO TOO.
THAT'S WHY I'VE BEEN...
...THINKING ABOUT HER ALL THE TIME.

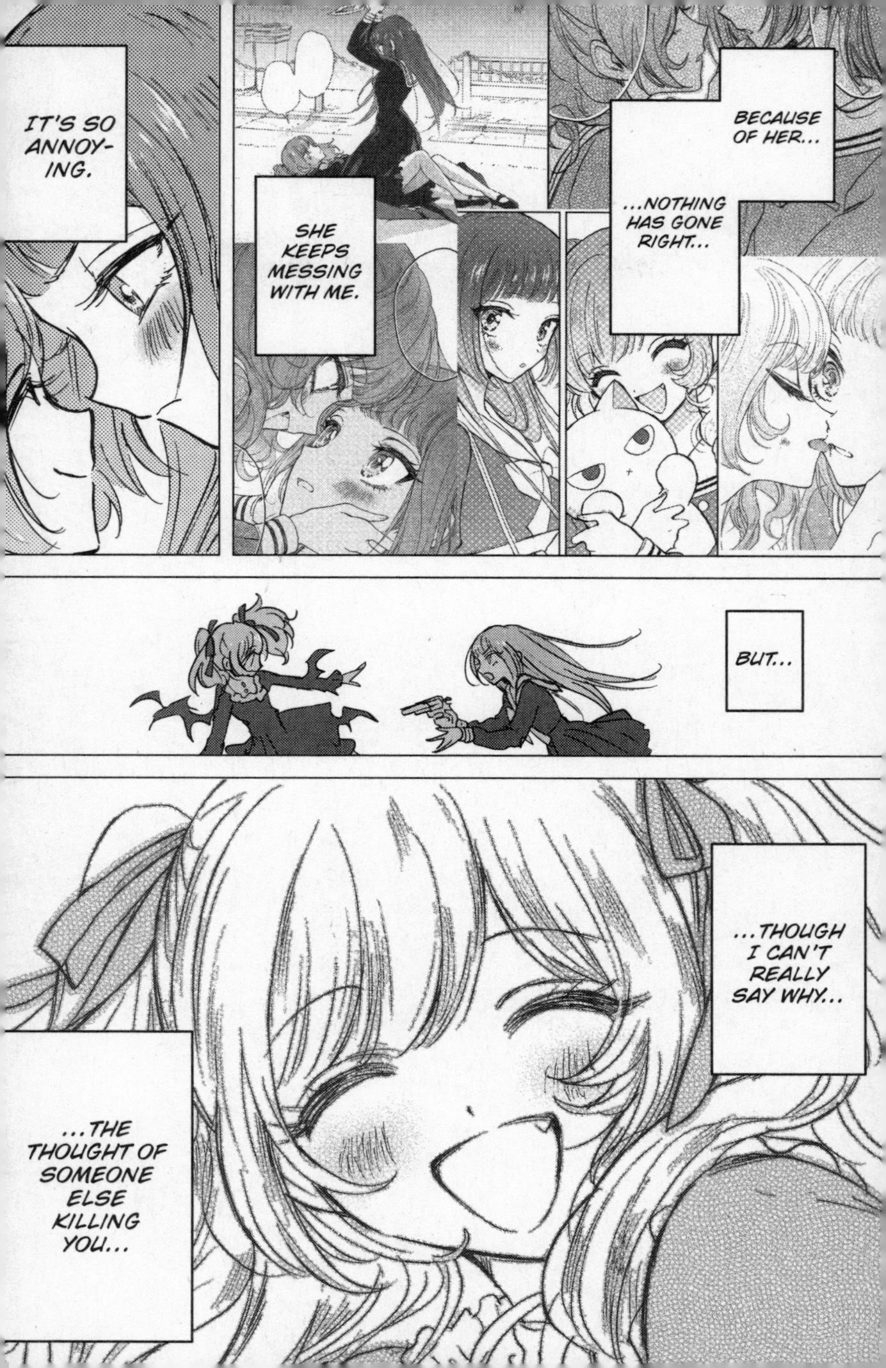
BECAUSE OF HER...
...NOTHING HAS GONE RIGHT...
SHE KEEPS MESSING WITH ME.
IT'S SO ANNOYING.
BUT...
...THOUGH I CAN'T REALLY SAY WHY...
...THE THOUGHT OF SOMEONE ELSE KILLING YOU...

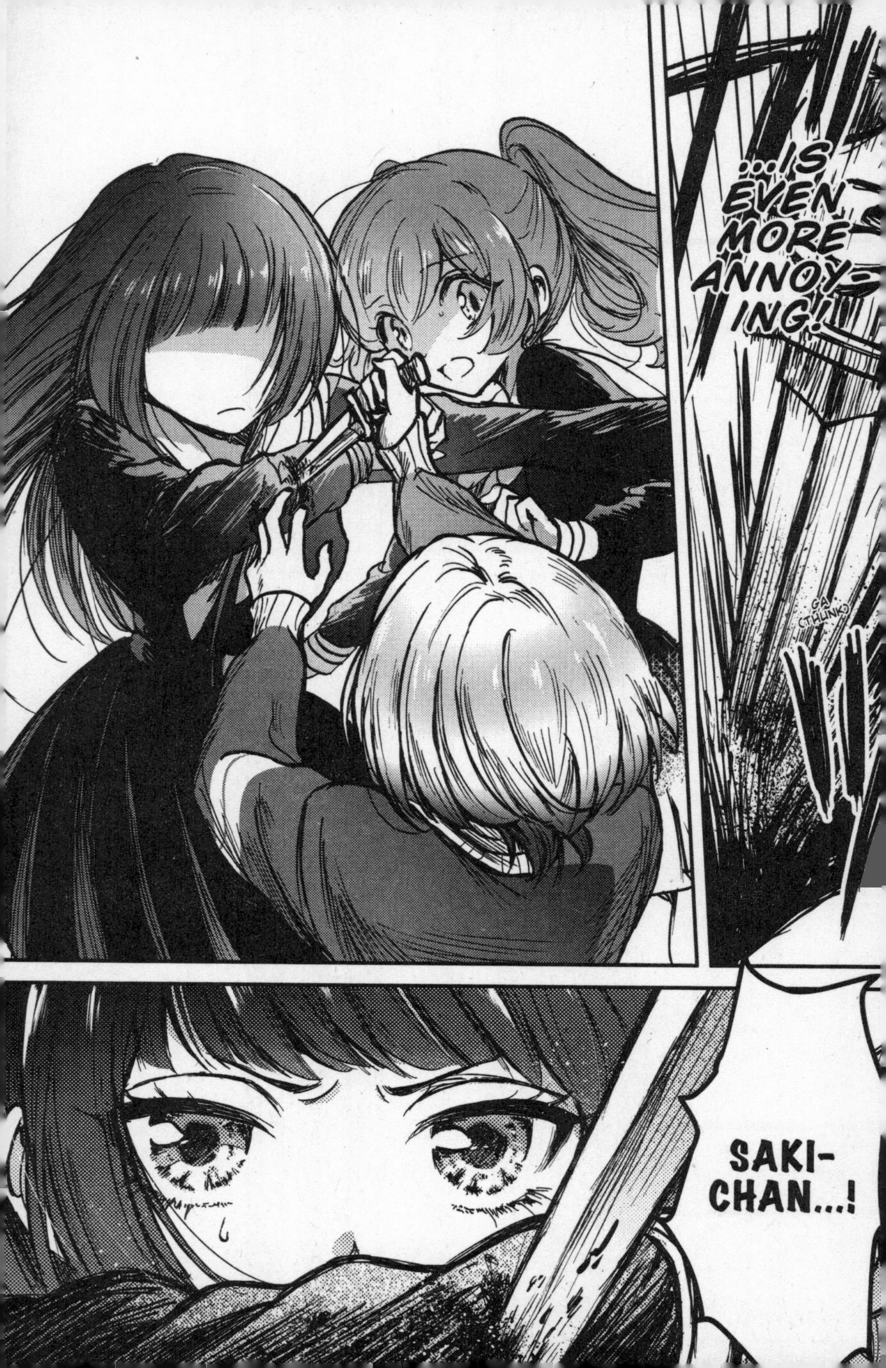
...IS EVEN MORE ANNOY-ING!
GA (THUNK)
SAKI-CHAN...!

Chapter 9

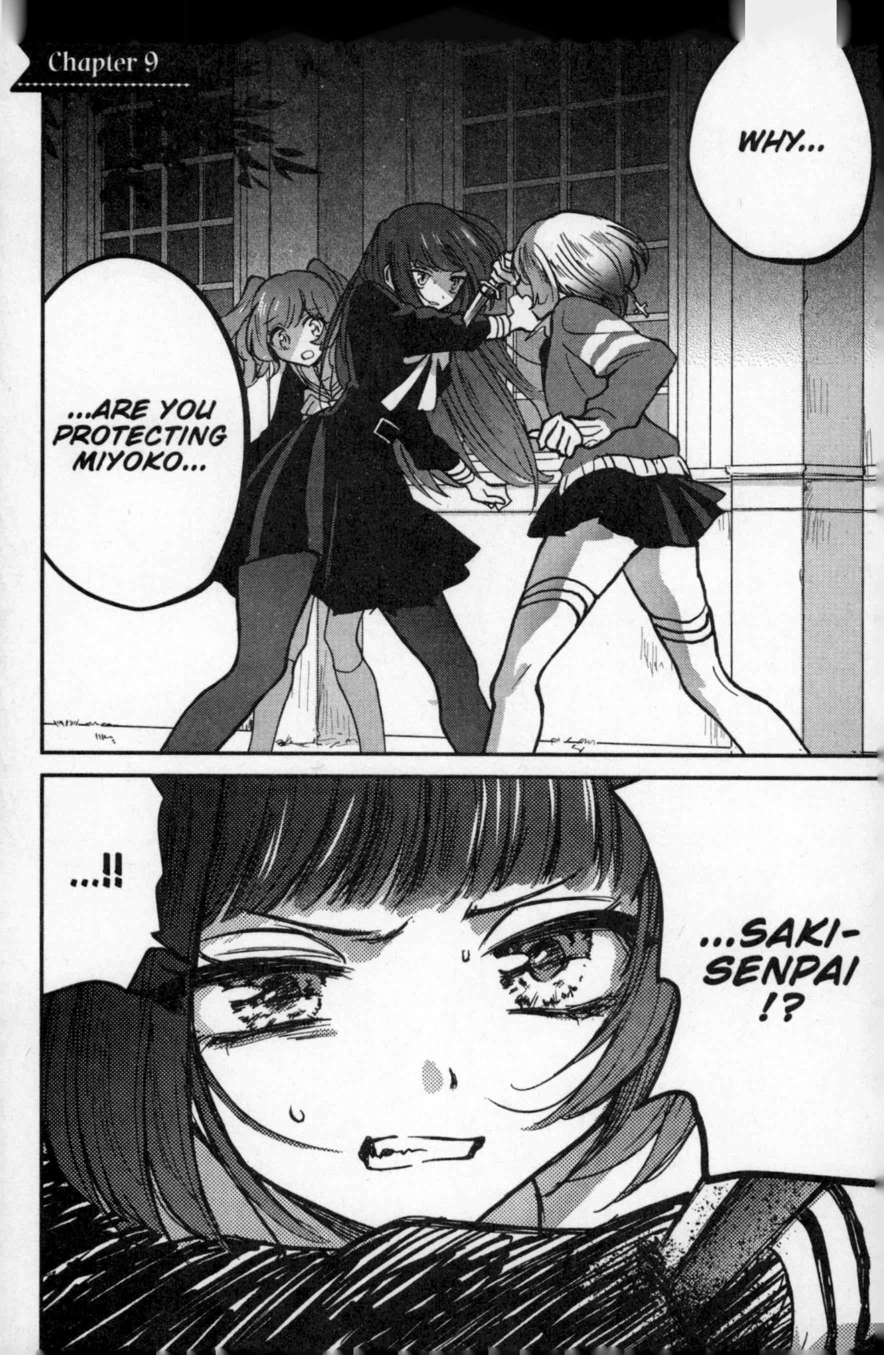
WHY...
...ARE YOU PROTECTING MIYOKO...
...!!
...SAKI-SENPAI!?

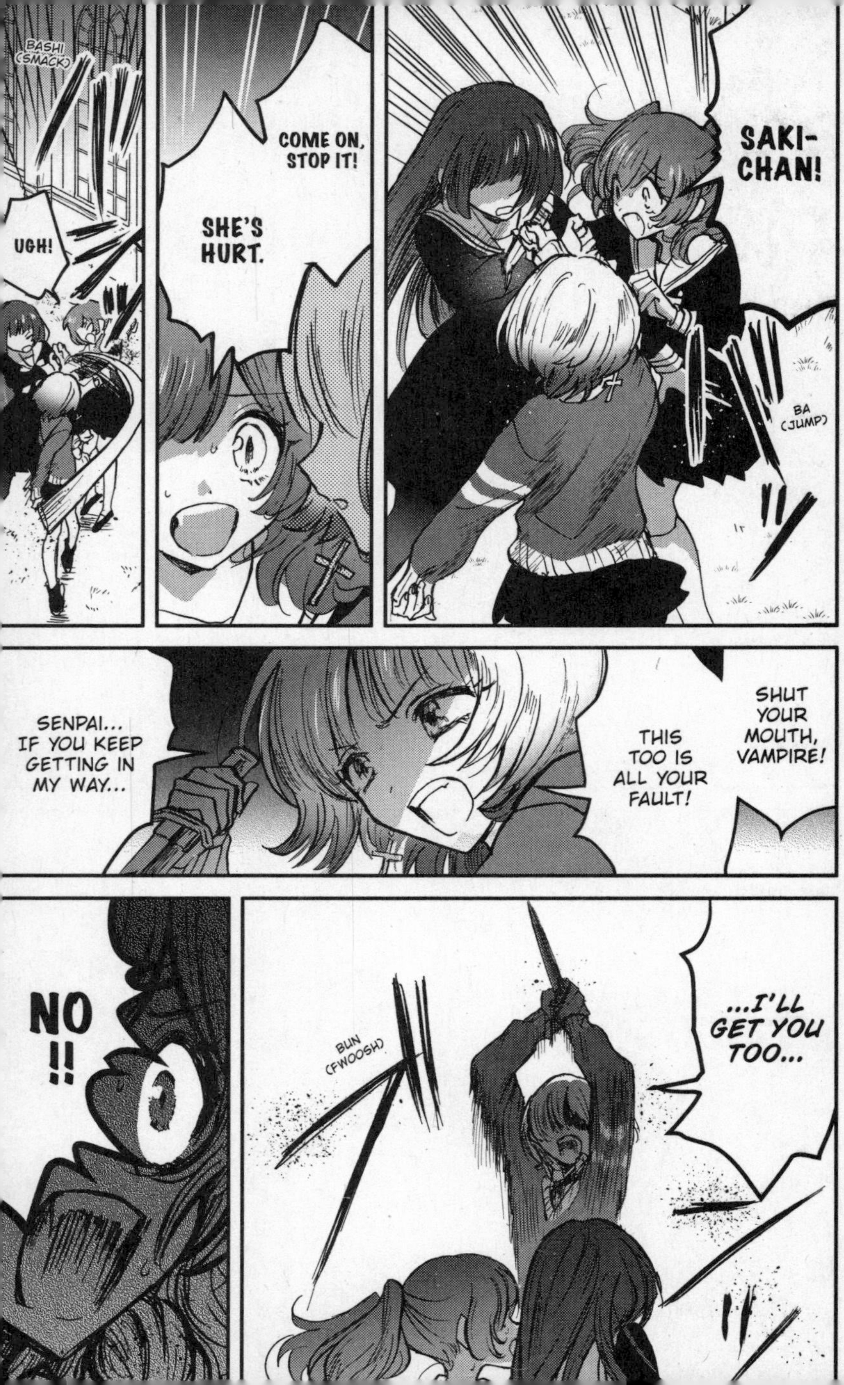
SAKI-CHAN!
BA (JUMP)
COME ON, STOP IT!
SHE'S HURT.
BASHI (SMACK)
UGH!
SHUT YOUR MOUTH, VAMPIRE!
THIS TOO IS ALL YOUR FAULT!
SENPAI... IF YOU KEEP GETTING IN MY WAY...
...I'LL GET YOU TOO...
BUN (FWOOSH)
NO!!

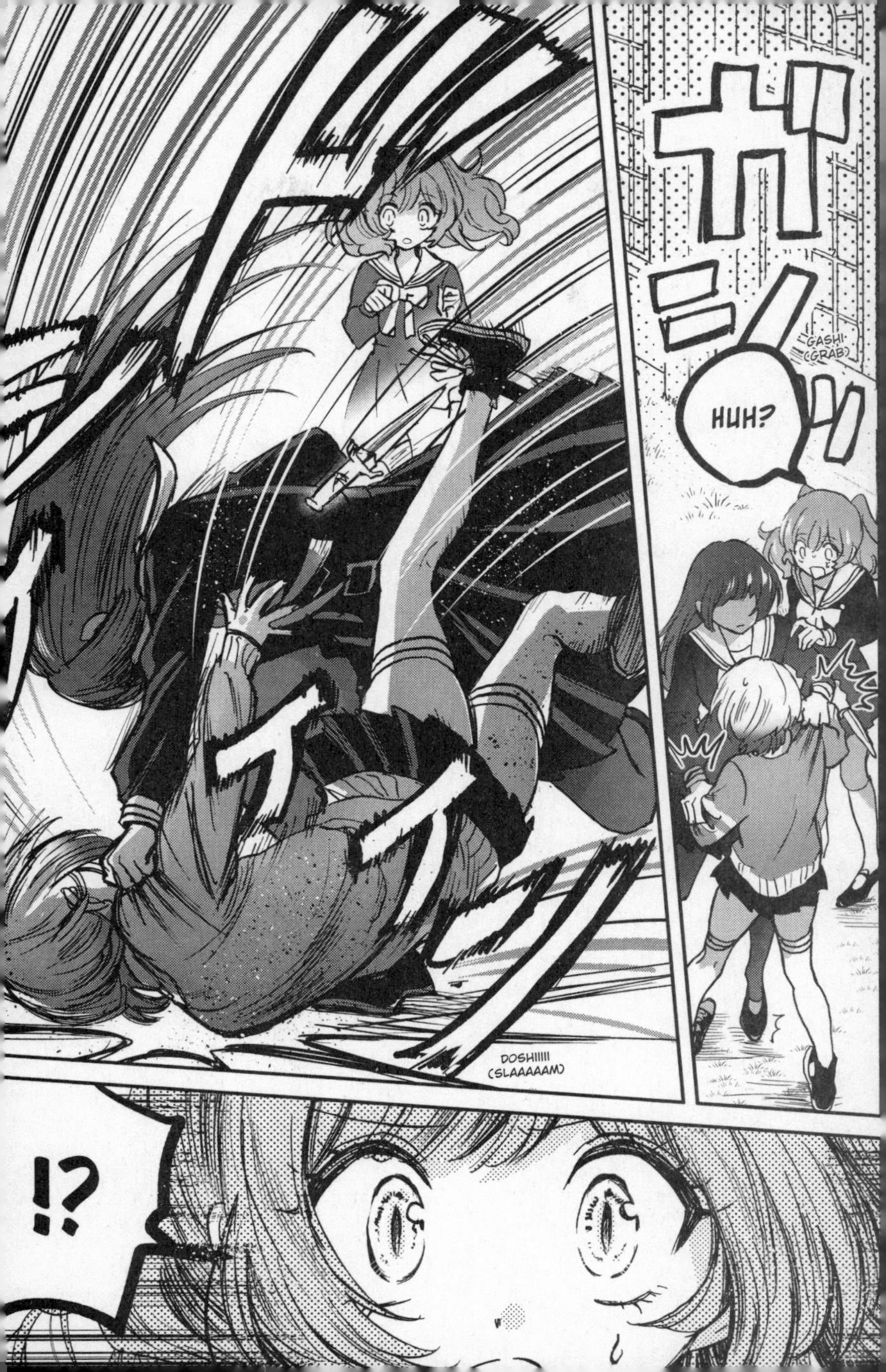
ガシッ
GASHI (GRAB)
HUH?
DOSHIIIII (SLAAAAAM)
!?

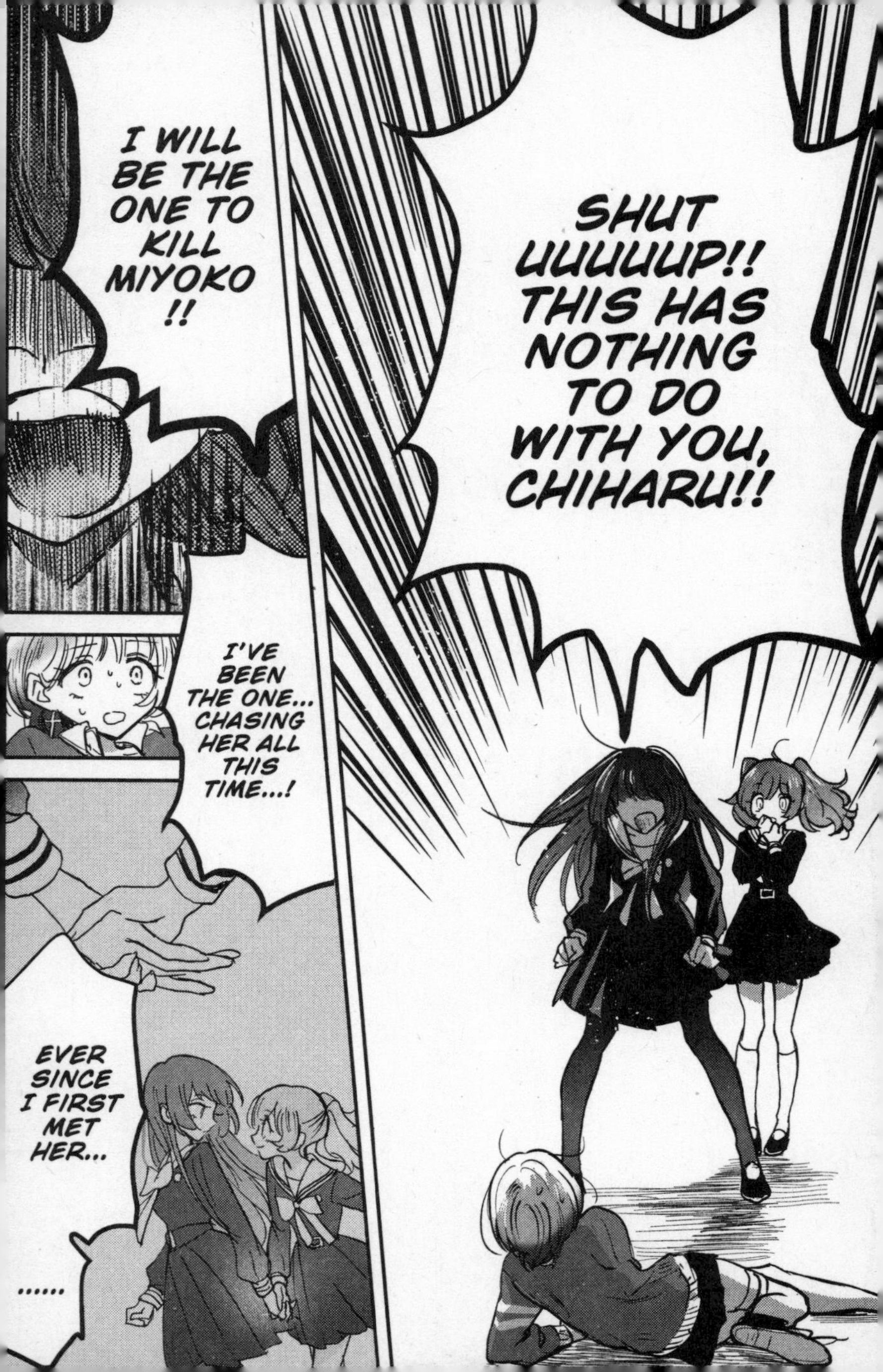
I WILL BE THE ONE TO KILL MIYOKO !!
SHUT UUUUUP!! THIS HAS NOTHING TO DO WITH YOU, CHIHARU!!
I'VE BEEN THE ONE... CHASING HER ALL THIS TIME...!
EVER SINCE I FIRST MET HER...
......

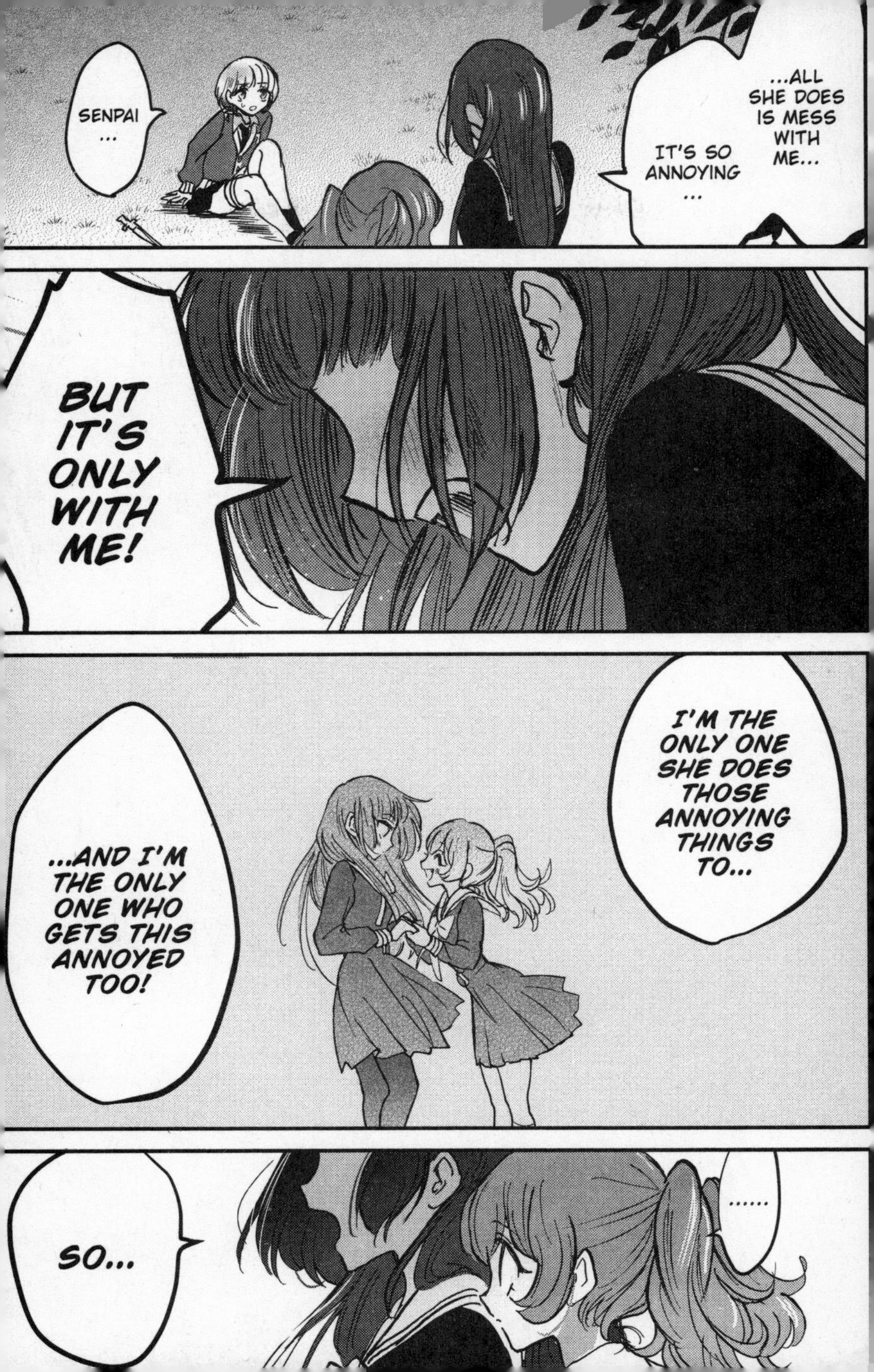
...ALL SHE DOES IS MESS WITH ME...
IT'S SO ANNOYING...
SENPAI...
BUT IT'S ONLY WITH ME!
I'M THE ONLY ONE SHE DOES THOSE ANNOYING THINGS TO...
...AND I'M THE ONLY ONE WHO GETS THIS ANNOYED TOO!
......
SO...

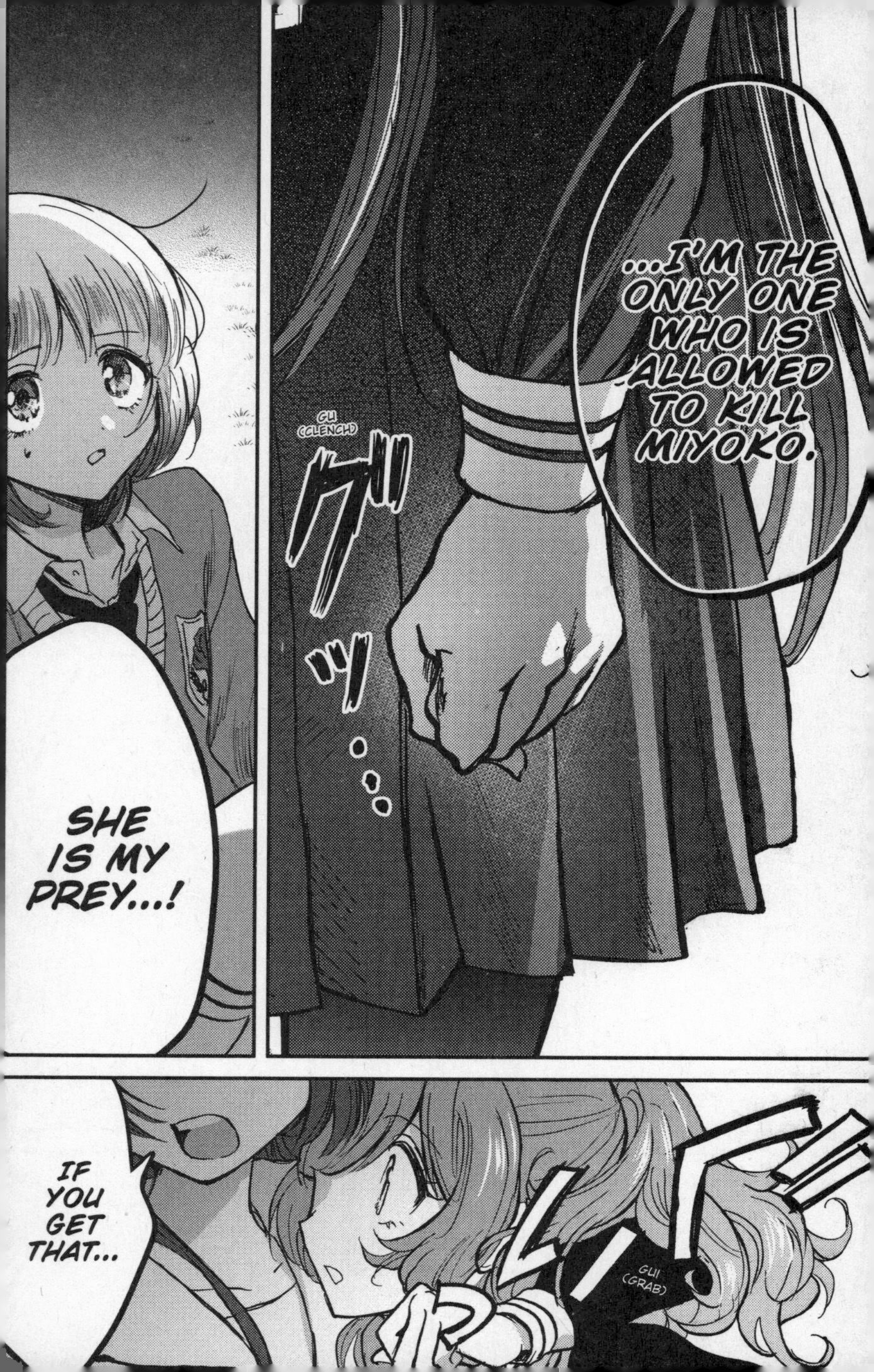
...I'M THE ONLY ONE WHO IS ALLOWED TO KILL MIYOKO.
GU (CLENCH)
SHE IS MY PREY...!
IF YOU GET THAT...
GUI (GRAB)

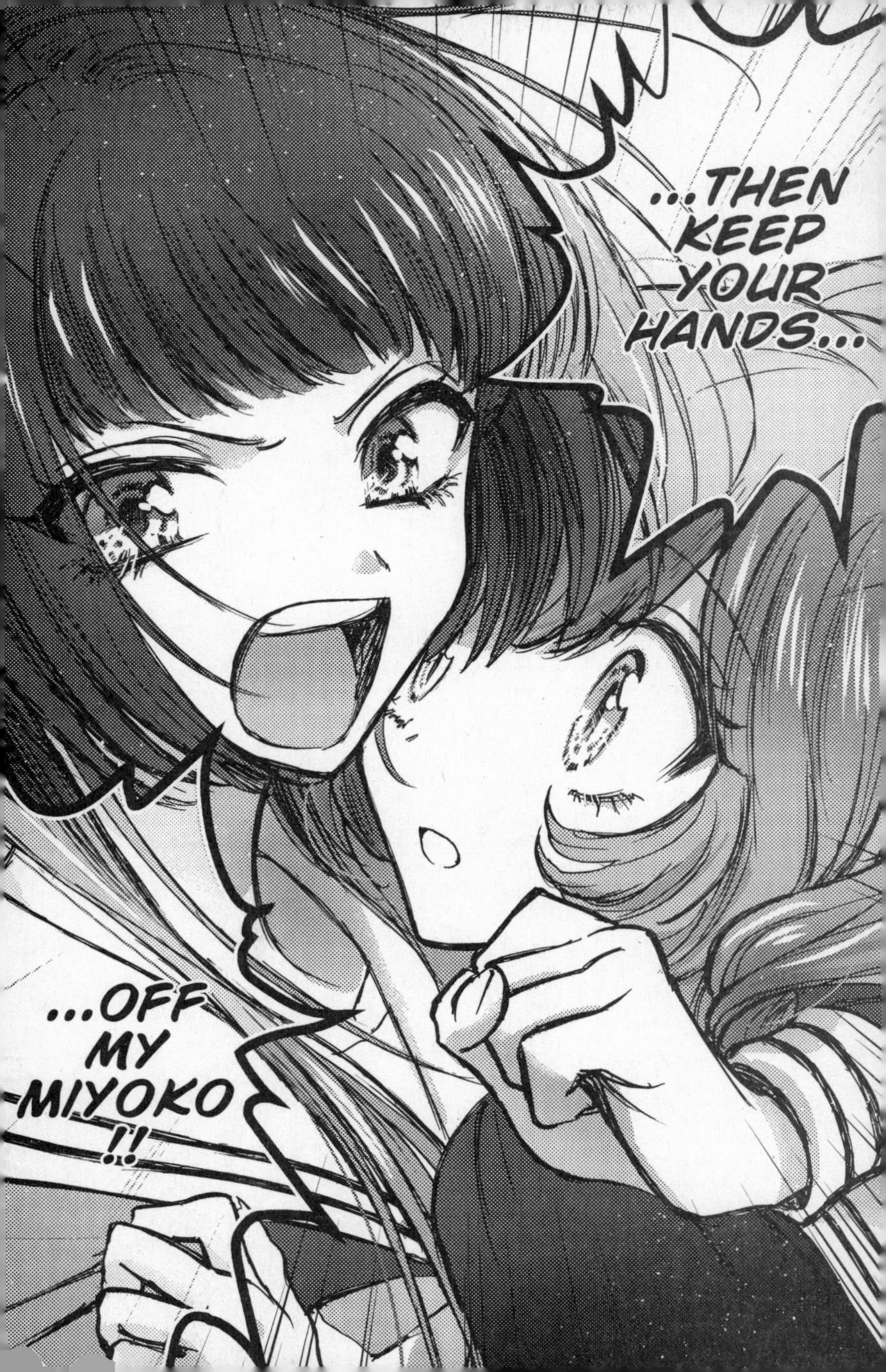
...THEN KEEP YOUR HANDS...
...OFF MY MIYOKO!!

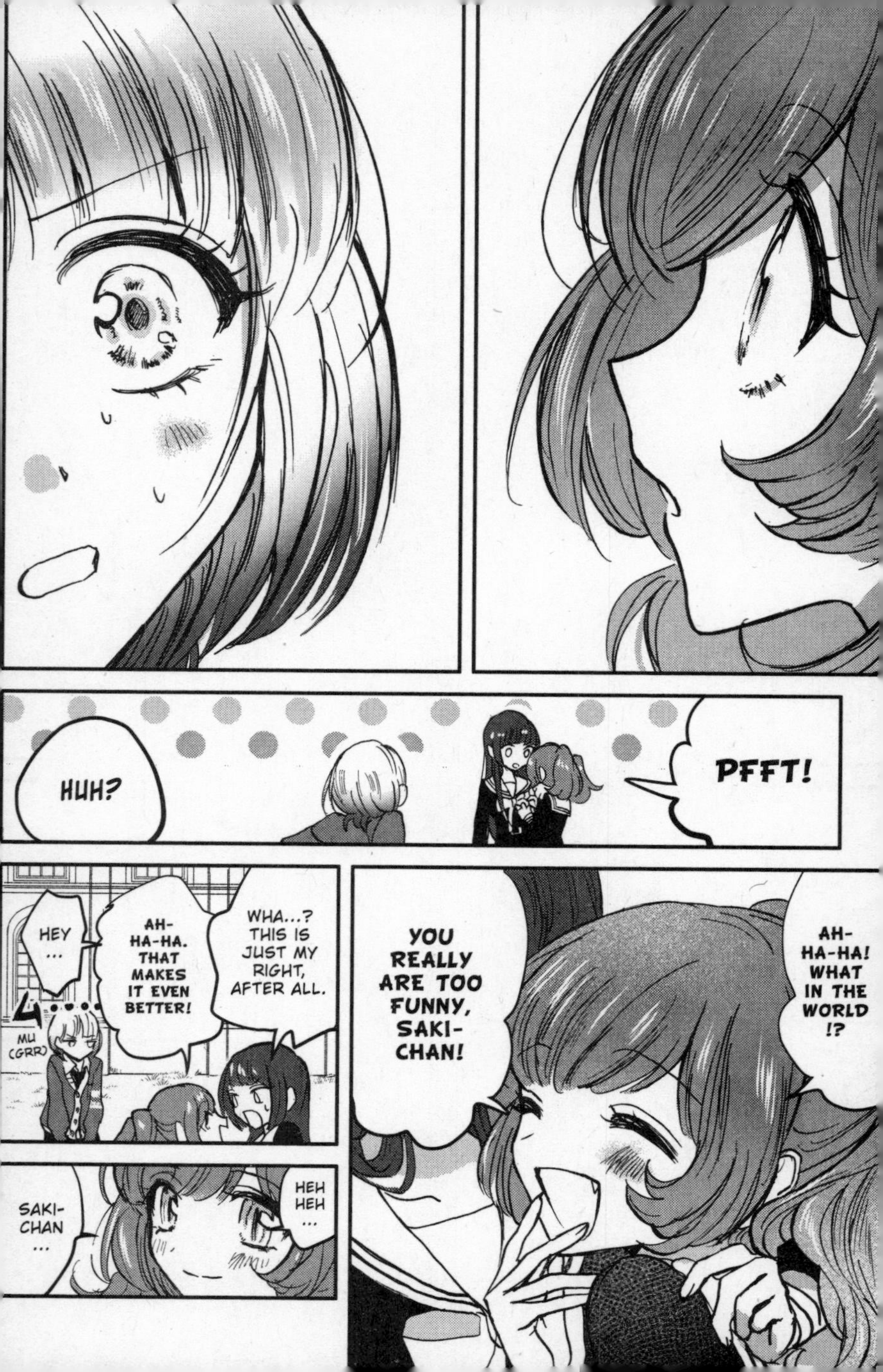
PFFT!
HUH?
AH-HA-HA! WHAT IN THE WORLD !?
YOU REALLY ARE TOO FUNNY, SAKI-CHAN!
WHA...? THIS IS JUST MY RIGHT, AFTER ALL.
AH-HA-HA. THAT MAKES IT EVEN BETTER!
HEY ...
MU (GRR)
HEH HEH ...
SAKI-CHAN ...

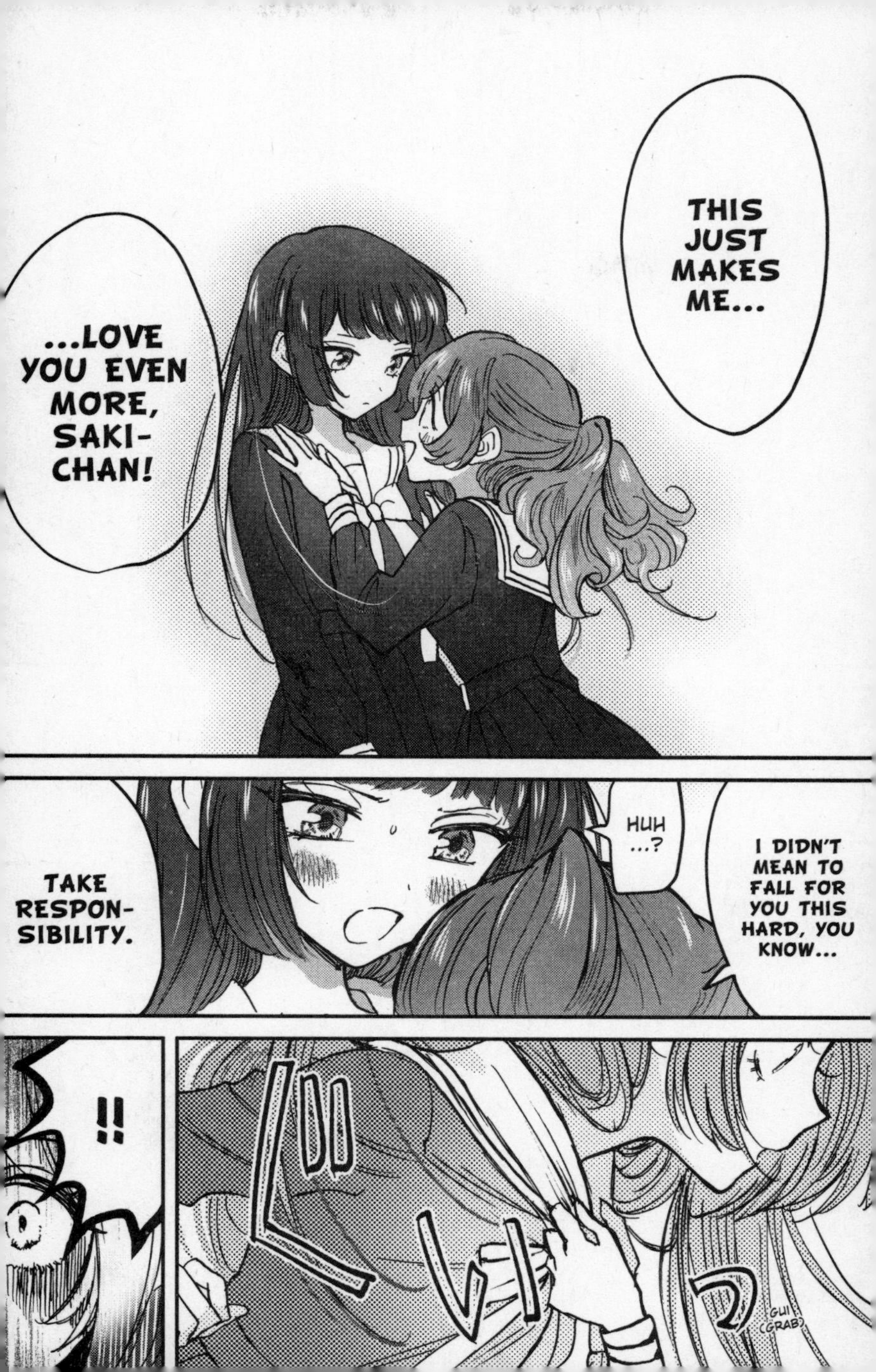
THIS JUST MAKES ME...
...LOVE YOU EVEN MORE, SAKI-CHAN!
I DIDN'T MEAN TO FALL FOR YOU THIS HARD, YOU KNOW...
HUH ...?
TAKE RESPON-SIBILITY.
GUI (GRAB)
!!

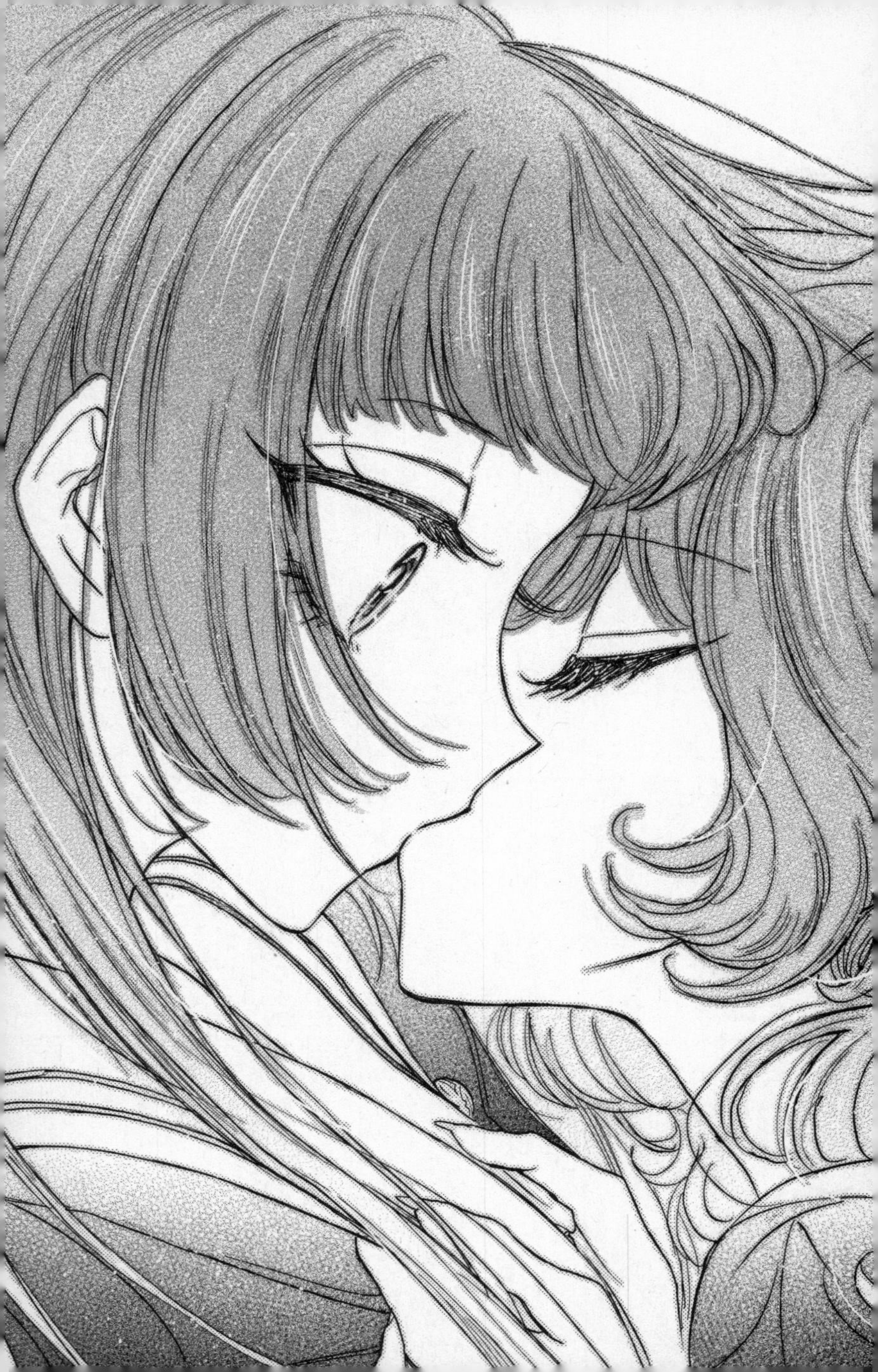

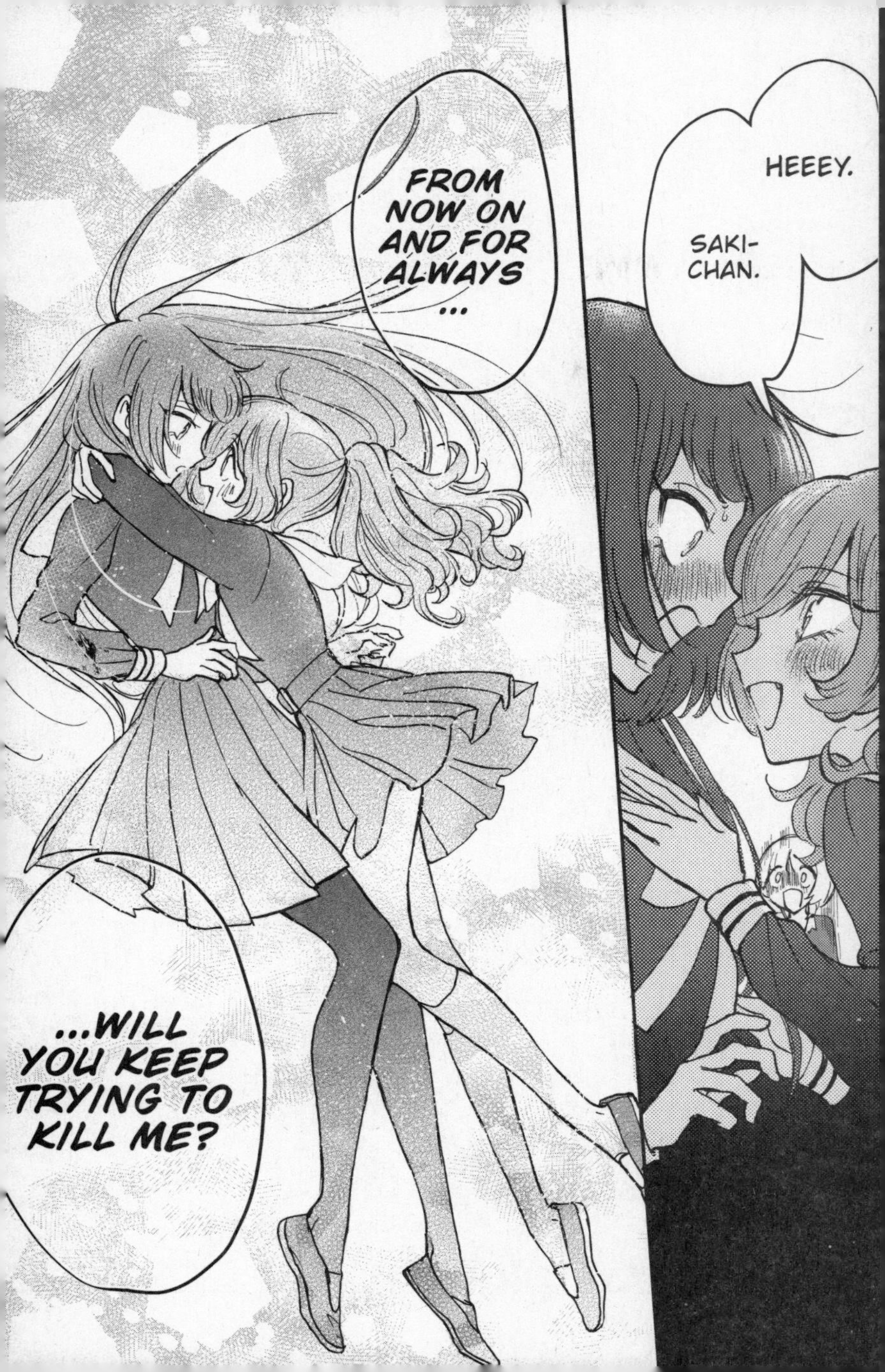
HEEEY.
SAKI-CHAN.
FROM NOW ON AND FOR ALWAYS ...
...WILL YOU KEEP TRYING TO KILL ME?

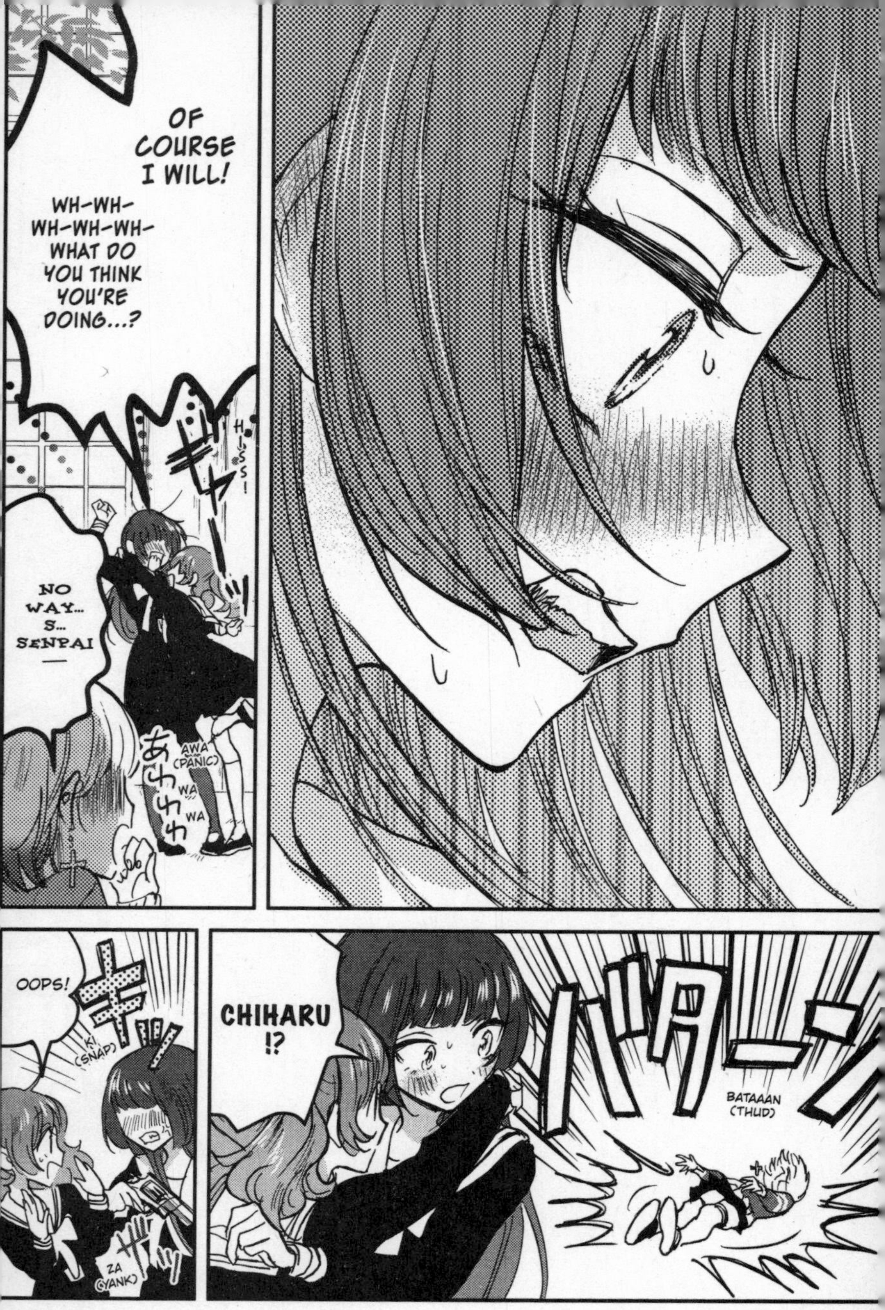
OF COURSE I WILL!
WH-WH-WH-WH-WH-WHAT DO YOU THINK YOU'RE DOING...?
HISS!
NO WAY... S... SENPAI—
AWA (PANIC)
WA
WA
BATAAAN (THUD)
CHIHARU !?
KI (SNAP)
OOPS!
ZA (YANK)

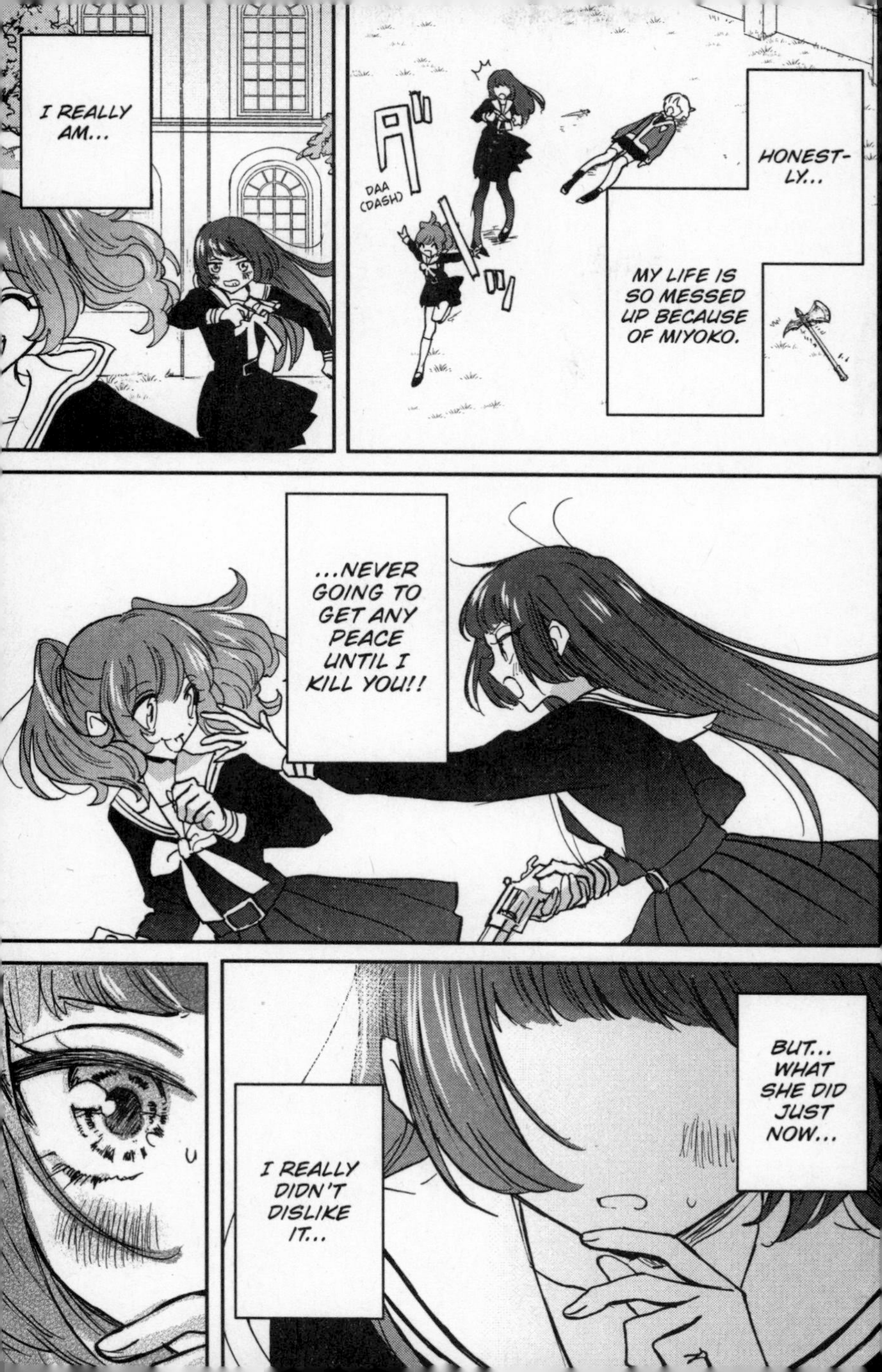
HONEST-LY...
MY LIFE IS SO MESSED UP BECAUSE OF MIYOKO.
DAA (DASH)
I REALLY AM...
...NEVER GOING TO GET ANY PEACE UNTIL I KILL YOU!!
BUT... WHAT SHE DID JUST NOW...
I REALLY DIDN'T DISLIKE IT...

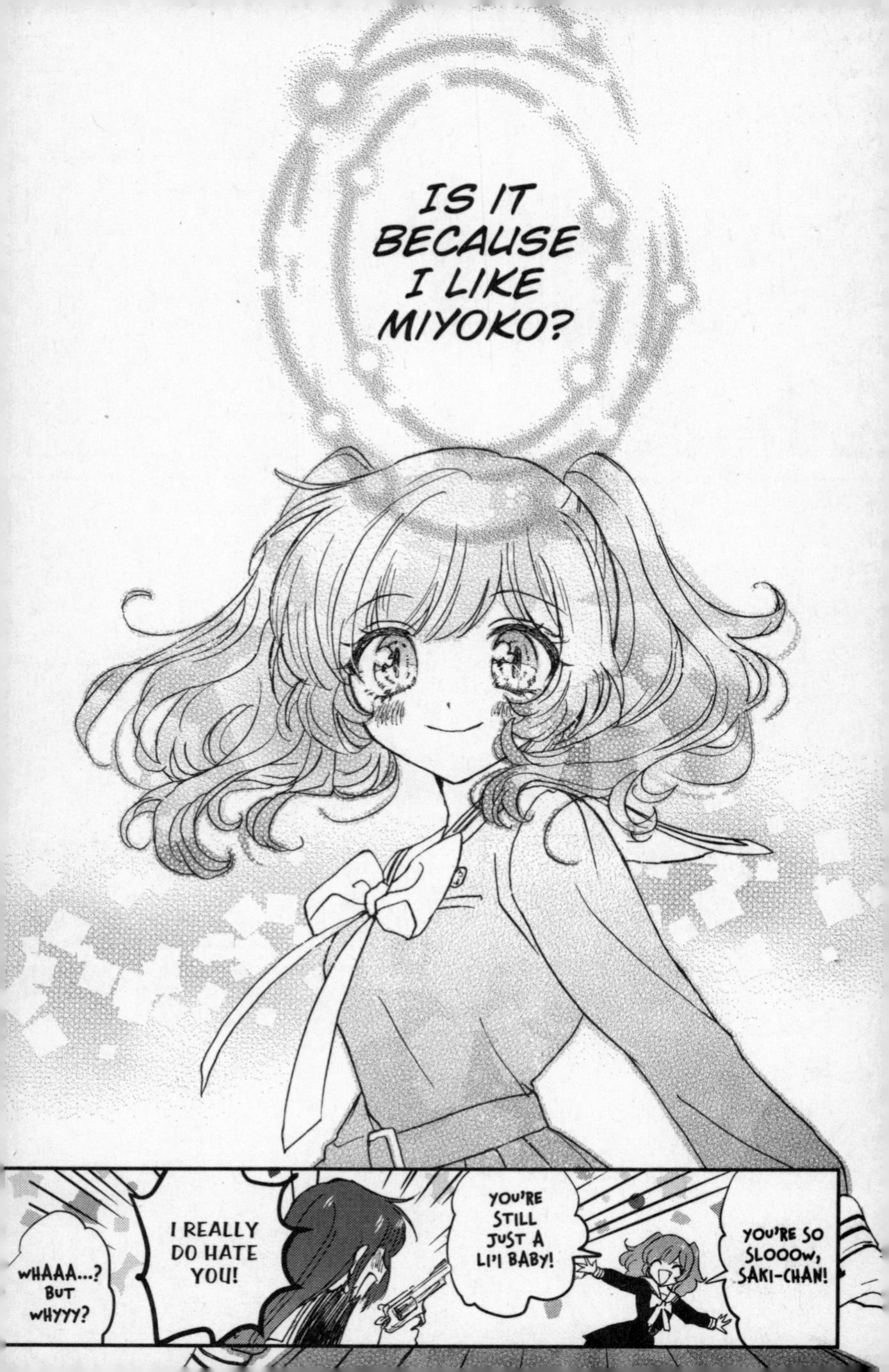
IS IT BECAUSE I LIKE MIYOKO?
YOU'RE SO SLOOOW, SAKI-CHAN!
YOU'RE STILL JUST A LI'L BABY!
I REALLY DO HATE YOU!
WHAAA...? BUT WHYYY?

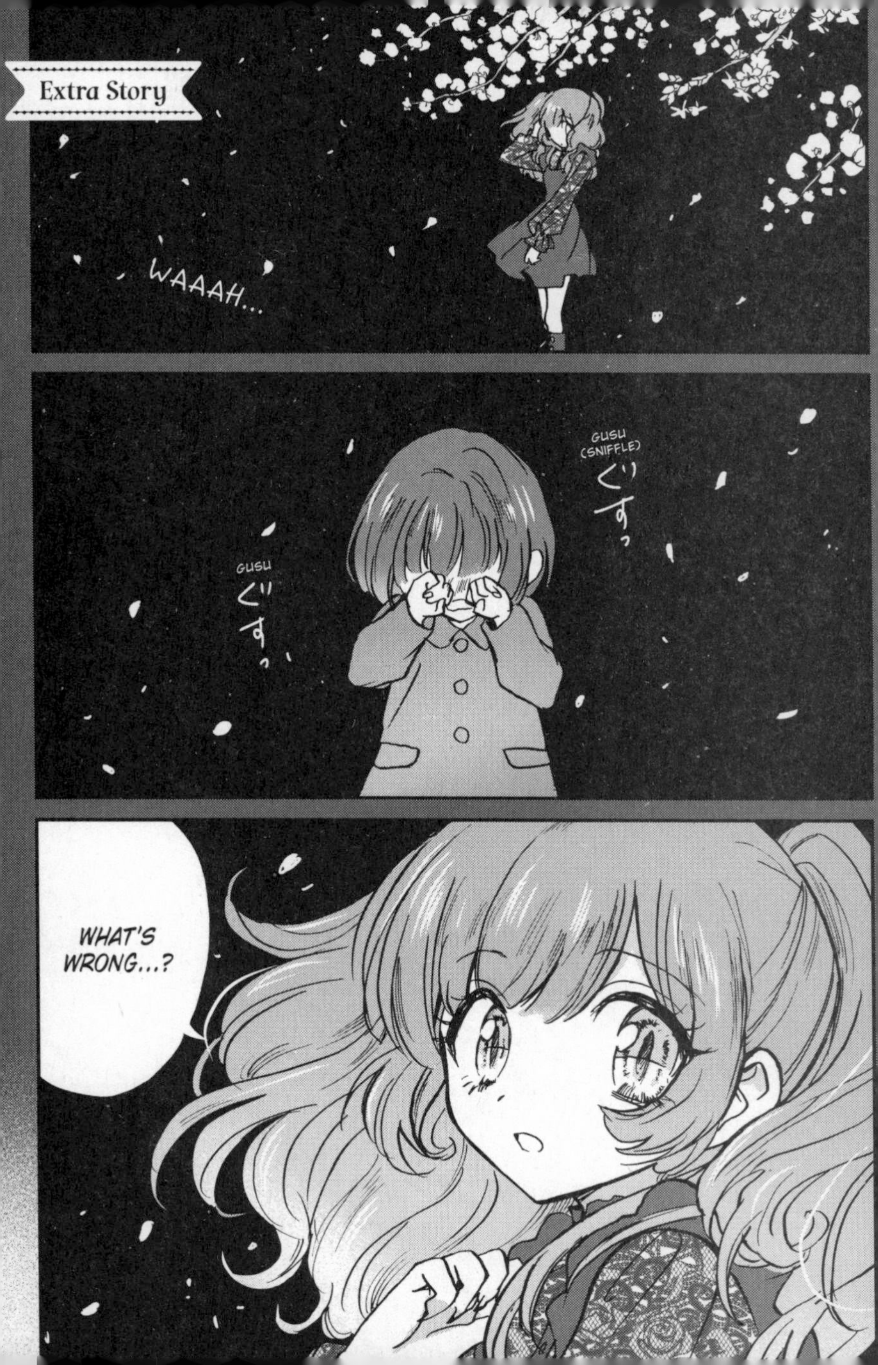
Extra Story
WAAAH...
GUSU (SNIFFLE)
ぐすっ
GUSU
ぐすっ
WHAT'S WRONG...?

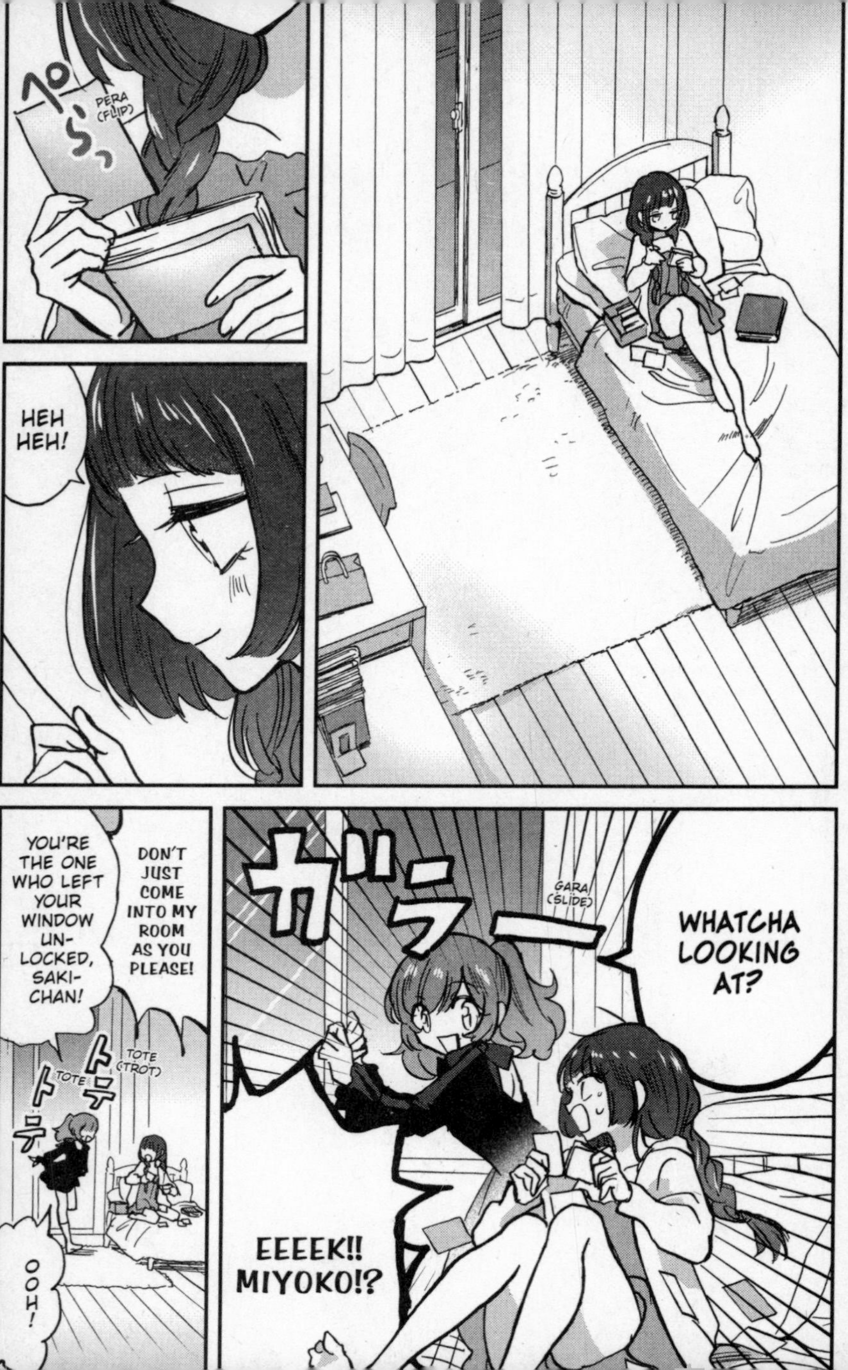
ペらっ
PERA (FLIP)
HEH HEH!
ガラー
GARA (SLIDE)
WHATCHA LOOKING AT?
EEEEK!! MIYOKO!?
DON'T JUST COME INTO MY ROOM AS YOU PLEASE!
YOU'RE THE ONE WHO LEFT YOUR WINDOW UN-LOCKED, SAKI-CHAN!
トテトテ
TOTE TOTE (TROT)
OOH!

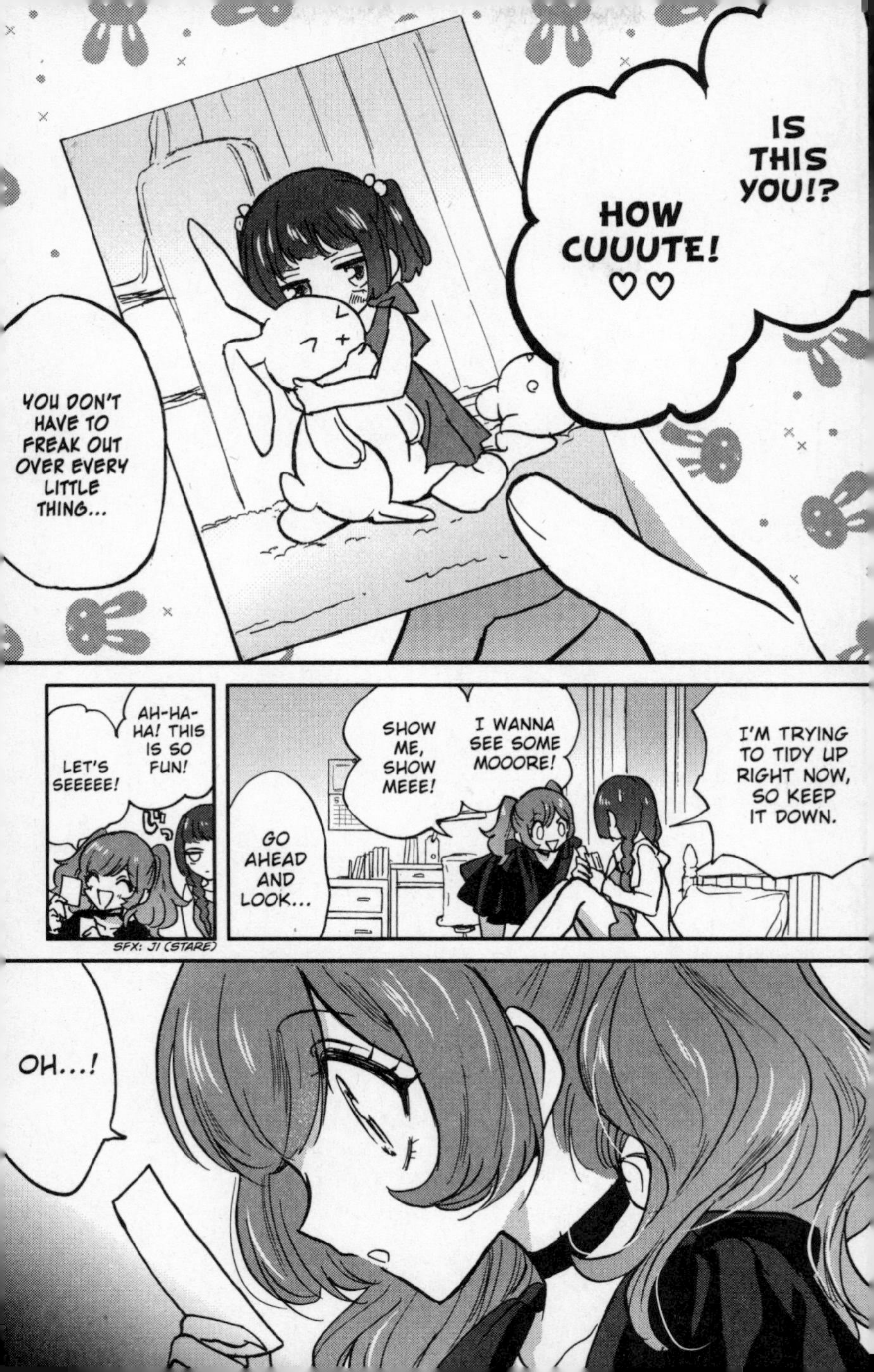
IS THIS YOU!?
HOW CUUUTE! ♡♡
YOU DON'T HAVE TO FREAK OUT OVER EVERY LITTLE THING...
I'M TRYING TO TIDY UP RIGHT NOW, SO KEEP IT DOWN.
I WANNA SEE SOME MOOORE!
SHOW ME, SHOW MEEE!
GO AHEAD AND LOOK...
AH-HA-HA! THIS IS SO FUN!
LET'S SEEEEE!
SFX: JI (STARE)
OH...!

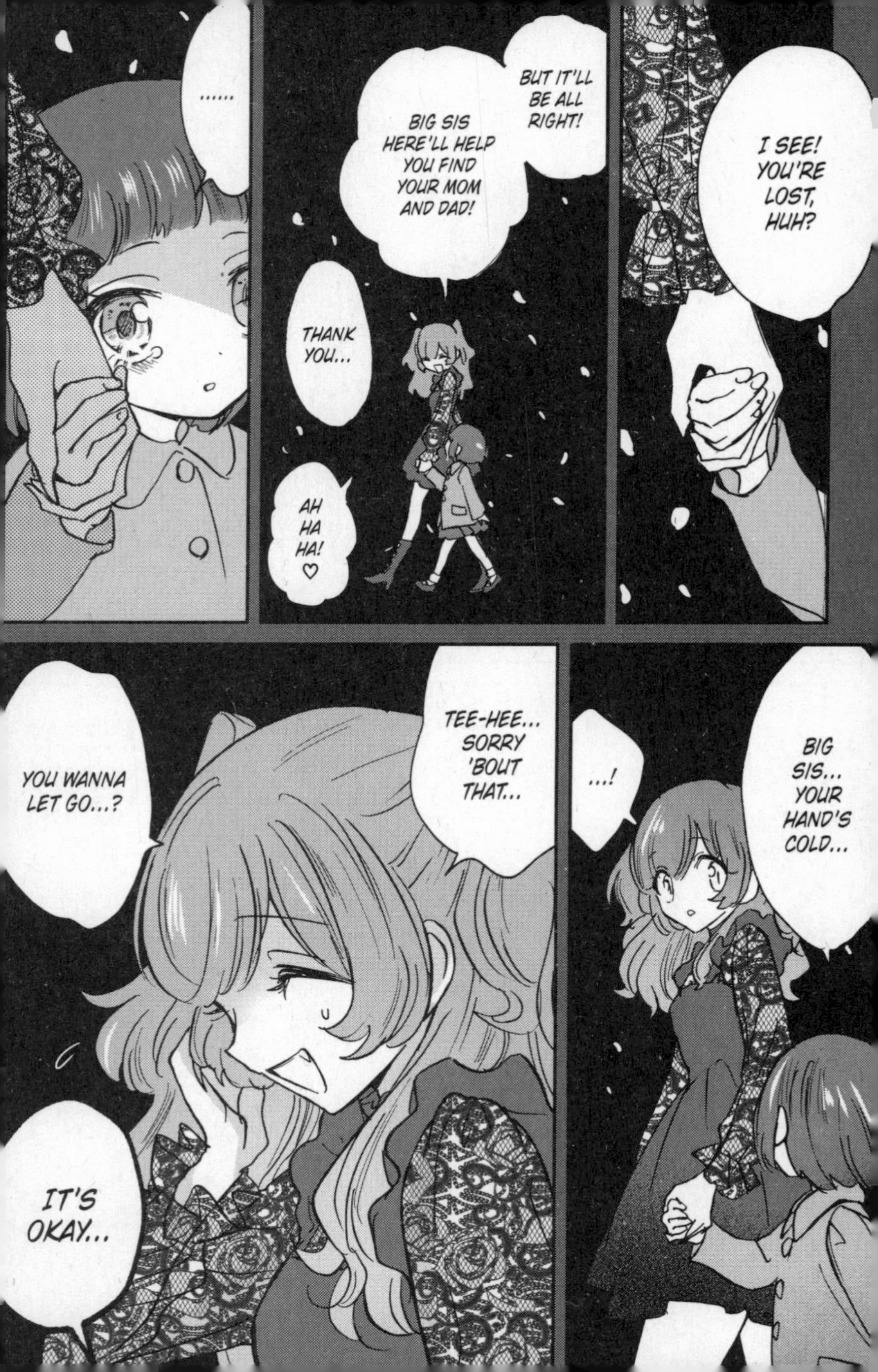
I SEE! YOU'RE LOST, HUH?
BUT IT'LL BE ALL RIGHT!
BIG SIS HERE'LL HELP YOU FIND YOUR MOM AND DAD!
THANK YOU...
AH HA HA! ♡
......
BIG SIS... YOUR HAND'S COLD...
...!
TEE-HEE... SORRY 'BOUT THAT...
YOU WANNA LET GO...?
IT'S OKAY...

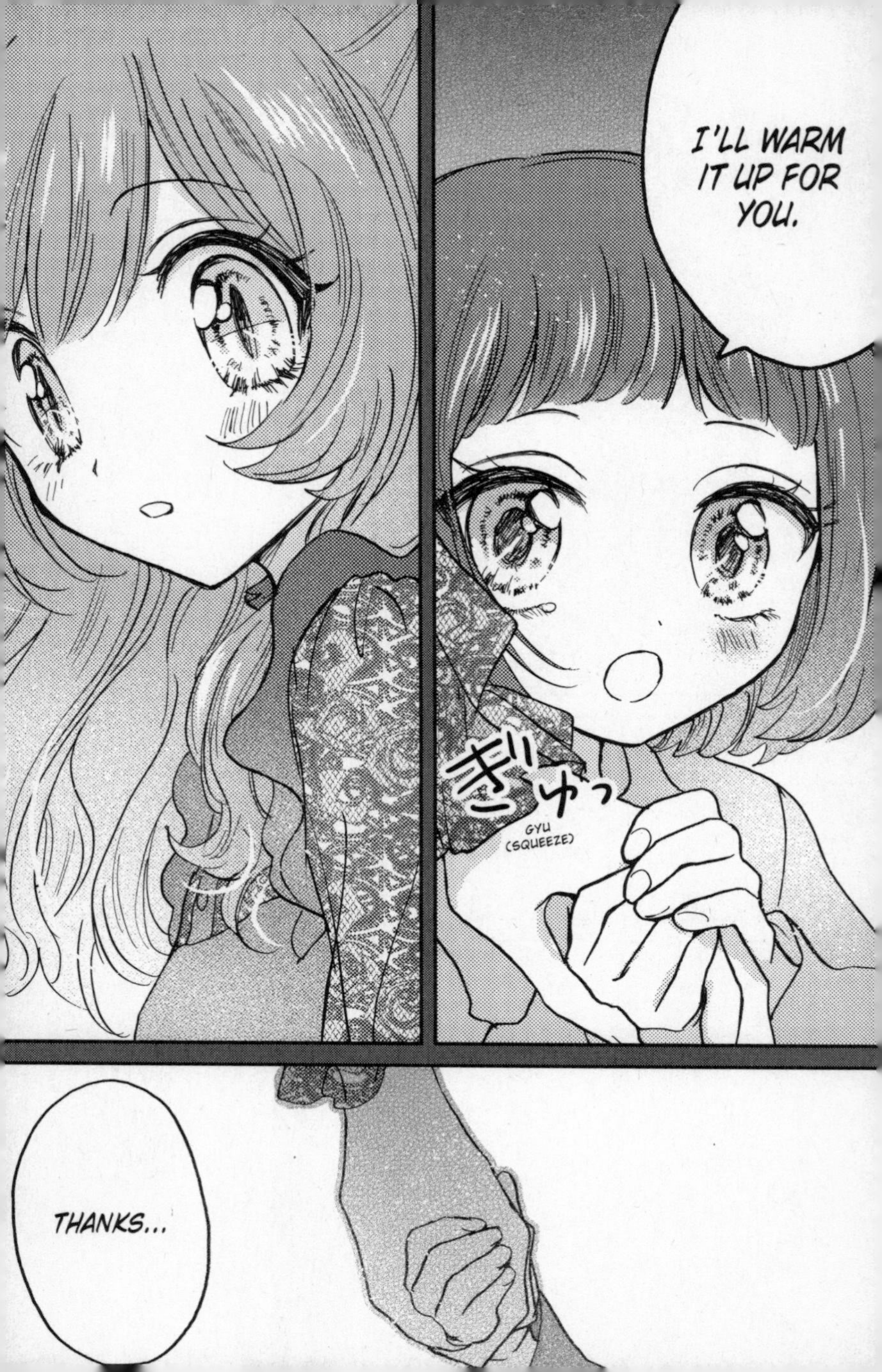
I'LL WARM IT UP FOR YOU.
ぎゅっ
GYU (SQUEEZE)
THANKS...

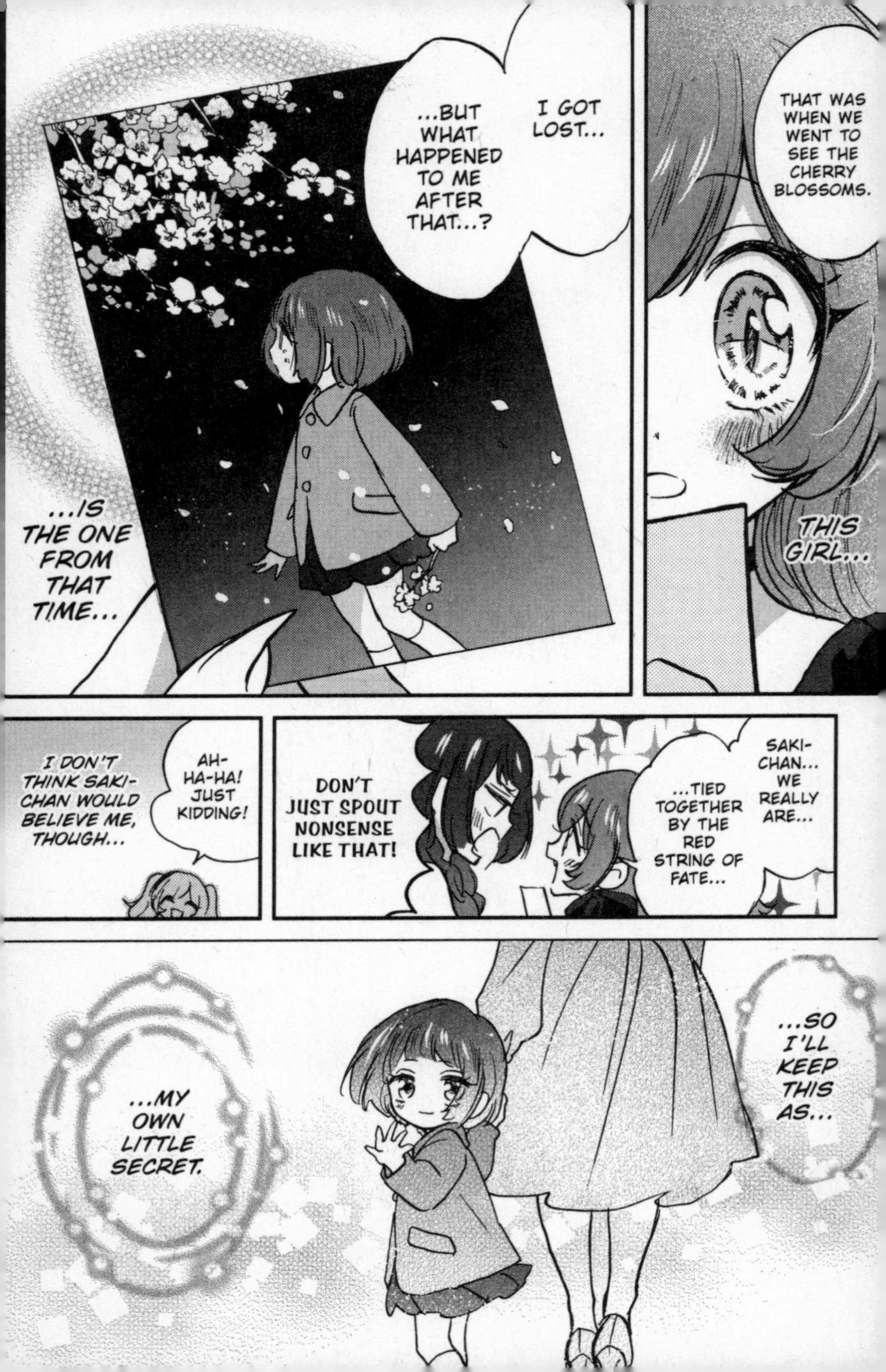
THAT WAS WHEN WE WENT TO SEE THE CHERRY BLOSSOMS.
THIS GIRL...
I GOT LOST...
...BUT WHAT HAPPENED TO ME AFTER THAT...?
...IS THE ONE FROM THAT TIME...
SAKI-CHAN... WE REALLY ARE...
...TIED TOGETHER BY THE RED STRING OF FATE...
DON'T JUST SPOUT NONSENSE LIKE THAT!
AH-HA-HA! JUST KIDDING!
I DON'T THINK SAKI-CHAN WOULD BELIEVE ME, THOUGH...
...SO I'LL KEEP THIS AS...
...MY OWN LITTLE SECRET.

Killing me! ❤

①

THIS IS WHAT I LIKE.

Thank you so much for picking up Killing Me! Volume 1!!

The phrase "Killing me" can be used to express something unbearable or totally absurd, but "You're killing me" can be used to mean you love something so much you might die, or something like that. ♡ Isn't that profound? To be completely honest, I reached my limit with English back in junior high, so I'm not really all that confident. Anyone who's actually good with English, please cut me some slack. And that's it for my afterword.

Akiyama

✝ Special Thanks ✝

· My editor, Yamamoto-san
· The designer, Seki-san
· The guest artists
· Hikari Komaru-san
· Scallion-san
· All of the readers

Thank you so much!!
I kneel to you.

Killing me!

1

TRANSLATION NOTES

Common Honorifics

No honorific: Indicates familiarity or closeness; if used without permission or reason, addressing someone in this manner would constitute an insult.

-san: The Japanese equivalent of Mr./Mrs./Miss. If a situation calls for politeness, this is the fail-safe honorific.

-chan: An affectionate honorific indicating familiarity used mostly in reference to girls; also used in reference to cute persons or animals.

-senpai: A suffix used to address upperclassmen or more experienced coworkers.

Page 32

Carmilla: Miyoko refers to herself as a "Carmilla type of vampire." This is not a usual form of categorization for vampires, but rather a direct reference to the title character of the 1872 Gothic novella by Joseph Sheridan Le Fanu, *Carmilla*. Preceding *Dracula* by 26 years, *Carmilla* is about a female vampire who preys upon a young woman named Laura. She makes romantic advances toward Laura and strong displays of affection, despite the two not knowing each other for long.

Killing me!
1

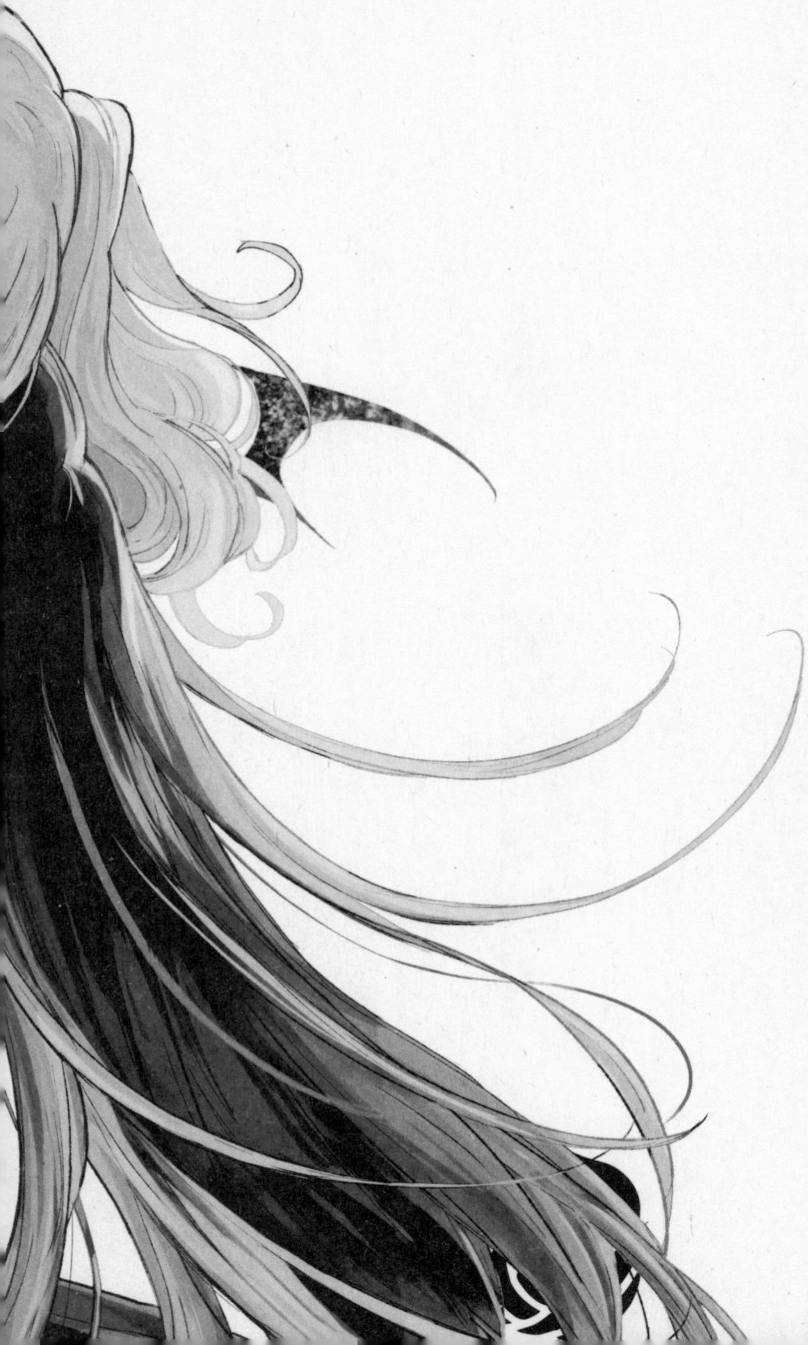

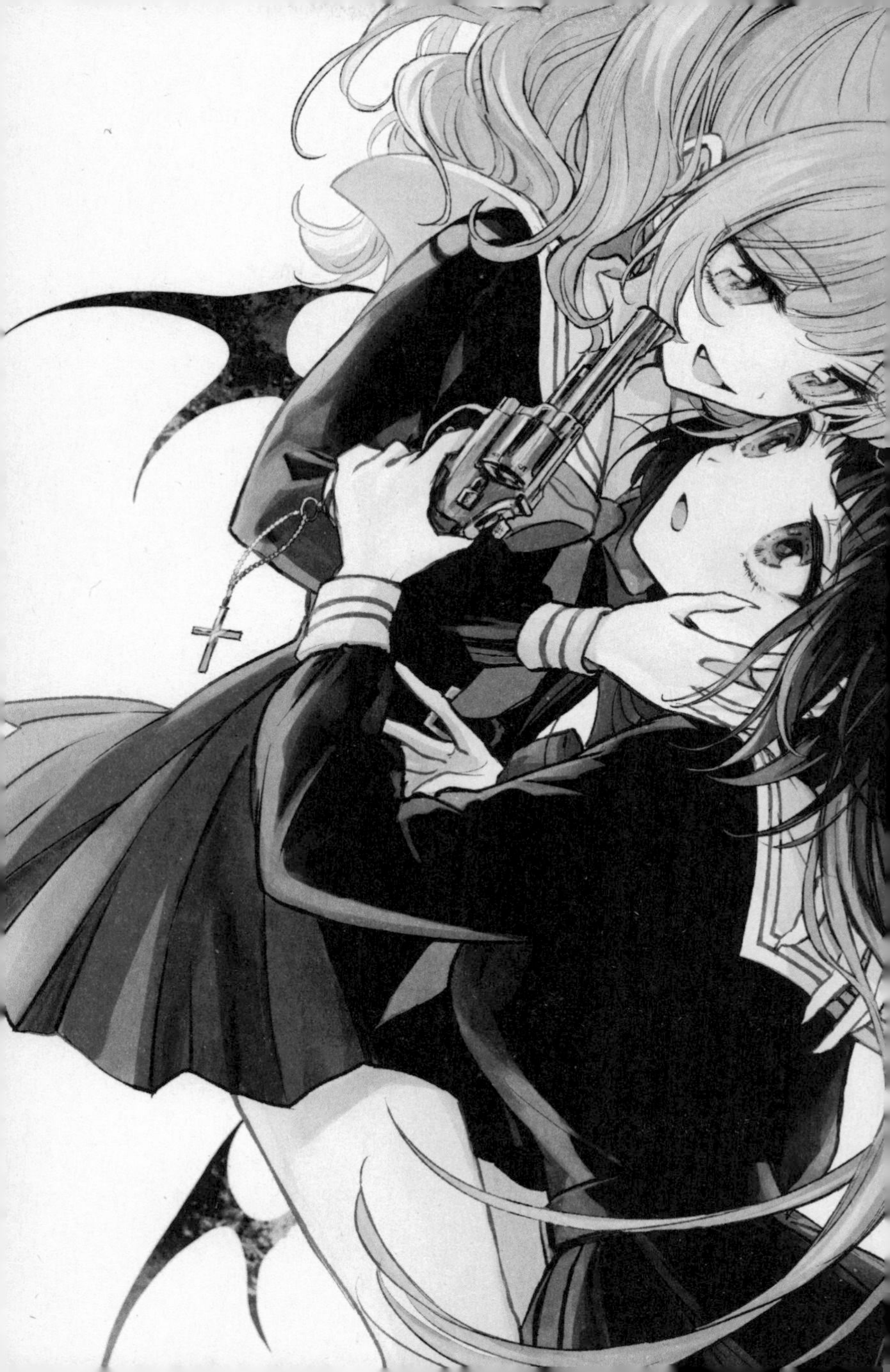

Killing me!

1

AKIYAMA

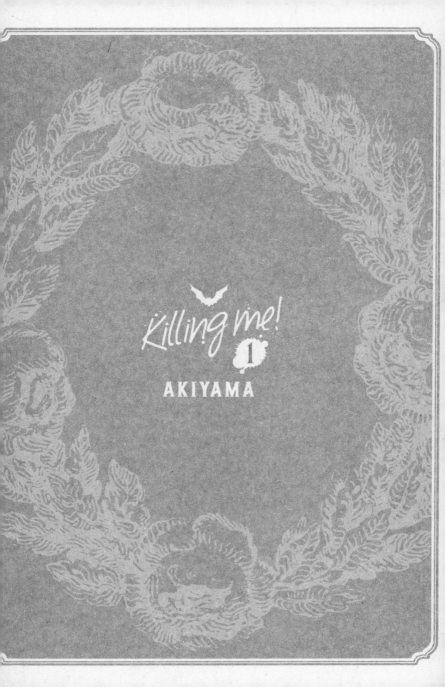

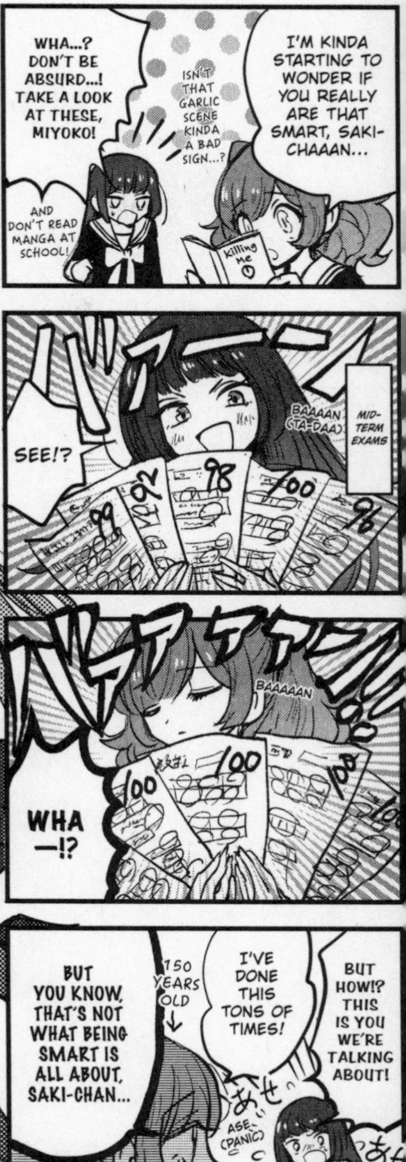
I'M KINDA STARTING TO WONDER IF YOU REALLY ARE THAT SMART, SAKI-CHAAAN...
ISN'T THAT GARLIC SCENE KINDA A BAD SIGN...?
WHA...? DON'T BE ABSURD...! TAKE A LOOK AT THESE, MIYOKO!
AND DON'T READ MANGA AT SCHOOL!
Killing me
MID-TERM EXAMS
BAAAAN (TA-DAA)
SEE!?
BAAAAAN
WHA—!?
BUT HOW!? THIS IS YOU WE'RE TALKING ABOUT!
I'VE DONE THIS TONS OF TIMES!
150 YEARS OLD
BUT YOU KNOW, THAT'S NOT WHAT BEING SMART IS ALL ABOUT, SAKI-CHAN...
ASE (PANIC)
ASE

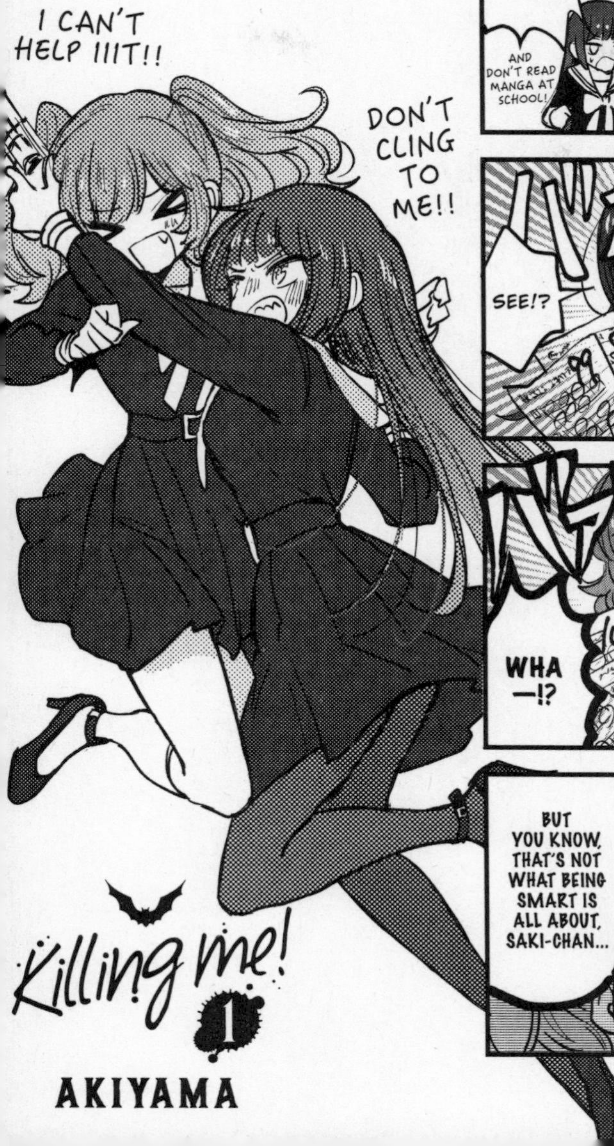
DON'T CLING TO ME!!
I CAN'T HELP IIIT!!
Killing me!
1
AKIYAMA

AKIYAMA

Hello there,
I am Akiyama. To me, a
girls' love, kill-or-be-killed
comedy about a vampire
and a young girl is kind of
like a Hamburg-steak rice-
omelette covered in curry—
packed with calories! I hope
you eat this story up!

Killing me

AKIYAMA 1

Translation: Leighann Harvey
Lettering: Alexis Eckerman

KILLING ME! Vol. 1
© Akiyama 2018
First published in Japan in 2018 by KADOKAWA CORPORATION, Tokyo.
English translation rights arranged with KADOKAWA CORPORATION, Tokyo
through TUTTLE-MORI AGENCY, INC., Tokyo.

English translation © 2019 by Yen Press, LLC

Yen Press
150 West 30th Street, 19th Floor
New York, NY 10001

Visit us at yenpress.com

facebook.com/yenpress yenpress.tumblr.com
twitter.com/yenpress instagram.com/yenpress

First Yen Press Edition: July 2019

Yen Press is an imprint of Yen Press, LLC.
The Yen Press name and logo are trademarks of Yen Press, LLC.

The publisher is not responsible for websites (or their content)
that are not owned by the publisher.

Library of Congress Control Number: 2019938441

ISBNs: 978-1-9753-5724-5 (paperback)
978-1-9753-5725-2 (ebook)

10 9 8 7 6 5 4 3 2 1

WOR

Printed in the United States of America

Guest + COMIC BY TAMAMUSHI OKU

AMBUSH

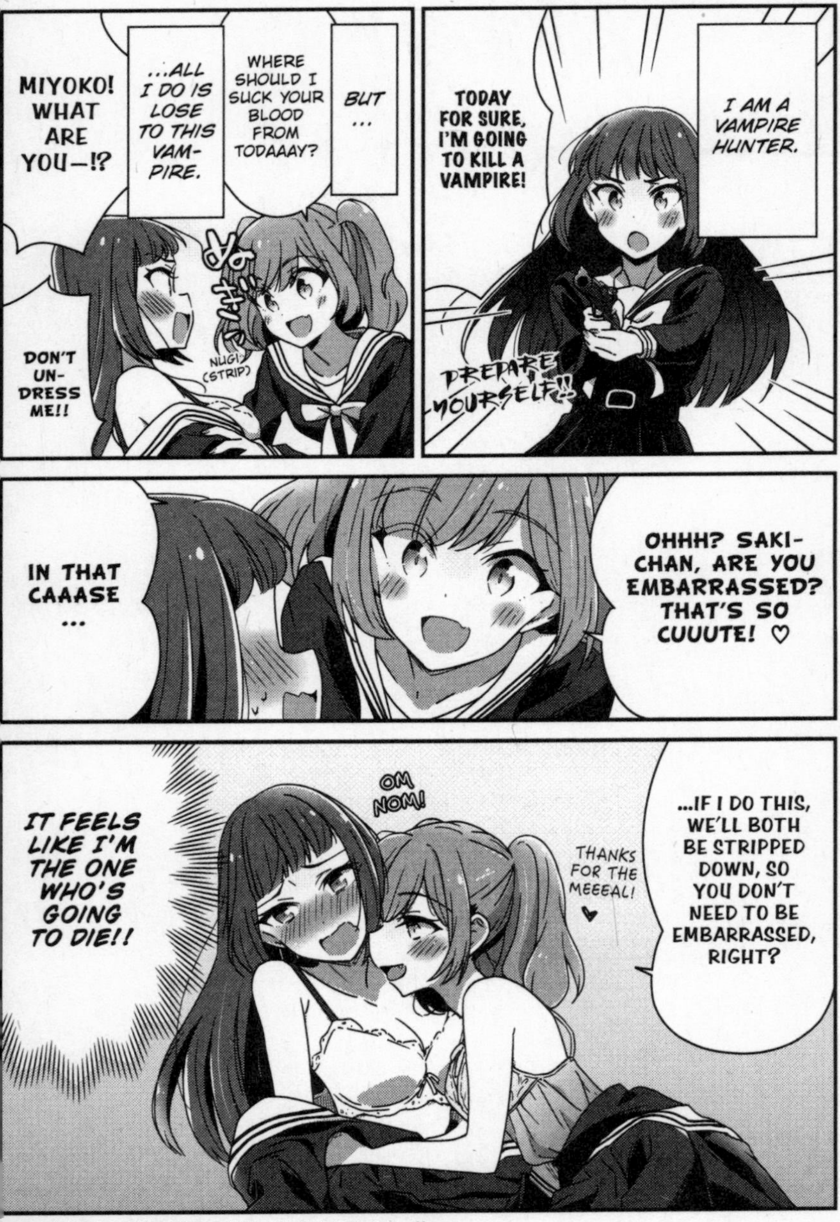
I AM A VAMPIRE HUNTER.
TODAY FOR SURE, I'M GOING TO KILL A VAMPIRE!
PREPARE YOURSELF!!
BUT ...
WHERE SHOULD I SUCK YOUR BLOOD FROM TODAAAY?
...ALL I DO IS LOSE TO THIS VAMPIRE.
MIYOKO! WHAT ARE YOU—!?
NUGI (STRIP)
DON'T UNDRESS ME!!
OHHH? SAKI-CHAN, ARE YOU EMBARRASSED? THAT'S SO CUUUTE! ♡
IN THAT CAAASE ...
...IF I DO THIS, WE'LL BOTH BE STRIPPED DOWN, SO YOU DON'T NEED TO BE EMBARRASSED, RIGHT?
THANKS FOR THE MEEEAL! ♡
OM NOM!
IT FEELS LIKE I'M THE ONE WHO'S GOING TO DIE!!

GIRLS HUNTING EACH OTHER DOWN—I THINK IT'S GREAT!!

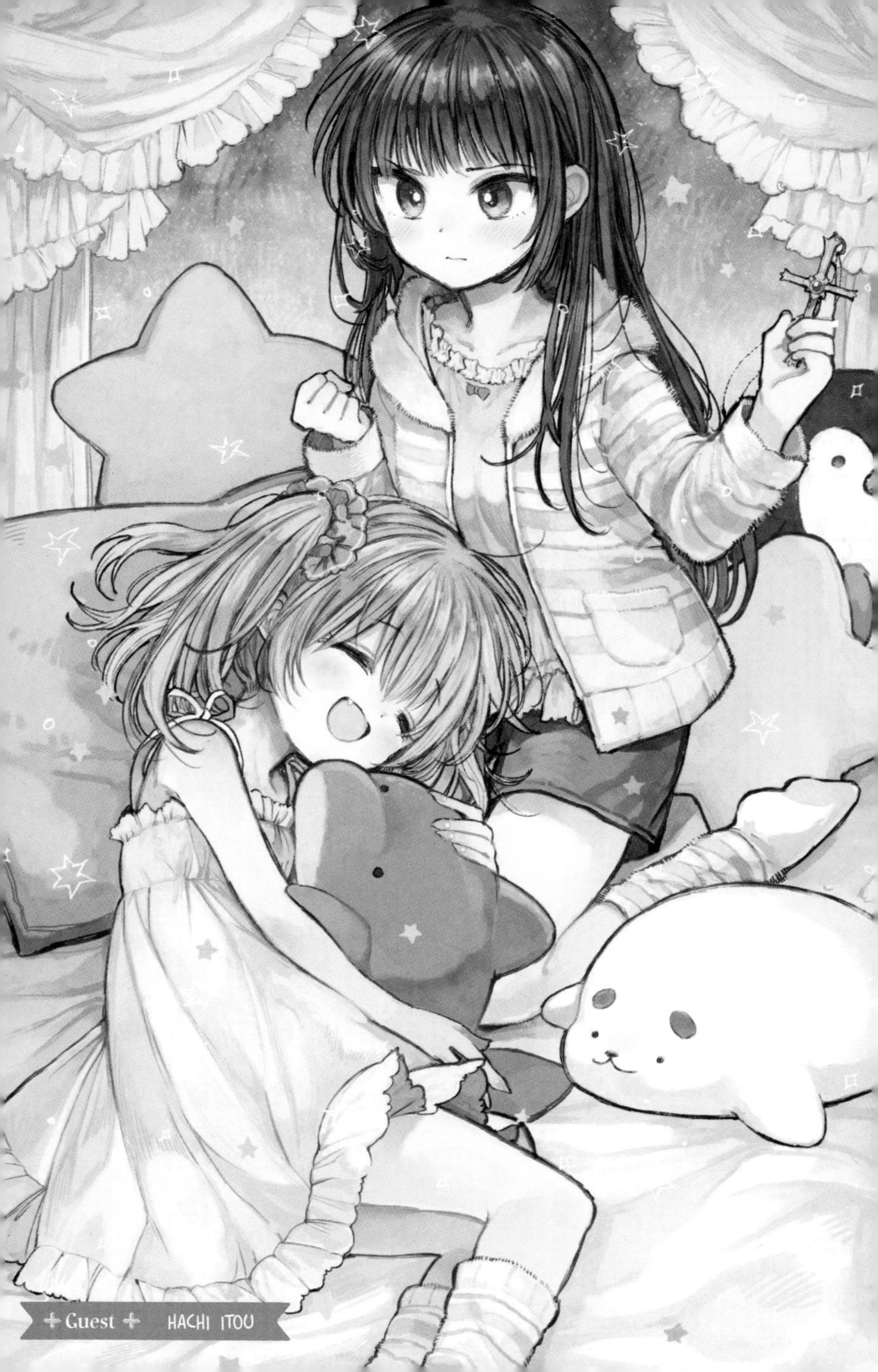
+ Guest +
HACHI ITOU

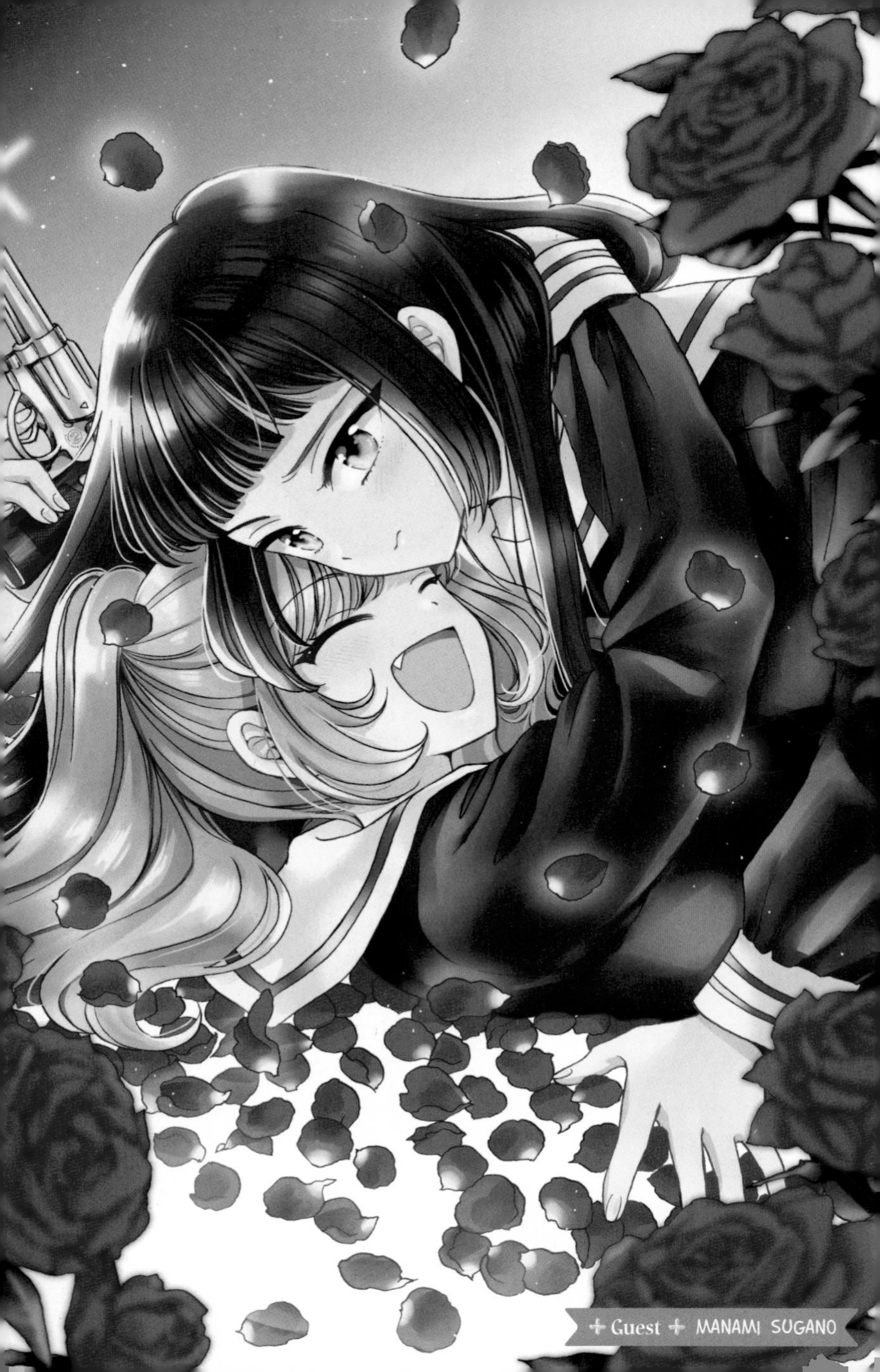
+ Guest + MANAMI SUGANO

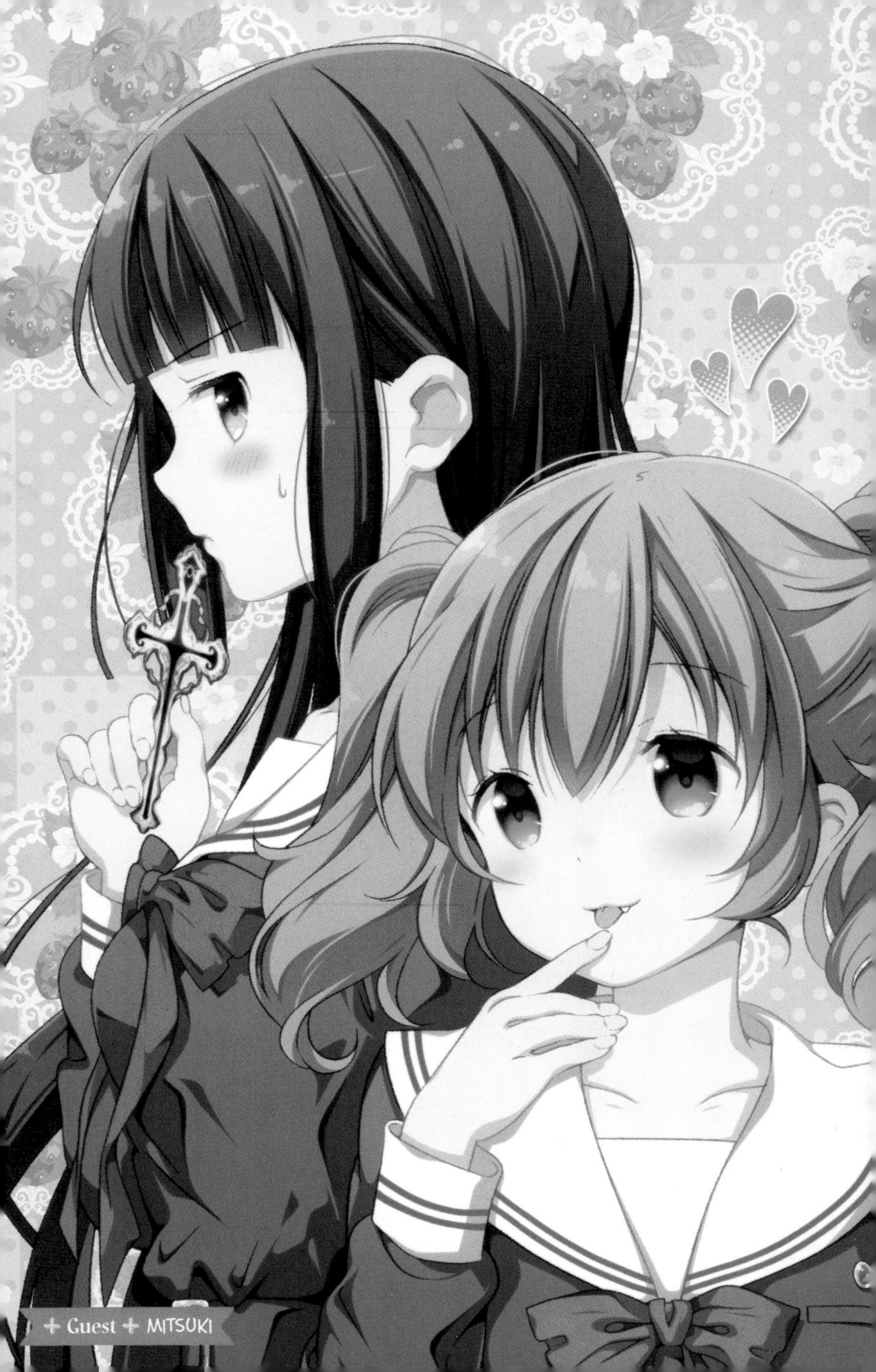
+ Guest + MITSUKI

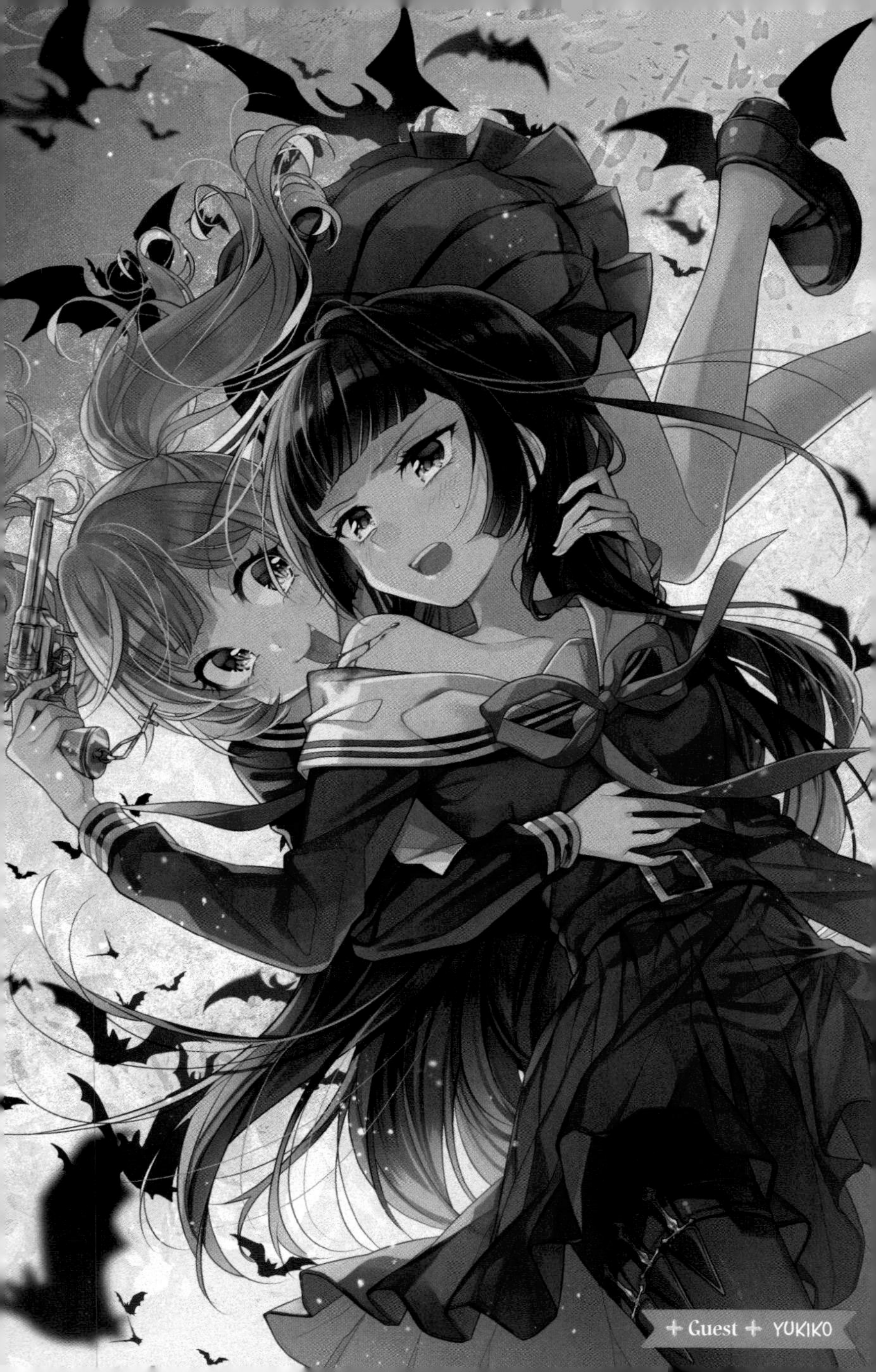
+ Guest + YUKIKO